Advance Praise for *Sacred Lessons*

"*Sacred Lessons* is much like the monarch butterfly; it points beyond itself to the connection for which we all long. The tenderness of this book carries the soul to repair what is severed and cherish the vulnerability of our kinship with each other. This fine book reminds us not to 'break the cycle' but to heal it."

—Fr. Gregory Boyle, Founder, Homeboy Industries

"Mike de la Rocha delivers a transformative memoir that unpacks the inherited weight of patriarchal expectations while exploring the tender evolution of fatherhood. Through vivid storytelling, de la Rocha reflects on moments of growth—like choosing empathy over rigidity when his son Mio expresses vulnerability—and delves into the subtle lessons he learns through shared experiences, from skipped soccer practices to emotional nights at WrestleMania.

"With raw honesty and introspection, he navigates the complexities of traditional masculinity, childhood trauma, and the generational patterns that shape our understanding of manhood. This memoir is not just a tale of being a son, or even a father, it's something more, offering a deeply personal yet universal perspective on what it means to love, nurture, and break cycles of emotional repression.

"For anyone seeking to redefine relationships and embrace a fuller spectrum of humanity."

—Dream Hampton, Award–Winning
Filmmaker and Writer

"This is a memoir of how sensitive men (most are) have had to toughen up to hide this crucial aspect to their soul's detriment. It's also about how love comes through even when one is conditioned not to express it. Mike de la Rocha is the writer to tell it. His male ancestry and his current state of a father reveals how true 'manhood' is multidimensional and emotionally complex. Thank you, Mike. Reading this I understand my own hardened-Mexican father much more."

—Luis J. Rodriguez, Author of *Always Running, La Vida Loca, Gang Days in L.A.* and *It Calls You Back: An Odyssey Through Love, Addiction, Revolutions & Healing*

"*Sacred Lessons* is a beautiful gift. To see and witness the vulnerability and authenticity of our parents, especially our fathers, pushes back against the cultural tide that dehumanizes parents trying to live a full experience in life. Mike de la Rocha offers us a glimpse into how we navigate that balance from moment to moment. Stepping into tenderness with our parents. Inviting them to mentor, hold and support our growth as adults. To be partners in this life journey. To benefit from the collective wisdom of our shared journey. It is ultimately the greatest gift we can give to each other. The power to truly see each other. And to hold space for each other. To love each other unconditionally."

—Cole, Founder, Brown Boi Project

"When you are born, no one gives you a book on how to be a son to a father carrying generations of their own challenges. Then when you become a father, no one gives you a book on how to be a dad and partner (much less a curriculum for loving your child in ways your own father never knew). And when your father dies unexpectedly, no one tells you what to do with all that grief and unexpressed love so rather than become toxic, it sets you free. Finally, a book that begins to do all that. A book that breaks your heart in ways that help you heal. *Sacred Lessons* indeed."

—Mark Gonzales, Award–Winning Author,
Storyteller, and Entrepreneur

"Through *Sacred Lessons*, Mike de la Rocha crafts a brilliantly colorful diptych that questions the many meanings of masculinity across generations; from his abuelo's gun-slinging machismo, to his father's stoic intellectualism, all the way to his son's sensitive love of WWE. As a new father myself, the pursuit at the core of the memoir, the transmutation of patriarchal traditions into loving, empathetic relationships, is something that is deeply relatable and applicable to my own healing journey. The myriad ways in which our family trees perpetuate both the strengths and the sins of a father are on bare, vulnerable display here, and the messenger is a trusted source that has long dedicated his life to liberation movements across racial barriers, cementing himself as a bastion of solidarity, and now, as a literary force."

—Vic Mensa, Musician, Actor,
Entrepreneur, and Philanthropist

Sacred Lessons

Teaching My Father How To Love

Mike de La Rocha

A REGALO PRESS BOOK
ISBN: 979-8-88845-415-2
ISBN (eBook): 979-8-88845-416-9

Sacred Lessons:
Teaching My Father How to Love
© 2025 by Mike de la Rocha
All Rights Reserved

Cover Design by Jim Villaflores

Publishing Team:
Founder and Publisher – Gretchen Young
Editorial Assistant – Caitlyn Limbaugh
Managing Editor – Aleigha Koss
Production Manager – Alana Mills
Production Editor – Rachel Paul
Associate Production Manager – Kate Harris

As part of the mission of Regalo Press, a donation is being made to the Ismael "Mayo" de la Rocha Scholarship, as chosen by the author. Find out more about this organization at: https://venturacollegefoundation.org/donate/

This is a memoir. The events are portrayed to the best of the author's memory. Some names and identifying details have been changed to protect the privacy of the people involved.

This book, as well as any other Regalo Press publications, may be purchased in bulk quantities at a special discounted rate. Contact orders@regalopress.com for more information.

No part of this book may be reproduced, stored in a retrieval system, or transmitted by any means without the written permission of the author and publisher.

Regalo Press
New York • Nashville
regalopress.com

Published in the United States of America
1 2 3 4 5 6 7 8 9 10

Para mi Papá, Ismael "Mayo" de la Rocha
y hajj ibrahim salih abdul-matin

By far the worst thing we do to males—by making them feel they have to be hard—is that we leave them with very fragile egos.
—Chimamanda Ngozi Adichie

Contents

Prologue: Teaching My Father How to Love xiii

Lesson I: Patience

Chapter 1: The Trouble with "I Love You" 3
Chapter 2: Forever a Mamá's Boy 11
Chapter 3: Meeting My Person 18
Chapter 4: Inheriting a Daughter 27

Lesson II: Forgiveness

Chapter 5: Muy Macho 41
Chapter 6: Besito Grande 55
Chapter 7: Running Toward Home 66
Chapter 8: The "Saint" and the "Wildman" 76

Lesson III: Love

Chapter 9: My Green Deen 91
Chapter 10: Surrendering to the Ocean 112
Chapter 11: Confronting Whiteness 124
Chapter 12: Wishing on a Star 136

Lesson IV: Compassion

Chapter 13: The Willingness to Let Go 153
Chapter 14: Seeing My Father Cry 169
Chapter 15: Becoming Cesar Chavez 182
Chapter 16: I Never Wanted to Hurt You...........................204

Lesson V: Acceptance

Chapter 17: Chosen Family...221
Chapter 18: The Wisdom of Children 240
Chapter 19: Why Can't I Ask for Help?..............................248
Chapter 20: Saying Goodbye...254

Lesson VI: Faith

Chapter 21: Coming Full Circle..263
Chapter 22: The Love of My Father.....................................281

Resources 287
Medicine: Author's Note 291
Acknowledgments 297
Ismael "Mayo" de la Rocha (1949–2015) 303

Prologue

Teaching My Father How to Love

This isn't the story I intended to write, but this is the story that needed to be written. These are the words that kept playing over in my head as I first tried to write a book about my father's life while still processing the greatest heartbreak I've ever known.

Like so many of us, I was not equipped to handle the death of a parent. Grief affects us all very differently, and there is no linear timeline or timetable for how to process or even get over such a profound loss. I was not prepared for the funeral arrangements and the long goodbye. I was not ready to accept a life without my father by my side. So I tried to make sense of his passing by writing *his* story.

Waking up in the early morning before the sun rose, I spent hours writing about his life. It was a sacred time that allowed me to feel closer to him. It was a special time that provided me with a quiet space to confront my own secrets, my own self-doubts, and even my own relationship with him.

As I wrote about his life, something just didn't feel right. As I continued to go to therapy to unpack my own trauma, I began to see that I was hiding behind my father's voice. I was running away from addressing my own issues because I was spending countless hours writing *his* story, not recognizing that his story was intimately connected to my own story.

Only when I realized that the book that needed to be written was the story I was too afraid to tell—the complicated story of my relationship with my father, of how outdated definitions of manhood continue to harm me and all those I love—was I able to begin to address and finally tell my truth, my history, my story.

Yes, this is a story about love. About the love between a father and a son. About the love that I so desperately wanted to be verbally expressed, and outwardly given. But this is also a story about the immense amount of love that's required to truly break the unhealthy patterns and societal pressures that have prevented me, and my father, from living out our full and authentic lives.

This book is for people, and men in particular, who are yearning to learn how to deepen their relationships with themselves and with those around them. It's a book that will help contextualize why so many of us men are the way we are. A book to drive us to have difficult conversations so that we can start to dismantle patriarchy in order to become more present and loving fathers, partners, sons, and brothers.

This book is about us, all of us, and the ways that we maintain or challenge a toxic environment where boys and men are taught to run away as far as possible from themselves. A book

SACRED LESSONS

that will make you laugh, a book that will make you cry, and a book that I hope will change you in some meaningful way.

And while I can point to my father overworking himself or having one too many health problems as the reason for his sudden passing, the truth is that the image of a "strong" man that he felt he had to subscribe to—a man who protects and a man who provides for his family at all costs—is what I truly believe ultimately contributed to his early death.

In trying to cope with the unexpected loss of my father, I took a hard look at myself. I examined my own relationships with my loved ones and with death in general. I grappled with the fact that my fear to address my father's passing, coupled with my own childhood trauma, was fueling the same unhealthy patterns that took my father away from me.

This is what this book is about. It's about living with loss and realizing that if I—if any of us—want to stop the cycle of violence, then we must redefine manhood and engage in the necessary and difficult self and collective work needed to heal our pain and our suffering.

These are the reasons why I felt compelled to write *Sacred Lessons: Teaching My Father How to Love*. These are the reasons why I consistently work on myself and why I participate in daily rituals intended to equip me with the tools I need to address decades' worth of personal and ancestral trauma. This is why I've dedicated my life to reimagining and rebuilding with others a more just and equitable society for everyone.

My hope is that this book will change you as much as it has changed me. That it will have you questioning everything. Because even till this day, I still find myself struggling to look inward. I still find myself struggling not to engage in old, harmful habits and behaviors that negatively impact me and my loved ones. And I still find myself having a hard time accepting why it was so hard for my father to tell me those three simple words that I always wanted to hear from him: "I love you."

So as the universe takes these stories where they're meant to go, my greatest hope is that this book will help men find the words that we're too afraid to say. That this book will help men confront our most hidden wounds so that we can learn how to address our worst pain, our worst memories, and our worst versions of ourselves if we truly want to heal.

Healing is a difficult journey, but a necessary one that we must take together. One that our children, our families, and even our own lives depend on. This is an invitation to forgive. This is an invitation to heal. This is an invitation to love once again. Join me.

Lesson I
Patience

Chapter 1

The Trouble with "I Love You"

"Mijo, I'll be fine."

"I know, Papá, but I want to be here with you."

"But you're busy. I'll be fine."

Even though it was hard to admit it, I was scared. This was my father's third back surgery in less than two years, and his insistence that he get it done so quickly worried me.

Of course I couldn't comprehend the level of pain he was in. The truth was that I wanted him to wait and get the procedure done at UCLA Medical Center, a more prestigious, well-known hospital. But like most of the men in my family, once my father's mind was made up, that was it. There was no turning back. And now we were both nervously looking at each other in anticipation of another major back surgery.

I had tried to convince my father not to go through with it. I had even introduced him to alternative holistic remedies, but soon it was clear that the pain was too unbearable for him to wait. So I bit my tongue and made sure that my father was in the right mental state before his surgery began.

As we waited for the nurses to come in and take him to the operating room, my father looked at me from his bed and gently said, "Mijo, I know you're busy, so you can go ahead and go. I will call you when they're done. The surgery's not going to last that long. I'll be fine. I'll give you a call as soon as I'm out."

Standing next to him, with my eyes glued to every movement he made, I replied, "No, Papá! I'll see you when you get out of surgery. I'm going to stay here with you and Mamá. Don't worry about it. I want to be here with you."

Just as I finished my sentence, the nurses came in to prepare him for the operation. And without saying anything more, I grabbed my father's left hand as the nurses began to wheel him into the operating room. It was an awkward but necessary moment. My father and I weren't accustomed to sharing any kind of physical contact, but in this instance, it was the only thing I could do to make sure he believed that everything would be okay.

As we approached the area reserved for hospital staff only, I looked one last time at my papá and told him, "Papá, everything's going to be okay. I love you." And without being able to respond, he just looked up at me and smiled. No words. No reply. Just a desperate look of acknowledgment and appreciation.

As the nurses whisked him away, I knew he would try and act tough. I knew that despite his best attempts to act fearless, despite his best attempts to look brave, he was afraid that the surgery wouldn't go well. I knew he would try to convince himself not to be scared. And I knew that he would be thinking about why he couldn't just find the courage to tell me that he loved me.

SACRED LESSONS

It was a bittersweet moment because all my life, both of us have struggled with sharing any kind of emotion with each other. And while I felt compassion in that moment of silence, the truth was that I was sad and angry that my father couldn't tell me he loved me. I knew that his own father had rarely, if ever, said those same words to him, but that didn't matter. All I wanted, all I've ever needed, was for my father to say, "I love you."

So, despite how I was feeling, I was there. I had to be there, and there was nowhere else in the world I wanted to be. I was exactly where I was supposed to be, in Ventura, the city where I grew up, holding my father's hand at Community Memorial Hospital of San Buenaventura.

As soon as the surgery began, I walked into the hospital waiting room, where my mother immediately looked at me and asked, "Is everything okay?"

"Yes, Mamá. Papá just went into surgery."

But my mamá knew me better than anyone else and understood that something was wrong. She could pick up on my fears without me saying anything. It was just that sixth sense. That motherly instinct that kicked in, and had her instantly trying to reassure me that the surgery would turn out fine.

"It's okay, Mijo. Your father is going to be okay."

Trying unsuccessfully to hold back my tears, I replied, "I know, Mamá. I just wish that he would have waited and got the surgery done at UCLA."

No longer keeping her distance, my mother moved closer and held me as she always did. "He's in too much pain. That's why he wanted to have the surgery done as soon as possible. Don't worry. Jesus will take care of him."

Jesus, the one name that always provided my mother with such calmness and assurance in the face of any doubt or danger.

The one person that she relied on more than anyone else. The one name that I didn't want to hear as I felt an utter sense of fear and uncertainty.

As I sat there in the waiting room trying to find anything to keep my mind off the situation at hand, I started thinking about my last words to my father: *Papá, everything's going to be okay. I love you.* I started thinking about how I usually rush those words when I say them to him. I started thinking about how this time around I made sure to make every syllable count, and to make sure that he heard every ounce of emotion I could squeeze into those three needed words.

You see, growing up, my father rarely told me and my younger brother Albert that he loved us. It wasn't that we didn't know he loved us. He absolutely did. It was just that he didn't know how to communicate his feelings. We took it as a foregone conclusion that he would just share his love in other ways, like coaching our Little League sports teams, taking us out to eat whenever we came home from college, or filling up our cars with gas when we came home to visit on the weekends. My father made sure to provide for us, and that was his way of telling us that he loved us deeply.

Maybe that's why I buy my son and daughter everything they want. Maybe that's why I have such a bad shopping habit. I learned from an early age, and in fact society taught me, that men show their love to their families by providing for them. It wasn't a question but a foregone conclusion that our society judges a man by his ability to financially support his loved ones. It's not our ability to be emotionally expressive. It's not our ability to be emotionally vulnerable with our children and partners. It's not our ability to ask for help. No, it's our ability to provide. No more, no less. And my father, like me, was no different.

SACRED LESSONS

I remember one time getting drunk with my father. Drinking together was the only time where it was okay for us to let down our guard and talk truthfully with one another. And during that rare moment, I asked him why it was so difficult for him to say, "I love you."

I distinctly remember him telling me, "Mijo, I don't ever remember your abuelo telling me that he loved me."

Shocked, I replied, "Papá, you don't remember abuelo telling you that he loved you? Not even once? Come on, he must have told you that he loved you."

Looking out into nothing, my father responded, "Maybe once or twice. But…"

After a slight hesitation, he continued, "As your abuelo and I have gotten older, he's started to tell me 'Mijo, te amo' in passing, but it always feels more like an afterthought. So the truth is that I didn't grow up hearing your abuelo or anyone else for that matter tell me that they loved me."

For some reason, more than likely because I was drunk, or maybe because I wasn't cognizant enough to know that I was breaking the male code of silence, I once again asked him, "You honestly don't remember abuelo telling you that he loved you?"

It seemed like minutes passed without a response until my father finally replied, "I guess your abuelo and I just don't know how to talk to each other."

"Don't know how to talk to each other?" I asked, even more confused.

But it was too late. My father was done talking and changed the subject before the conversation got too heavy, too truthful, or just too emotional. My father's response, like his feelings, was hidden from the world, and known only to him and him alone. Knowing my father, I knew that I wasn't going to get anything else from him that night, so I didn't push him to answer any more questions. And then I did what all the men in my family do during these rare moments: I relinquished my agency and retreated back into the bottle.

The inability to express his emotions was at the root of my father's complicated relationship with my abuelo. That was the reason for the difficulty my father had in sharing his thoughts and feelings with me, my brother, or my mother for that matter. And I believe to my core that that was one of the main reasons why I ended up in a hospital waiting room for the third time in less than two years hoping for another miracle.

Growing up in Ventura, California, and even till this day, I've always been acutely aware of how lucky I am to be the eldest son of Ismael "Mayo" de la Rocha, a man who taught, mentored, and transformed the lives of tens of thousands of students as a beloved community college professor for over forty years. A man who played an absolutely critical role in the massive social movements of the 1960s and '70s. A man who, if you asked him what his greatest accomplishment in life was, would immediately respond to you by saying that being a loving and present father to his two boys was his greatest legacy.

I guess that's the oxymoron of my story. Despite knowing that my father loved me and my brother more than life itself, I'm still trying to understand—and accept—why my papá had such a hard time telling me those three insignificant yet massively significant words: "I love you." And through my own introspection and self-work, I've realized that I can't blame my father for not learning how to verbally express himself to me or to those closest to him. I can't blame my father for how society indoctrinated him to be emotionless. I can't blame my father for the fact that his own father didn't tell him that he loved him enough, if at all.

SACRED LESSONS

In my family, it's not normal for the men to verbally express our affection to one another. *I can't tell you that I love you, but I can show you that I love you* was the unspoken rule. This is how it's always been for us de la Rocha men in México and in the United States. It's why, despite my mind telling me not to grab my father's hand while he was going into surgery, I did it anyway. It's why I know that my father wanted to respond to me before going into his surgery, but he just couldn't reply because he didn't know how.

The unfortunate part about all of this is that I almost didn't grab my father's hand because I was too worried about what the people in the hospital—or to be more specific, what the *men* in the hospital—would have thought about me. I've been so conditioned to believe that showing any kind of affection is a sign of weakness that I struggled to hold my own father's hand before his surgery because I didn't want to look too weak or too powerless. As I was fighting my own internalized homophobia, I didn't want to look too "gay" or too "feminine." I didn't want to look like I wasn't "man" enough.

This is the pain that I carry, and I know that my father carries. The pain of not being able to be ourselves, our whole and authentic selves. The pain of not being able to just let go. The pain of always having to perform for everybody in order to pretend that we're somehow "strong" enough. This is a form of trauma that leads to depression and worse. This is the kind of damage that still unfortunately affects both me and my father. This is why I'm in therapy and why I'm always trying to be loved by everyone else, even more so than myself.

Despite all this, in that moment, in the hospital room, none of it mattered. In that moment, my body instinctively knew what needed to happen. In that moment, I needed to hold my father's hand no matter what to provide him with a sense of reassurance and support. And in that moment, I knew that nothing would ever be the same again. I knew that something had to change. I knew that something had to be broken.

Chapter 2
Forever a Mamá's Boy

For as long as I can remember, I've always been a mamá's boy. From the moment that I took my first breath, I've had a special bond with my mother. And while this is a story about a father and a son, no story is complete without a mother.

Since the moment I was born, I've had to fight hard to survive. I was born premature, a "preemie" baby, born two months too early. I guess you could say that from day one, I came out swinging and fighting, not only to survive but to belong.

From the very beginning it was a pretty tough pregnancy for my mamá. Being the firstborn and oldest of two, my parents didn't know what to expect with me. To make matters worse, my mother developed toxemia, a condition during pregnancy characterized by high blood pressure, damage to the liver and kidneys, and swelling in the legs, which, if not treated properly, can lead to very serious, often fatal, complications for both the baby and the mother.

The entire pregnancy was a very traumatic experience for my parents. At seven months, my mom was in excruciating pain, with her feet and hands so swollen that she could barely walk on her own. The irony is that even though society portrays men as the tough ones in our families, my mamá, like most women, could endure a level of pain that would be unbearable for most men. This is why my father, no matter how macho he thought he was, was terrified the day my mom insisted that he take her to the hospital.

"Hon, we need to go to the hospital," my mother said with desperation in her voice.

"Just go to bed, you'll be fine," my father replied.

"Hon, I need to go to the hospital now, right now!"

"Go to sleep. You're not going to have the baby right now," my father said irritably. "It's too early to have the baby. Go to sleep. You'll be fine."

Upset and crying, my mother firmly looked at my father one last time and said, "You're either going to take me to the hospital now or I'm going to drive myself. I can't take this pain anymore. We need to go—now!"

Finally grasping the magnitude of what my mother was saying, my father reluctantly got out of bed and grabbed his keys to his blue 1970 Datsun 280Z to drive him and my mother to the old Saint John's Hospital that used to be located on F Street in Oxnard, California.

As soon as my parents arrived at the hospital, the nurses took my mother into an intensive care room to check on her high blood pressure. After a few minutes of running tests, the doctor pulled my father aside and told him, "Sir, if you hadn't brought your wife into the hospital tonight, she would have died. You're both extremely lucky. We're going to have to keep

SACRED LESSONS

her here for the next couple of days to make sure that she and your baby are okay."

Stunned, and more than likely ashamed for not believing my mother, my father finally uttered the words "thank you" to the doctor.

The next day, my Naná Daria, my maternal grandmother, was coming to town to surprise my mother. She had no clue what had happened the night before, and when my father picked her up at the Greyhound bus station, he just told her that my mom was in the hospital. Worried, and now even more of a nervous wreck than she already was, my grandmother didn't say a word to my dad as the two of them drove in silence to the hospital.

Upon seeing my naná, my mother immediately burst into tears. My mom, like me, was extremely close to her mother, and seeing my grandmother provided her with a sense of relief and assurance that she would be fine. My mother never knew her father because he left her and her family when she was just two years old. My Naná Daria raised my mamá, my aunts, and my uncles all by herself as a single mother living in a gritty working-class neighborhood in East San Jose, California.

My mom, Gloria de la Rocha, is the second youngest of eleven children. A devoted Catholic, she worked multiple jobs when I was young so I could attend private Catholic school. And even though her dream of me becoming a priest never materialized, my mom made sure that I was raised Catholic and afforded opportunities that she never had as a child. That's why for almost fifty years, my mom has dedicated her life to being a teacher for Head Start, a federally funded preschool program for poor and underserved children.

Growing up was hard for my mother. To make ends meet, she started working at a very early age, picking plums in the fields, cleaning houses with my grandmother, and doing whatever it took to help my naná pay the rent. Eventually, my naná would rely on my mother for everything. So, with her mother by her side, my mom was overcome by a sense of calmness in the midst of the increasing pain that was sweeping through her body.

Like my father, my mamá doesn't know how to stop working. She's the type of person who gets to work first and is the last person to leave. The person who takes work home with her and then finishes it after making food for the entire family and putting all the kids to sleep. The kind of person who's the most dependable employee, and thus given the most responsibility, oftentimes with the least amount of pay. That's why, despite being in terrible pain, my mother worked until her body couldn't work anymore. Working gave her a false sense of control in a world that undervalued and underappreciated her. Working allowed her to love strangers and the children who reminded her of herself. Working allowed her to live her Catholic values and fulfill her life's purpose.

On September 11, one day after my grandmother arrived and a day that would live in infamy some twenty-something years later, everything changed. On that day, my father noticed the nurses and doctor frantically reviewing my mother's charts and not for one second taking their eyes off her blood pressure monitor.

Finally, the doctor approached my father with a look of fear. "Sir, I need to speak with you."

Worried, my father responded, "Of course. Is everything okay?"

"No. I'm afraid that every time your wife has a contraction, her and your child's heartbeats slow down dramatically. We've

SACRED LESSONS

given her multiple medications, but her body is reacting negatively to everything we give her. She's in very serious danger."

"Serious danger? Is she going to be okay? Is the baby going to be okay?"

And without responding to my father's questions, the doctor simply replied, "I'm sorry, but we are going to have to operate on her immediately."

Without giving my father a second to say anything else, the doctor continued, "Given the dire circumstances, we can't save both your wife and your unborn child. I know that this is an extremely difficult question to ask, but if we can only save one life...would you want us to save your wife or your child?"

The moment he finished answering a question that has haunted me for my entire life, my father ran outside to his car and vomited profusely. As for my mother, she was immediately taken into the operating room for an emergency C-section surgery without fully knowing what was happening.

After an intense time of uncertainty, the operation was finally over. My father, who couldn't stop pacing back and forth in the hospital waiting room, ran toward the doctor who was walking toward him. "Doctor, Doctor, is everything okay? How's Gloria? How's the baby?!"

With a look of relief, the doctor replied, "We were able to save both your wife and your baby. They are both doing fine and are under observation. We have your son in the intensive-care unit so we can keep an eye on him, and you'll be able to see Gloria shortly."

Unable to shed the macho stereotype embedded in his psyche, my father hid his tears and graciously said, "Thank you so much, Doctor. You don't know how grateful I am."

"You're welcome. I know how hard this was for you and for your family, so please just try and get some rest. One of the nurses will come and get you to visit Gloria and see your baby boy soon."

Two months premature, I was so small that I could literally fit into the palm of one of my father's hands. In fact, the situation was so uncertain that my mother and I had to stay in the hospital for over a month. And despite this, once my mother and I were taken out of the intensive-care unit, my father went straight back to work. He didn't know what to do, so he did the one thing that he could control: He worked nonstop to distract himself from the situation, to avoid what he was truly feeling. Despite the detriment to his own health and well-being, my father felt like he had no other choice but to leave.

Now that I've had children of my own and felt the pressure of providing for my family, I've come to realize that my father was acting exactly the way that society had taught him to act. Rather than spending as much time as possible with my mother and me in the hospital, he simply reverted to his predetermined role as the "breadwinner." And despite what my father truly wanted to do, which was to be with his family in the hospital, in his mind he couldn't stay. He had to work. He had to economically provide for his family, no matter the cost to him, or to us.

Forty years later, I finally got the courage to ask my mother how she felt during that particular moment. "Mamá, how did you feel when Papá went straight back to work after I was born?"

Laughing, my mom said, "Well, I had Naná with me, so I was okay."

Knowing that would be her response, I jokingly replied, "I thought you would say this."

SACRED LESSONS

Still chuckling, my mother said, "They gave your father time off, but your father loves to work. So he went back to work. I was okay with it because I know that your father loves teaching."

Thinking that the story had ended with my father spending most of his time away from us, my mother continued, "But your father actually took time off from work after Naná left."

"He did? I didn't know this," I said, trying to hide the shock in my voice.

"At first, he would come home late from work and watch you so I could have a break. He was a very big help. But then…"

"But then…?"

"But then Papá took three months off of work so he could spend time with you."

With a big smile on my face, I said, "I never knew."

And with those words, my mother reminded me of my father's love. She reminded me that despite learning to work nonstop from my abuelo, and from all the men in his life, my father actually took time off to be with me. That from the very start, my father was being the present and loving father that he wished he would have had growing up. That deep down inside, even though it was hard for him to say it, my father really did love me.

Chapter 3
Meeting My Person

As the music began and the wedding party started walking down the aisle, Claudia leaned over to me and whispered, "Everyone says to look at the bride when she first makes her entrance, but make sure to look at my cousin's reaction when he first sees her."

We both stood up as the processional concluded and "Here Comes the Bride" began to play. Looking at the groom as his soon-to-be wife walked down the aisle, the hairs on my arms stood up. Underneath my black Ray-Ban sunglasses, I started to cry.

In that instant, I completely understood why Claudia had told me to focus on him. I understood why I couldn't control my tears. I couldn't stop reminiscing about our own wedding, about how I had that same look on my face when I first saw Claudia walking down the aisle in her gorgeous white dress and beautiful turquoise necklace.

As Claudia held tightly on to my arm, I couldn't help but wonder how lucky I was to still be in a relationship with a person

SACRED LESSONS

I'd met almost two decades ago. A person who, like my father said about my mother, had come when I least expected it but when I needed her the most. It is Claudia who has been my foundation through some of the toughest and greatest moments of my life, and I am honored to still call her my wife, and my best friend.

Claudia is one of the most caring and loving people I have ever met. A selfless person who wears her heart on her sleeve, she is brilliant and beautiful all rolled into one. We first spoke at her sister's wedding eighteen years ago. Our meeting will be forever ingrained in my heart because from that day forward we literally saw each other nonstop until I proposed to her one year later.

I always tell Claudia that I treated our relationship differently because she was not only the sister of a dear friend of mine, she also had a child from a previous marriage. And even though I had previously dated a woman with a child, I promised myself to never get involved with a woman with a child again, but here I was once again choosing to love. Consequently, I was on my best behavior from the very start. It was probably this decision, as much as any other, that cemented our partnership and allowed us to grow together despite the many hardships that come from being married and running a business together.

There's a saying that we often gravitate toward partners who are like our parents. And I must say that Claudia fits that saying perfectly. She has a lot of the same qualities and values as my mother. Both are extremely compassionate and giving. Both are incredibly smart and talented. And both are by far two of the best mothers and wives that any child and partner could ask for.

Claudia is my anchor and the person who holds me accountable more than anyone else. Like my mother's relationship with my father, she is the one person who's not afraid to tell me the hard truths. She is, and will always be, "my person," the one always looking out for the best interests of me and our family. She is the primary, and most important, relationship in my life. She is my teammate, my lover, and like I said before, my best friend.

Now don't get me wrong, marriage is hard, and I often get defensive when we argue, but we made a commitment to stick together through thick and thin. We made a commitment to work on our own issues and to admit when we are wrong. So, like my father, and his father, we find a way to work it out. It may not be pretty. I have made plenty of mistakes, and I'm still learning. But together we are always growing and evolving as a couple.

That's why the moment I decided to marry Claudia, I knew I had to do something special, not just for the two of us but also for me and my father. So I did what my papá wished he could have done if my mother had known her father. I asked him to be there when I asked my soon-to-be father-in-law for his permission to marry Claudia. Of course, this is a very patriarchal tradition that I fully admit to and struggled with then, and even now. But I knew how much it would mean to my father.

Wondering whether or not to say anything, I finally got the courage and timidly said one Saturday afternoon, "Papá, can I ask you something?"

"Yes, Mijo, what is it?" my father asked as he cut up pieces of freshly barbecued carne asada in the house that I grew up in for most of my adolescent life.

"I wanted to see if you could help me out with something."

Sensing the hesitation in my voice, my father put down his knife and looked straight into my eyes.

SACRED LESSONS

Nervously, I asked him, "I wanted to see if you could come to my house next weekend to help me ask Luis for his permission."

"Permission? Permission for what, Mijo?" my father replied.

"To marry Claudia."

It's not an exaggeration to say that even though I was confident he would say yes, I was still terrified to ask. I was afraid of not looking "strong" enough. And more than anything else, as I shared before, it just wasn't common for me to be so vulnerable with my father.

Instead of my father giving me a hug, like I knew he probably wanted to do, he just looked at me with a smile and said, "Absolutely, Mijo. I would love to be with you when you ask Luis for his permission to marry Claudia. I'd be honored."

One week later, my father arrived at my condo in North Hollywood for another carne asada BBQ, but only this time Claudia's parents, Luis and Mary Lou, were present.

My mom and dad had developed a great relationship with Claudia's parents and absolutely loved the fact that they were hardworking Latino immigrants. Luis was born and raised in Atengo, Jalisco, México, while Mary Lou was from Nicaragua, a country that my father loved and even spent time teaching in during the late 1980s.

From their first meeting, our parents developed a special bond. You could tell that they genuinely cared for each other and enjoyed spending time together. In fact, for my father, he saw himself in Claudia's family. He took immense joy in the fact that they only spoke Spanish. He loved that they had a large, tight-knit family who enjoyed throwing parties where everyone would be drinking and dancing all night long. And he completely loved being around la familia Torres because every time he got to be around them, he felt as if he were hanging out with his familia back home in Atascaderos, Chihuahua, México.

For my father, I know that my marrying Claudia brought him a sense of relief, because he didn't want me to forget about my cultural roots and upbringing. I know that, like I do every day, he questions his parenting skills and whether raising me and my brother in a predominately white environment was the best decision for me, and frankly, for the entire family. And I know that marrying Claudia reassured him that he had succeeded in making sure that I would remember who I am, a beautiful brown person of Mexican descent.

During my childhood, my parents chose to speak only Spanish to me. In fact, I didn't learn a single word of English until I went to preschool. As a baby, I would spend hours in my swing singing—no, yelling—the song "Los Pollitos Dicen," which translates in English to "The Chickens Say," at the top of my lungs. It filled my parents with such joy to see me express myself so comfortably in my native tongue that they even gave my brother his middle name, Tomás, after my favorite song from *El Show de Cepillín*, a hugely popular children's show that featured Cepillín, the most famous clown in all of México and arguably all of Latin America.

However, as I got older, English dominated everything around me, and it became harder for my parents to communicate with me only in Spanish. This tension came to a boiling point when my mother received a phone call from my preschool teacher requesting a meeting with her and my father.

Upon arriving at the school, my parents found me playing all by myself in the sandbox. Alone. Frightened. Crying. My mother instinctively wanted to run and comfort me, but my father immediately grabbed her arm. Trying not to get into

SACRED LESSONS

an argument in front of the teachers and students outside, my father simply said, "Leave Michael alone. We need to find out what's happening first and then we can come and get him. He's fine. Come on. There's teachers outside. He's going to be okay. Gloria, let's go. We have to meet with his teacher."

Knowing the words were eerily reminiscent of the ones he'd said when my mom was having contractions two days before I was born, my mother simply bit her tongue and walked beside my father as they entered the building to meet my preschool teacher.

During the meeting, my parents learned that none of the kids would play with me because I couldn't speak a single word of English. Even worse, the teacher informed my parents that the kids were calling me "ET," the name of the extraterrestrial alien from the hit Steven Spielberg movie. Destroyed, my father—who was reliving his own childhood trauma of being beaten in school for speaking Spanish—kept quiet as my mom thanked the teacher for sharing what was happening to me in school.

That night my parents had one of the most difficult conversations of their lives. That night they decided to stop speaking Spanish with me. And at that moment, English became the predominant language in my household, and in my life. It was a decision I know my parents regretted making but felt forced to make. It was a decision that has dramatically impacted my sense of self and identity since that fateful evening.

My parents could have found a middle ground and tried to keep speaking Spanish with me at home. But they choose not to do that. And although they had their reasons, which I may or may not agree with, I am forever grateful that they chose to take me to Boyle Heights every weekend so I could continue to communicate in Spanish with my grandparents and relatives without any ridicule or judgment.

To this day, I still struggle to speak Spanish because of the embarrassment that I feel from those earliest memories. I'm heartbroken that I can't shake the insecurity I feel because my language was stripped from me. Ironically, I can understand everything in Spanish and can even speak almost perfect Spanish with older people and children, but I still feel a sense of shame for not being able to fully communicate in my first language.

I know that my dad, probably more so than my mom, regrets this decision not only because he felt pressured into it, but because it contradicted what he was teaching in college, a deep love and appreciation of our Mexican culture, especially the beauty of our language. So yes, it's not an understatement to say that my dad was ecstatic when I told him I was going to marry a Latina from a traditional Spanish-speaking family who would ensure that Spanish would be a part of our lives forever.

Fast-forward to that Saturday afternoon as I sat there drinking Coronas in my backyard with my father and soon-to-be *suegro*. As I heard our parents speaking in Spanish, I began to get extremely nervous. It wasn't just because I was gonna ask Claudia's dad for permission to marry his daughter, but it hit me that even though Luis spoke some English, I would have to ask the most important question of my life to my future father-in-law in Spanish.

As the minutes, and then hours, quickly passed, I knew that if I was going to do something, it would have to be soon, before the sun set and everyone came into the condo. So, to speed up the situation, my father and I began drinking excessively, until we felt brave enough to finally go inside and pop the eternal question to don Luis: "Can I have your permission to marry your daughter?"

SACRED LESSONS

Right before the sun began to set, my father grabbed a tequila bottle, which he was known to do at parties, and in front of everyone looked at my future father-in-law and said, "Luis, ¿Quieres entrar para tomar un trago de tequila?"

Even though we hadn't spoken in detail about how the conversation would go, my father seemed more anxious than I was. As the three of us entered the house, I subtly closed the sliding door behind me so no one outside could hear us. We crammed into my tiny kitchen, and I grabbed three shot glasses and started to pour tequila as I turned to Luis and in my broken Spanish mumbled, "Luis, I want to ask you something."

"Por supuesto, dime."

Translation: "Well yes, what do you want to ask me?"

And before I could say another word, my father moved right in between Luis and me and started speaking in Spanish, "Luis, I hope you know how much we adore your family. This last year we have grown to love Claudia more and more as a daughter."

As he continued to speak, my father's voice started to crack, and I could see Luis trying vehemently to stop any kind of tears from forming in his eyes.

"I guess what I'm trying to say is that I would like to ask for your permission. I would personally like to get your blessing for my son Michael to marry your daughter Claudia."

Sensing that all of us were about to cry uncontrollably, Luis quickly said yes. As we all raised our glasses to take an unforgettable shot of tequila, I remember smiling so big inside because my father looked not only relieved but extremely proud.

Given that we wanted to keep the wedding proposition a secret, the entire conversation happened in the blink of an eye. What I remember is don Luis being extremely grateful that we came to him in such a traditional way. It was a surreal moment where two patriarchs came together to decide what was best for their children. It was the old-fashioned way. It was the deeply patriarchal way. It was the one way that I felt I could honor the sacred tradition of marriage being the way to bring two families together.

One week after that conversation, I proposed to Claudia and my life changed forever. I'll save all the details for a later time, but let's just say that it was a very special moment underneath the stars of Venice, Italy. With the song "One" by my favorite band U2 playing under a night sky lit by fireworks, I got on my knees and asked Claudia to marry me. It was the moment when I decided to commit not only to myself but to someone else. It was the moment that transformed me into the person I am today. It was the moment I try to remember every single time my ego tells me that it's too difficult to stay.

French Romantic writer Victor Hugo once said, "The supreme happiness of life consists in the conviction that one is loved." And no greater words were ever spoken. As I reflect on my unfolding life journey with Claudia, I am humbled and grateful that our paths crossed when they did. I met "my person," who not only compliments my personality but pushes me to be my best self. Someone who not only challenges me, but who chooses, day in and day out, to love me. And there is no greater gift, no greater feeling, no greater conviction, than knowing that I am truly loved.

Chapter 4
Inheriting a Daughter

Patience. It's such a tricky word. It's an attribute you don't often associate with men because of all the societal conditioning that teaches us to be anything but patient. The closest men in my life, my father and my grandfather, are two of the most impatient people I know. Through them, I've learned to act swiftly and decisively. Rationally and emotionlessly. And like them, patience is something I've had to work really hard to develop.

As I've gotten older, I've started to learn the wisdom of patience and of allowing the space for what's supposed to unfold to unfold. I've started to see how grind culture and the desire for immediate gratification has contributed to my father's health challenges, and to me getting sick too often. And I've come to realize, by watching my father struggle with his increasing health problems, that slowing down is literally a matter of life or death.

As I've reflected on the reasons why I've decided to work on being calmer and more collected, I've realized that my daughter, Mayela, more than anyone else in my life, has taught me the benefits of slowing down. Maybe it's because I've seen time go by so quickly through watching her grow up. Or maybe it's because of my love for her, which has taught me to be open and more understanding with her and, by default, everyone else in my life. Regardless, my first child has been nothing short of a test in fortitude and the importance of me challenging my own habits and behaviors.

In many African and indigenous cultures around the world, there's a saying that children choose their parents from the spirit world. For me, I absolutely believe this to be true. Children come into this world knowing all of our gifts as well as the lessons that we still have left to learn. They know what buttons to press and what issues are still left unresolved. As for Mayela, she is not only the glue in my relationship with Claudia but also the sweet little girl who came into my life to teach me the importance of patience.

I vividly remember meeting Mayela for the first time when she was almost two years old. After five months of dating, Claudia finally decided it was time for me to meet her daughter. So, on a warm, sunny weekend, I met Mayela and Claudia at the Grove, a trendy outdoor shopping mall in Los Angeles.

Crouching down so I was eye level with her, I said, "Hi. I'm Michael. What's your name?"

Hesitantly, she replied, "Mayela."

"It's nice to meet you, Mayela. Your mom has told me so much about you. Are you hungry? Do you want to go and get something to eat?"

As she tightly gripped Claudia's hand, she looked up to her mother for approval and then nodded to me with a resounding "Yes."

SACRED LESSONS

I still have a picture of meeting Mayela for the first time. It's a picture of us at a table, with our heads lying on our arms as we made funny faces at each other. I was smitten with Mayela from day one. And from that moment forward, I knew that I was committing myself to not just Claudia but also to her beautiful little girl.

From a very early age, Mayela has consistently provided me with insight and clarity. She has helped me understand her mother's perspective as well as how my actions are contributing to making any situation better or worse. And she has been my inspiration to do everything I can to slow down for the benefit of not only myself but also for our household, and for my relationship with her and her mother.

I've always treated Mayela as my daughter because she *is* my daughter. For almost her entire life, she's grown up having two dads and two households. She has grown up with four sets of grandparents and going back and forth during holidays and birthdays. And I've seen the inherent challenges of her growing up with two different families. The difficulty that she had alternating from our house to her biological dad's house. The weekly conversations we used to have as two families when she was younger to ensure that we were always on the same page. And till this day, the uncertainty about whether we made the right decisions and the right choices all along the way.

Being a parent is a constant test of patience. From worrying about Mayela's well-being to doing all that I can to give her everything she needs, parenting is hard. There's no textbook for how to parent, no manual to read that explains how I should handle certain situations until I experience them firsthand. Instead, parenting is a continual trial-and-error journey where I've learned to communicate better with Claudia, follow my natural instincts, and have faith that we are doing the best we can to raise her.

Through my relationship with Mayela, I have been challenged to stop projecting my own unmet needs as a child, or even my anxieties as a parent, onto her. As we both have gotten older, I've been forced to become more cognizant of the fact that I'm sometimes nitpicky about the little things, like her taking too long to get ready or her room being messy, because I'm fighting that little child within me that got in trouble for the exact same things. Now don't get me wrong, I'm still a work in progress, and I still get upset at these things, but more than anything, Mayela has tested my patience with not only her but also with myself.

Up until recently, I've struggled with finding enough time to spend with her and the rest of my family. The demands of work often forced me away from them, and I felt guilty for missing quality time with them. In the past, I would justify this by saying that I had to work nonstop to provide for them, but this was always a half-truth. As Mayela has gotten older, I've realized that I can't get back the time I've lost with her. I've realized that I have to make a conscious effort to spend more quality time with her, such as Claudia and I planning our family vacations around her school schedule. And I've realized that prioritizing her, my son, and my wife is what matters most to me.

There is absolutely nothing that Claudia and I wouldn't do for Mayela and our son Mio. We've made sure to provide them with everything they need to be successful in life: a loving home, food on the table, and the best possible education we could afford. And while this is something I know we are committed to doing, I must admit that we, or mostly I, sometimes fall short.

With college on the horizon for Mayela, Claudia and I sacrificed buying our first home so we could pay for her to go to one

SACRED LESSONS

of the best private schools in Los Angeles. We made sure to spend as much time as possible with our parents so she could learn the importance of family. And we made sure to consistently remind her of how brilliant and beautiful she is despite what society or anyone else may try to convince her to believe.

I thought that by doing all these things she would be set up for success, that she would grow up and always be that confident little girl who didn't care about what other people thought about her. That little girl who was open to trying new things and being the best nine-year-old drummer I've ever heard, who absolutely loved fashion and wasn't afraid of taking on the world. That little girl who was living her dreams.

Unfortunately, I was wrong. As Mayela got into one of the most "prestigious" high schools, it became clear that her self-esteem was taking a beating from attending a predominantly white private school. It made her doubt her brilliance and dim her light. Till this day, I try my best to not beat myself up about this. I remind myself that I was doing what I thought was best for her. I was paying a fortune for her private high school because she was supposed to have access to the best teachers and a network that would benefit her later in life. I was doing all this because that's what society told me I needed to do.

Hindsight is always twenty-twenty, and I now know that her high school may have prepared Mayela academically, but it did little to encourage her to love herself. Mayela's sense of self-worth was dramatically impacted by the fact that she was only one of two Latinas in her entire class, and only one of a handful of students of color in the entire school. I should have known better from my own experience that going to a predominantly white high school would affect Mayela's self-esteem, but instead,

I pretended that things were somehow different, or even worse, that things had actually changed.

Mayela is a beautiful dark-skinned woman who gets treated very differently than me because of her gender and because of the color of her skin. As a light-skinned Chicano, I'm afforded opportunities that I know are not given to dark-skinned people like my daughter. As a straight man who grew up in a middle-class neighborhood and attended middle-class schools, I know that I was given a head start in life. And despite my social status and access, I was unsuccessful in shielding my daughter from the painful reality of race and gender.

Toni Morrison said it best when she said, "The very serious function of racism is distraction." My false thinking that a predominately white school would be better for Mayela was a distraction from what she really needed. Because of its overwhelming whiteness, the school was incapable or unwilling to provide my daughter with the resources, the tools, and the environment she needed to thrive as a young woman of color. And my internalized racism, and the false belief that the white school was better for her, was why I didn't even notice that it was negatively impacting her sense of self until it was too late.

Ever since she was a child, Mayela had dreamed of going to UCLA. I would frequently take her to the campus that changed my life and share with her crazy stories of my early days as a student organizer and being elected the undergraduate student body president. She grew up seeing my closest mentor and some of my best friends, all people that I met at UCLA. She knew how much the campus meant to me, and how much I wanted her to go there. And if I'm being completely honest, I agreed 100 percent to enroll her in a private school because of the high probability that she would be accepted at my alma mater.

SACRED LESSONS

It was in this backdrop when it all came to a head. After four years of intense college-prep classes and endless nights studying for exams, Mayela was finally applying for college. She had done everything she was supposed to do. She had gotten good grades. She had written an excellent essay. And she was the daughter of an influential alumnus. Even though I was pretty confident she would get into UCLA, my nervousness was palpable.

As we all sat around the dinner table waiting for Mayela to open her UCLA college acceptance email, I put my hand on her shoulder and said, "I'm so proud of you, babe. Whatever happens, know that Mamá and I are so, so proud of you."

And before she clicked on the email, Mayela looked up at me with those same innocent eyes that I had seen for the first time sixteen years earlier at the Grove and replied, "I know, Michael."

As she sat at the corner of the dining room table, with Claudia, Mio, and me standing around her, Mayela slowly opened the email. Within seconds of her not screaming with excitement, I knew that she hadn't gotten into UCLA. And before she could look up at us with tears in her eyes, I started crying.

At that moment, I hated that I couldn't do anything to comfort my daughter. I hated that there was nothing I could say, or nothing that I could do, to change the situation. I was angry. I was bitter. And I was pissed off that I had let my guard down for a split second and believed that we could somehow run faster than our race. I hated the fact that I couldn't do anything to shield my daughter from the cold reality of the world.

For weeks I beat myself up and questioned whether I had done enough to get Mayela into UCLA. I wondered if putting her into private school was the best decision. I wondered if there was an extra phone call I could have made or an extra class she could have taken. And in the end, I had to accept that my wife and I had done everything we could to give her a fighting chance. I had to have faith that everything would turn out fine. I had to know that Mayela had done her absolute best and that we had raised an incredibly resilient and smart girl who would succeed no matter what college she decided to go to.

In the end, my daughter was very fortunate and ended up enrolling at another incredible university in Los Angeles. As Mayela started her first year of college, my wife reminded me about the importance of having patience with her transition. She reminded me of how COVID-19 had forced her to miss out on several life-defining moments, such as going to prom or having her first job in high school. And she reminded me about how I had to be patient with the fact that the ongoing pandemic was still impacting Mayela's sense of safety and affecting her decisions, including her wanting to go to a college that was close to home.

As Mayela started her second semester, it became clear that she was struggling with the transition. So, I decided to pick her up one evening and take her out to dinner so we could have some time to talk about what was going on.

As we were driving to a nearby pizza place, I asked, "Mayela, how's school going?"

"It's okay."

Knowing this was the typical teenager response, I pressed a little more. "I mean, tell me more about your new classes. Do you like them? Are there any classes that really interest you?"

"There's one political science class that I really enjoy. The teacher is great, and I'm learning a lot from it."

Sensing an excitement that I hadn't heard from her for quite some time, I probed some more. "What kinds of things are you learning?"

SACRED LESSONS

"I'm learning a lot about race and how racism affects us all."

Without me saying a word, she continued, "I didn't know that a high number of youth of color, specifically African American youth, die every year because many youth of color haven't been taught how to swim. My teacher is really helping me see how racism impacts everything. He's helping me see how race has shaped my life."

I don't want to say that this was the first adult conversation I'd ever had with my Mayela, because it wasn't, but it was definitely one of the most impactful. At that moment, I breathed a sigh of relief, because no matter what the future may hold for her, I realized that Mayela was exactly where she was supposed to be. She was learning the lessons that she was supposed to be learning. And no matter what, this college journey would make her stronger and wiser. And in my heart of hearts, I knew she would be okay.

After she finished talking about her class, I pushed a little more to gain some additional insight into what had happened during her first semester in college. "So how were your grades last semester?"

Caught off guard, Mayela immediately replied, "Mom didn't tell you?"

Acting dumb, I said, "No. What happened?"

"Are you serious, Michael? You don't know anything?"

I didn't respond directly to her question, but instead I shook my head. "No."

She then proceeded to let me know about the difficulty she'd had during her first semester and how hard it was for her to make new friends. We spent the next hour talking, with me letting her know that what she was feeling was completely normal. I told her that I had had the same challenges in college and that it was important for me, as it is for her, to ask for help. I shared that it was also critically important for her to take advantage of tutoring and the specialized services that colleges offer students of color.

As we ate our pizza and basked in the time that we got to spend together, all I could think about was that I wished my father would have had the same talk with me when I was struggling in college. I kept thinking about how much I had grown in my relationship with Mayela, and how much I appreciated that we could be honest and open with each other.

As I dropped Mayela off at her college dorm room, I gave her a big hug before she got out of the car and made sure to tell her that I loved her. And in that moment, I was reminded once again of how quickly time passes. Here I was dropping off my daughter at her college dorm when it seemed like only yesterday that I was playing dolls with her or taking her to karate practice. As Mayela walked away, Claudia's words rang in my ear once again: *Michael, be patient with her. She's going to be okay.*

All I could do was smile in that moment as I thought about how blessed I was to have Mayela in my life. Like I shared before, she and her mom came into my life at the absolute perfect time, when I was finally ready to commit to having a family, and when I was finally ready to give and to receive love.

Whether it was destiny or luck, I know that Mayela is one of the greatest gifts I have ever received in my life. She has made me a better father, a better husband, and a better person. And there is no greater joy than watching her grow into the mature and intelligent woman that she is today.

Mayela has taught me how to slow down and how to enjoy life. She has taught me how to be resilient and how to be more patient. And while I may want to hold on to that shy and rambunctious little girl that I met almost twenty years ago, I know that truly loving Mayela means that I must trust her decisions and learn to let go of any expectations. In the end, no matter what happens, I must have the confidence to know that she has a solid foundation to thrive in whatever career she chooses or wherever life may take her. And that sense of assurance—or dare I say faith—is all I, or any father, could truly ask for.

Lesson II

Forgiveness

Chapter 5
Muy Macho

All my life I've heard, and struggled not to internalize, the statement, "Real men don't cry." And no one in my family, actually no one in my life, exemplifies this statement more than my abuelo Alberto de la Rocha.

My grandfather was born on November 27, 1918, in Atascaderos, México, in the same house and in the same pueblo as my father. The fifth born of ten children, my abuelo was what you would describe as *puro* Mexicano, meaning he was from that generation that always wore a cowboy hat with a buttoned-up shirt, dark polyester pants, and worn-down boots.

Formally educated through the third grade, my abuelo had no choice but to have a hardened exterior because his father, my great-grandfather Raúl, was a man who raised his children with an iron fist. Nobody, and I mean nobody, would dare talk back to my bisabuelo or else they would be severely punished. On top of that, life in el rancho was just different from life here in the United States. Over there, you settled things the old-fashioned way: mainly through fistfights or gunfights. And for whatever reason, trouble always had a way of finding my abuelo no matter what side of the border he was on.

In his early twenties, my grandfather left for the United States to work alongside other Mexicanos who were part of the Bracero Program, a temporary guest worker program in which almost five million Mexicans worked in the fields across the US from 1942 to 1964.

My grandfather, along with his younger brother Moises and about twenty other relatives, would work before the sun came up and hours after the sun went down in the scorching-hot fields of California. I could say a whole lot more about his experience, and about how my abuelo lived in the most inhumane conditions, but let's just say that this moment in history contributed to my grandfather's alcoholism and bouts of rage. America was never kind to my abuelo, or any other brown person for that matter. This is the reason why my abuelo finally decided to leave the bracero camp and run away.

After laboring for about five years in the strawberry fields of Oxnard, California, my abuelo was fed up with being overworked, underpaid, and living in a filthy housing barrack. So one day in the middle of the night, he quickly packed up all his belongings and left. He didn't care that it was against the law to leave. He didn't blink an eye at the fact that he would be severely beaten if he was caught. And even though he didn't know where he was going or what he was going to do, my grandfather knew that he had no choice but to leave.

My abuelo ended up traveling forty miles south to Boyle Heights in East Los Angeles. Once there, he found work cutting aluminum for the screen windows that were being put in all the new tract homes. It was the 1950s, and my abuelo worked

SACRED LESSONS

day and night to save enough money to bring his family to Los Angeles. Over the next twenty years, my abuelo managed to purchase a home, a liquor store, and even a small, grungy bar. And while I could write a whole other book on all the illicit activity that transpired during this time, let me just say that I remember not seeing my grandfather for over five years when I was younger because he was on "vacation," code for being in prison.

It was these experiences that contributed to my father and grandfather's very complicated relationship. You see, my father never really knew my abuelo until he immigrated to America at the age of seven. As a result, they never really developed a close father-son bond. In fact, even when my father moved to Boyle Heights, he rarely saw my grandfather because he was always working. The only time he would see him would be at 5:00 a.m. for breakfast or on weekends when he would go to work with him. This, coupled with the fact that my abuelo would come home late at night and then yell at my naná for no reason, led to my father distancing himself from my abuelo from a very early age.

I always knew that there was a tension between my father and my abuelo. There was never an outright argument between them, but there was a lot said in their silence and in their body language. I never asked my father anything because it was too taboo of a subject to broach. Instead, I learned about their difficulties through my mother, who would share stories of how my father was always trying to get the approval of my abuelo. My father had tried to make my grandfather proud of him by being a track star in high school, being the first in his family to go to college, and being my abuelo's most reliable and dependable child. He wanted my grandfather's validation so much that he even named his second son, Albert, after my grandfather. But

43

in the end, nothing worked. My abuelo never once went to one of my father's track meets or even visited him when he was in college.

This lack of attention and approval hurt my father very deeply. He, like myself, simply wanted the love of his father. Although he never mentioned this to me or my brother, he did express these feelings to my mother. More than anything else, my father did everything in his power to make sure that our relationship didn't mirror the fractured relationship that he had with my abuelo for so long. He made sure that my brother and I knew that we could depend on him, no matter what was going on in our lives. And he made sure that he was present, and that he was attentive to all of our needs.

Regardless of their strained relationship, my abuelo and I developed a very special bond and connection. Whether it was because I was the firstborn grandson or because I used to visit him often as a child, my grandfather and I just clicked. Every time we saw each other we would both immediately light up. And even though I could barely speak Spanish and he could barely speak English, we were able to communicate in a way beyond words. Even to this day when I close my eyes, I can vividly see him making that trademark de la Rocha smirk when he would see me walk into his rancho in Clovis, California.

I absolutely loved and adored my abuelo. Since my mother never knew her dad, I only ever had one grandfather. He was the epitome of a patriarch and the person who taught me not only how to survive in America, but also how to hold on to my cultural identity. He was a stoic and hardened man. A hustler and a womanizer. But also one of the most gentle and loving souls, who modeled for me the importance of prioritizing family.

SACRED LESSONS

Despite the armor around his emotions, my abuelo was actually the first man in my family I ever saw cry. It was at my parents' house as my grandmother took her final breath. I was holding my Naná Cuca's left hand while my grandfather gripped her right. As we both said our goodbyes, the hardened man became a baby and we both cried as we kissed her one last time. It was a surreal moment that I will cherish forever. It was a moment of anguish and of letting go. The first moment that I saw the love of my grandfather on full display.

This moment not only deepened my relationship with my abuelo, but it also transformed my father's relationship with him. During those final months of my grandmother's life, their resentments slowly started to fade away and a new relationship began to form between the two most important men in my life. Watching my father and my abuelo repair their broken relationship provided me with one of life's greatest lessons: that forgiveness doesn't have an expiration date. And despite the pain of their past, the death of my grandmother propelled my father and abuelo to do what they had been conditioned to never do as men: let go and try to heal their broken relationship.

As a son and as a grandson, this was a sight to behold. I wasn't used to my dad expressing any kind of emotion with my grandfather, let alone wanting to spend time with him. My father certainly did not forget all the years of fighting, but he did learn how to forgive my grandfather. Watching my abuelo and father rebuild their relationship showed me the power of commitment. It showed me how both men had to compromise and how both men had to want to build a new kind of relationship despite the constant pull of their past.

And nothing showed this more than a time when I went to visit my parents and saw my papá actually having a conversation with my grandfather over the phone.

"Hola, pops. ¿Cómo estás?"

And with his gritty, beat-up voice, my abuelo responded, "Estoy bien, hijo. No más aquí, cuidando los caballos."

Shockingly my father didn't end the conversation as he was accustomed to doing but instead asked, "¿Qué planes tiene para hoy?"

My grandfather then replied, "No tengo planes, solo quiero descansar."

Five minutes later, after chit chatting with my grandfather about his plans for the week, my father hung up the phone and went back to lying in his reclining chair. I was stunned, because my father didn't like to talk to anyone over the phone, not even to me or my brother. And even though it was my mom who handed him the phone, my papá didn't fight her and uncharacteristically had a brief conversation with my grandfather.

If it weren't for the persistence of my mother, I don't know if my father would have tried to make amends with my abuelo. It was the pain of not knowing her own father that motivated my mom to push my dad to do all he could to build a healthy relationship with my grandfather. It was my mom who made it a point to regularly check in on my abuelo and to make sure that my dad spoke to him. It was my mom who knew the healing power of time and of forgiveness. It was my mom who willed this to happen.

It may seem silly, but it's not typical for me, or my father, or really any of the men in my family to have long, detailed conversations in person or over the phone. And while my cousins and I are trying to change this pattern, we still have a long way

SACRED LESSONS

to go. I know that deep down inside we want to connect more, especially with our fathers, but more often than not, we end conversations before they become too uncomfortable for us. We end them right at the point when we need to lean in and let go. We end them right when we're on the cusp of breaking free from traditional gender norms of how men are supposed to act.

This is the kind of protective shell that I witnessed melt away during the years following my Naná Cuca's passing. And while my father's conversations with my abuelo weren't an hour long or even more than five minutes, it was enough, more than enough for my father to show my abuelo that he cared for him and was trying to make up for lost time. It was a defining moment in my life, because I saw what was possible and that men could indeed change.

Months before my grandfather passed away, my mother and I drove to see him at his ranch. Seeing my abuelo so weak and frail was painful to witness. As he battled dementia and willed his body to hold on just a little bit longer, my grandfather was having a hard time remembering people and finding the right words to express his needs. One moment he'd be laughing, and the next moment he'd be imagining he was in his twenties going to some dance in Chihuahua to meet girls and get drunk with his best friend Enrique.

As we sat together and laughed, he tried his best to remember me, then he suddenly spontaneously started singing what can only be described as his own personal corrido, "Tu bien sabias que yo era muy pobre y borracho, pero siempre bien macho."

Translation: "You knew that I was very poor and a drunk, but I've always been very macho."

It was a tender moment that said so much. It was my abuelo's statement to his wife, or some other person trapped in his memory. It was his declaration of manhood. It was his reminder to us all that his manliness was what mattered most to him, the perfect song for him to sing as he neared the end of his life.

A few months later, I took my wife and baby boy to have breakfast with him for his 104th birthday. We sat there laughing as my grandfather ate his entire plate of food and looked healthier than I had seen him in years. He was very alert and talked to us the entire time. I made sure to sit next to him and to take as many pictures as possible. He had survived so much, and I just wanted him to know that I valued him deeply and appreciated all that he had done for us.

Unfortunately, this would be the last time I would see my grandfather alive. It was a bittersweet memory, but one that I am so grateful I got to have with him and my family. It ended with "I'll see you soon, abuelo" rather than "goodbye." And in those moments today when I need him the most, I honestly feel him with me on a very sensory and spiritual level.

There's something about death that either brings families closer together or destroys them. I wish there was another way, and I'm sure there are other possibilities, but in my experience, the loss of a loved one often has two roads: healing, or adding more fuel to a burning fire. When my grandfather passed, the latter unfortunately happened to my family.

Without my father around, there was no one to mediate after the death of my abuelo, no one to be the voice of reason, no one to bring us back together. I tried my best to be the middle person, to put compassion ahead of my ego, and my family before my pride. I tried, but in the end, I wasn't successful.

This was one of the most painful moments of my life. A time when I was supposed to be celebrating the life of an extraordinary

SACRED LESSONS

man and expressing what my abuelo meant to me and my family instead became a time when my heart was utterly broken.

During the days leading up to my abuelo's wake, things started to get really toxic. My uncles and aunts were not talking. My immediate family didn't know the details for the funeral. And all I wanted to do was say goodbye to my abuelo in a dignified and heartfelt way.

A few days later, I texted my Uncle Javier, who was planning the funeral with my Aunt Guadalupe: Javier, my mom, brother, and I have decided that I will speak on behalf of my father at the wake. Please let us know if there is a reception or if you need anything else.

A few minutes later his reply came in: Guadalupe has the schedule made up. Can you call her and let her know? Also, can I count on you guys to be pallbearers?

I immediately replied: I will be a pallbearer and I'm sure that my brother will too. I don't understand what's so difficult about me speaking. I shouldn't have to ask Guadalupe for permission. She wouldn't do this to my dad, and she shouldn't do this to me. If she doesn't put me on the program that's on her conscience. The fact that no one approached the oldest grandson to speak is disappointing.

As the years of pain started to bubble over the surface, my uncle responded: There's a misunderstanding; all grandkids were sent invites to speak through Messenger. Guadalupe paid for all the services and funeral expenses, and she's calling the shots. I don't think that she cares that you weren't personally approached. We were denied something much greater, and no one gave a shit. I'll pass your text on to her, though.

The pain was palpable. Rather than respond in anger, rather than respond from a place of hurt, I waited a few hours to gather my thoughts and composure. Finally, after taking a long walk outside in the crisp night air, I texted my uncle back and said: I pray that your heart heals, Javier. I will see you soon.

Two days later, I was at Rose Hills Cemetery in Whittier as we laid my grandfather to rest. The tension among my family had reached a breaking point. My Uncle Albert, who had spent the last ten years watching over my abuelo, was absent. My niño was not even making eye contact with my aunts and uncle. And I was still unsure if I'd be speaking at the wake.

Upon arriving at SkyRose Chapel, I was anxious and worried. I swallowed my pride and went up to the front row and gave my condolences to my aunts and uncle. I made sure not to make a big deal about the fact that there weren't any seats reserved for my mother, brother, and me up front. And as I sat there quietly holding my wife's hand, I tried my best to keep my emotions from getting the best of me.

I'd be lying if I didn't say that I was hoping everything would be okay. That my aunts and uncle would have stood up and embraced me. That my name would have been called by the priest for me to share some words about my abuelo. But none of this happened. Instead, I made sure to be the first person to stand up when the wake was over so I could be the first person in line at the open casket to say my final goodbye to my beloved grandfather.

I stood there, looking at the lifeless shell of my grandfather in his casket, and whispered, "Abuelo, thank you. Thank you for everything. Thank you for your sacrifice. Thank you for your love. Thank you for your life."

Tears rushed down my face, and the line behind me grew longer and longer. I silently continued, "You can go and rest

SACRED LESSONS

now, Abuelo. You have done your best. You can't do anything to fix the situation. It's up to us now. Te amo."

As I bent over to give one last kiss to the person who had sacrificed so much for me and my family, I was heartbroken, mourning the loss of my abuelo as the last of his generation. And I was mourning the loss of another opportunity for my family to let go of their pain so that we could all heal together.

There are always two sides to a story and then the truth. For me and my family, there are many perspectives and many reasons why things happened the way they did. Many fingers were pointed, many feelings were hurt, and many words should have never been spoken. Despite all of this being true, it didn't make the situation any better.

As the weeks went by and I was able to get a clearer perspective on everything, I learned to find the wisdom in all the emotions. I learned to sit still with my feelings and to try my best to find the lessons in the situation. And in doing so, I've realized that I'm trying to break unhealthy patterns that have been passed down to me, passed down to all of us, for generations. I'm still working to dismantle bad habits I've inherited, not just for my son and daughter but also for my father and abuelo, who I learned these habits from in the first place. I've learned that the division within my family is a result of our unwillingness to listen, our inability to express what we truly feel, and ultimately our inability to forgive and to let go.

I can now see the pain that each one of my uncles and aunts is carrying. I can now see the unfortunate battles for control. I can now see that we're not as different as I once may have thought. I now realize that I was triggered by what was said and by what was done during the final months of my abuelo's life. My reaction was more about my own ego and the work that

I still needed to do internally, not just externally. The fighting among my aunts and uncles had nothing to do with me and everything to do with their own trauma and need for healing.

As time passes and emotions subside, I think about the relationship between my father and my abuelo. I think about the hurt, about the pain, about their reconciliation. And in these moments, I still hold on to hope. I still hold onto the belief that my family will someday come back together, that we will learn to forgive and to let go, and that my abuelo's wish for his family to stay together will eventually come true.

Till this day, I celebrate my abuelo for his enduring love and sacrifice. I continue to speak with him daily, because his physical body may be absent but his spirit is always with me. And that's why I wrote the following on my social media on the night that he passed away.

> It is with a heavy heart that I share that my grandfather, Alberto de la Rocha, the patriarch of my family, has passed away.
>
> Last night, as I did my ceremonial offerings to prepare him for his journey, I was approached by two coyotes—symbols of wisdom and family, trickery and resourcefulness—and was reminded of a son guiding his father, and a father needing his son.
>
> O Great Spirit, guide my abuelo as he makes his journey home to you. Forgive him for his sins, and let his heart suffer no more. Let him bask in the beauty of your eternal love, and thank you for giving him to us for such a long time.

SACRED LESSONS

The last of his generation, my abuelo joins his wife and all his brothers and sisters in the realm of our ancestors.

He lived to be 104 years old.

A blessing, a blueprint, a life fulfilled.

He gave all that he had to give, and then some.

A man who defied expectations and brought his family from the sierras of Chihuahua to the barrios of Boyle Heights.

My grandfather did not have an easy life, but he never once complained.

He sacrificed for his children.

He sacrificed for his grandchildren.

He sacrificed for his great-grandchildren.

And he leaves behind nothing short of a miracle.

I can't put into words what my abuelo means to me.

The complete and utter definition of a Mexicano.

A gun-slinging, unassimilated, tequila-drinking, sombrero-wearing, Spanish-speaking, stubborn old man.

They don't make them like my abuelo anymore— or maybe they do, I don't know.

But what I do know for sure is that my grandfather taught me to appreciate, cherish, and love my culture.

He was my direct connection to México.

He was my source of pride and the person who taught me to love myself.

So today I will focus on his journey to the spirit world.

I will spend time reflecting on his beautiful life.

I will share stories and memories of him with my son and my family.

I will thank him for his hard work and dedication.

I will remember his fortitude and his vision.

And I will honor him for his life and his sacrifice.

Abuelo, mi sangre es tuya

Te extraño y te amo

I am grateful

For your life

For your legacy

For tu corazón.

Chapter 6
Besito Grande

"Papá, what's wrong? Why are you crying?" I asked my little boy, Mio.

My son was lying on the couch with his head thrown into the cushions crying uncontrollably. If we didn't leave soon, we would be late to his soccer practice, and I was starting to become irritable because he wasn't responding to any of my questions.

In the past, I would have demanded that he get up. I would have counted to three, and I would have threatened to take his Nintendo Switch or iPad away from him to force him to go to practice. It was what my parents did to me as a child, and I guess it was instinctual for me to respond in the same way. It was the unspoken and spoken rule: *Do what I say or else...* or better yet, *Do what I say, or you won't get what you want.* A very male, aggressive response, but nonetheless my go-to response in the immediate moment.

As a child, my father instilled in me the importance of finishing what I started. He taught me that it was important to be a person of my word and to be consistent in my actions. As it relates to sports, and life in general, he taught me to never let my teammates down, by always giving my best no matter what, which also meant never missing practice. Nothing, from being too tired to being too hurt, was an excuse for me to miss practice. Nothing.

So as my son lay face down on the sofa, memories of my own childhood flooded my mind. And right when I was about to yell at my son, right when I was about to project all of my childhood frustrations onto my little boy who clearly was not feeling well, I paused and remembered a passage from Terrence Real's *Us: Getting Past You and Me to Build a More Loving Relationship* (Goop Press, 2022), a book that my partner and I had begun reading together. A book that had chosen us as we continued to heal from our past traumas and attempted to let go of our own fears of inadequacy and rejection.

In the book, the author talks about the "adaptive child," a concept that describes how the survival mechanisms that we learned as children dictate how we react to situations when we're adults. The book made me realize that my reaction to many challenging situations was based on the way I was taught to act as a child. That unconsciously I'm still acting like that scared little boy who was conditioned to make others feel comfortable at the expense of my own feelings and needs. That I still put other people's needs before my own mental health and well-being. And that I learned how to code-switch as a child in order to fit into a society that had repeatedly told me that I don't belong.

As I sat next to my son, I attempted not to react or to project my own expectations onto him. I attempted to stop my automatic reaction and learned behavior from the past. So, rather than get upset, as I was accustomed to, I took a deep breath and

SACRED LESSONS

said in a calm voice, "Mio, you're not in trouble. Just please use your words to tell me why you don't want to go to practice. I need to know what's wrong. Why are you crying?"

After asking him at least two more times, consciously restraining myself from raising my voice, my son finally found the strength to open up and express his true feelings. With tears streaming down his face, he said, "Papá, I just don't want to go to practice. I practice every Monday and Wednesday, then you and I practice together on Tuesdays and Fridays, and then I have my soccer games on Saturday. Thursdays and Sundays are my only days off, and I just feel too much pressure. I just want to stay home today. I'm really tired."

With a sense of relief, especially because my son was able to express his feelings in such a profound way that most men my age can't even do, I replied, "Thank you for explaining yourself. Thank you so much for telling me how you feel."

As I was about to tell him that we still needed to go to practice, because that was what my father would have told me when I was his age, my son sat up and looked at me with his big brown puppy dog eyes expecting what he, and I, both assumed I would say: "Okay, now go get your stuff, Mio. We have to go to practice."

Knowing this was what educators call a "teachable moment," I gently looked at him and said, "We don't have to go to soccer practice today. I'm really proud of you, Mio."

At that moment, I not only surprised him, I surprised myself. As I gave him a big hug and kissed his forehead, I felt a huge weight lift off him as he held me longer than usual. And right when I was about to let him go, I looked at him one last time and said, "Dame un besito grande."

Translation: "Give me a big kiss."

As a child, my father rarely showed me any physical affection. As I shared before, he would show me his love in other ways, but I made a promise to myself that if I ever had a son, I would make sure to give him as many kisses as I could to make sure he knew that he was absolutely loved by his father. This was my way of challenging traditional gender norms that pressure men to either hide or not share any physical contact with other men. At this moment, I could give Mio a kiss that I wish I would have gotten more regularly from my own father. I could begin to heal my inner child.

This was a transformative moment in my relationship with my son. I was able to almost suspend time and get a perspective outside of myself. I was an observer watching my own movie, consciously choosing my next move. As it was happening, I remember thinking that I could react the way I always did, or I could stop and assess why I was feeling a certain way before I did anything else. And thankfully for him, and for me, I chose a different path.

Parenting is a gift and, at the same time, the hardest job on the planet. It's not just about learning how to raise my children but learning how to re-raise myself. For me, parenting forces me to confront my past. It forces me to examine why I do certain things with my children. Again, without judgment, but with an absolute awareness that I get to choose how I'm going to parent my kids and that I don't have to do what was done to me. I could either learn from my childhood, or I could repeat the same patterns that I unconsciously and consciously inherited from my parents. The choice is mine. The choice is always mine.

It was against this backdrop that seven months later, my son, my mom, and I were getting ready to go to WrestleMania, the biggest event in sports entertainment history, or at least that's

SACRED LESSONS

what the WWE likes to say. It was reminiscent of when I was Mio's age, because I too had loved everything about wrestling. The drama, the storylines, the superstars, everything. From the iconic Hulk Hogan to Bret "the Hitman" Hart to the Ultimate Warrior, I used to beg my parents to stay up late so I could watch every single wrestling match. And like my parents did with me as a child, here I was taking my son to his first live WWE event.

For the past couple of years, Mio has really gotten into wrestling. He watches every single match he can find and knows every character's backstory and history. We even play wrestling with his plushies: I pretend that I'm the announcer, and he designates wrestling superstars to each one of his plushies as they compete to become the next WWE champion. It has literally become our routine that every evening we play plushie wrestling on the couch. I absolutely love watching his imagination soar as he plays entrance music for every character as they enter the make-believe wrestling ring, complete with post-match interviews and more.

I cherish these moments because I know that someday he won't want to play plushies with me anymore. I know he's going to outgrow this phase of life and that someday it won't be cool to play with his dad. I hope that something else will take the place of wrestling, so I can keep spending "Papá-Mio" time with him, but I won't know until that inevitable time comes. I feel like it's happening way too soon as he's starting to shoo me away when I watch him walk through the school gates every morning. He's almost at that childhood stage where he's embarrassed by his parents and wants to stay as far away as possible from us. So, no matter how tired I am, I make sure to play plushie wrestling with him every single day.

Playing with Mio reminds me not to take life too seriously. He reminds me to never lose that childlike wonder and imagination. It's a win-win situation where I get to be a kid all over again and he gets a dad who will play along with all his crazy ideas. And, just as important, making the time to play with Mio shows him that he matters to me. That's why I walk him every day to and from school, why I never answer my phone when we're playing plushies, and why I play for as long as he wants. I want him to know that he means everything to me.

As we walked into SoFi Stadium for night one of WrestleMania with our brand-new WWE T-shirts on, there was an air of electricity as over eighty thousand fans were shouting for the spectacle to begin. I was doing my best to capture every minute of it on my iPhone, because I wanted to remember that day forever. As the matches went on, I secretly recorded Mio yelling when his favorite wrestlers entered the ring. I couldn't help but laugh as he got so emotionally invested in every aspect of the performance. He was having the best time of his life, and I felt so lucky to be able to experience that special moment with him.

As we prepared for night two of WrestleMania, I started to think about the influence that the WWE had on my own views of myself. I wondered about the subliminal impact that wrestling had on how I internalized what it meant to be a man. From the nicknames of the wrestlers themselves, such as Randy "Macho Man" Savage, Andre "the Giant," and "Stone Cold" Steve Austin, to the overt messages that men settle disagreements through physical violence and intimidation, wrestling helped define manhood for me. It reinforced what I had learned from my father and my grandfather: that "real men" are tough, powerful, competitive, and dominant over everything and everyone.

SACRED LESSONS

Every day as we play plushie wrestling or watch one of the hundreds of WWE matches that we've already seen, I question whether I'm doing enough to counter the hypersexualized and brutal aspect of the WWE. Am I doing enough to teach him that this is all just a show and that he doesn't have to subscribe to the so-called socially approved gender roles for men and women, boys and girls, that are constantly portrayed not just in wrestling but in life in general? Am I doing enough to avoid reinforcing the dominant belief that this is how a young boy should act and feel? Am I doing enough to teach him that fighting and violence are not productive ways for him to express his feelings and emotions?

As we sat on the second level of a sold-out stadium for night two of WrestleMania, I looked around at the audience and noticed that most of the fans in the seats were my age, men in their thirties and forties. Men with their children and couples enthusiastically cheering at every twist and turn. It was almost like I was participating in an intergenerational rite of passage, with men like me on the edge of our seats screaming alongside our little boys at the top of our lungs. It was as if WrestleMania had given me, and much of the male audience, the permission to be kids again and not to worry about how anyone would view us. In a weird way, it became a safe, even sacred space for everyone.

While I was contemplating all of this, the violence and the brutality reached a crescendo. A match called "Hell in a Cell" finally ended, and everyone got ready for the headlining match to begin. The final match featured Cody "the American Nightmare" Rhodes, the son of legendary wrestler Dusty Rhodes, versus Roman "the Tribal Chief" Reigns, one of the most dominant and feared world champions in WWE history. The storyline for this epic match had been building for months, with fans, wrestlers, and even the press almost unanimously behind and believing that Cody Rhodes would become the next big WWE superstar, winning a championship that had eluded his illustrious father.

With his crisp new Cody Rhodes T-shirt on, Mio was ready for the match to begin and jumped out of his seat as the theme music for "the American Nightmare" blasted over the loudspeakers. The anticipation in the stadium was palpable as each wrestler walked into the ring complete with pyrotechnics and the pageantry of a historic main event. After almost an hour of the two wrestlers beating each other up, with each one coming close to victory on multiple occasions, the match ended with a shocking finish as Roman Reigns won and kept his undisputed universal championship streak going for a record eight hundred–plus days.

As I yelled in excitement, not aware of anything that was happening around me, I looked over and noticed that my son's hands were over his eyes. And like months ago when I saw Mio on the couch before his soccer practice, I asked, "Mio, are you okay?"

As soon as those words came out of my mouth, I realized that Mio was crying. Stunned, I immediately sat down next to him and tenderly held my poor little baby boy. I looked at my mother in shock as my son sat there crying for the next ten minutes. I held him, gently kissed his head, and tried to reassure him that everything would be all right. I told him that it was all a show and that the WWE was simply building up the rivalry for Cody to eventually become champion. Just then, I noticed that another little boy around the same age as Mio was crying right behind us. Like me, his father was also trying to comfort him, and I felt a weird sense that my life was coming full circle.

SACRED LESSONS

Here I was holding my baby boy who couldn't stop crying at an event that epitomized "toxic" masculinity. Here I was in the middle of what many critics argue is one of the main reasons why young boys and men settle disagreements with violence, consoling a little boy whose heart was utterly broken because his favorite wrestler had just lost.

And right then it hit me that the way we define gender had started to shift and change for the better. In that moment, holding my son and watching another father hold his son, I realized that both of us were not telling our sons to stop crying. We were both allowing our children to process and release their emotions. We were both trying to disrupt the cycle of violence that feeds off of men holding on to their feelings and blowing up in harmful ways at a later time. And we were both teaching our sons a different way to be a "man."

Once Mio stopped crying, I grabbed his hand so we could start making our way out of the packed stadium. Before we left, I hugged him a little tighter and gave him another "besito grande" so he knew that everything would be okay. As we made our way out of the stadium and waited in a sea of WWE fans, I began to contemplate how much this moment was indicative of the ways that our culture was battling itself. I began thinking about how the WWE supports the dominant view of masculinity, one that emphasizes aggression, violence, power, and dominance. But I also began to recognize that something else was happening. As tough and as hard as the WWE tries to be, it's almost unconsciously homoerotic and queer when it's at its best. It's a space that's as close to men showing a spectrum of gender fluidity as anything else on mainstream media.

During the two days, almost two hundred thousand people in attendance at WrestleMania watched men wearing bright colors, even a wrestler named Seth "Freakin" Rollins in an all-pink dominatrix outfit, while other matches had wrestlers fighting each other with barely any clothes on. We saw burly "manly" men not even flinch as they caressed each other after their matches. And we witnessed men defying societal expectations by openly expressing their emotions, an act traditionally discouraged and often ridiculed, receiving the loudest cheers and reaction.

As we drove home, with Mio still visibly upset from his favorite wrestler losing, I thought about the contradiction in the entire two-day extravaganza. I thought about how multiple truths do indeed exist in the WWE, and in life in general. That the WWE, and our male-dominated culture, is indeed built around rigid masculine stereotypes, but that we are also living in a time when we are seeing more nuanced and accurate portrayals of "manhood" all around us. How we are living in a time when the younger generations are challenging all of us to be more flexible in what we consider socially acceptable behavior for those of us who consider and call ourselves "men."

That night after I tucked Mio into bed and turned off the lights, I stood at his door and watched him as he fell asleep. I started to get emotional imagining my father doing the exact same thing when I was young. I started to wonder if my father would have wanted to give me a "besito grande" when I was scared or needed reassurance that everything was going to be okay. I started to wonder if my father wished that he could have told me, "Mijo, it's okay to cry." I started to wonder if the weight of patriarchy and not being able to express his emotions ultimately contributed to his deteriorating health.

As I slowly closed Mio's bedroom door, I realized that I had to work on letting go of that scared little boy inside of me. I had

SACRED LESSONS

to stop projecting my own fears and childhood traumas onto Mio and accept that he's his own person. He will have his own wins and his own losses, his own triumphs and his own heart-breaks. My childhood is my childhood and not his. I have to trust that Mio is learning how to express himself, and therefore learning how to share his own unique and authentic truth with the world.

As I started to walk away, I heard my little boy quietly say, "Papá? Papá? Are you there?"

I turned around and quickly ran to his door. "Yes, Mio, I'm here. Are you all right?"

"Yes. I just wanted to say good night. I love you."

Chapter 7
Running Toward Home

"Hello, Mijo, it's your father calling," my father said in his phone message the day after his surgery.

Given the cheerful tone of his voice, I was optimistic that his back surgery had been a complete success. I was planning to drive back home to Ventura to check up on him and make sure everything was okay.

"I'm just calling to tell you that everything's fine and that you don't need to come back to the hospital. I know that you're busy with work, so don't worry about me. I'm fine," he said in his typical matter-of-fact way.

After a brief pause, he continued, "Your mother's here with me, and they're sending me home later today or tomorrow."

And with an air of confidence, my father finished his message by saying, "Just stay in LA and get your work done. I will call you when I get back home."

After listening to his entire message, something told me to drive to Ventura anyway. It was only an hour away, and as much as my father tried to act like everything was "fine," I knew that having his boy around would make him feel better.

For some reason or another, my GPS made me go the back way to Ventura, and I suddenly found myself driving through Simi Valley and then Fillmore. Right when I was about to call my mom to let her know I was about twenty minutes away, I passed El Pescador Restaurant, which reminded me of the time that I planned arguably one of the greatest surprise birthday parties of all time.

Six years prior, my father thought that my mother and brother were inviting all of my aunts, uncles, and cousins over to Ventura to surprise me weeks before my actual birthday. My mother and brother had convinced my father that I would be totally surprised since my mom's side of the family loved to come visit my parents during the summer, and therefore I wouldn't be expecting a surprise birthday party for me.

Given the fact that my father absolutely loved hosting parties, as well as hanging out with my Auntie Dolores and my Auntie Rose, he was beyond ecstatic. He had spent the entire week before meticulously cleaning the front yard and the backyard. He even bought a couple more coolers so there would be enough room for all the alcohol that would be consumed over the weekend.

After a week of cleaning the entire house, my mother's side of the family had finally arrived. My father had stocked up on bottles of tequila and as many Coronas as you could imagine. He even ordered ten-plus pizzas from his favorite pizza restaurant, Pizza Chief, located down the street on Telegraph Road.

That night we ate every slice of pizza and drank every can of beer and bottle of tequila that my father had purchased. We spent the whole night laughing and just basking in the love of being around each other. The next morning, still buzzed from drinking too much alcohol, we woke up earlier than expected and went to Los Comales, our go-to Mexican restaurant in Saticoy, to eat some homemade menudo, the Mexican cure for any hangover.

Despite the magic of the menudo, my brother Albert and his Niná Becky and her husband Pete wanted to make sure that they got rid of their headaches faster, so they did what they always do: they ordered more beer. There we were at eight o'clock in the morning, right when the restaurant first opened, drinking Tecate with menudo, the breakfast of champions.

After coming back home to rest for a little bit, my cousins, along with my aunts, who were also in on the surprise, left early with my mom to set up decorations at the restaurant. A few hours passed, and the time had finally come for us to leave, so I yelled upstairs, where my father was busy working on his computer, "Papá, are you ready to go?"

"Yes. One minute," he replied.

Eager to get going, I waited a few more minutes and then once again said, "Papá, are you ready to go? I don't want to be late."

As my father walked down the stairs, I could tell he was worried that we were leaving too early and that my eagerness to leave so soon would ruin "my" surprise. Trying to waste more time, he stopped in the middle of the stairs and asked me, "Mijo, do you want to stop by Salzer's before we go to the restaurant?"

I smiled because Salzer's is one of my favorite independent music stores in the world, and my father knew without a doubt that this was the perfect way to make me late for anything.

Trying hard not to laugh, I replied, "That's okay, Papá. Maybe we can go after we get back from dinner. If we don't

SACRED LESSONS

leave now, we're going to be late, and I don't want to miss our reservation."

Sensing that my father was thinking of something else to delay our departure, I continued, "Papá, you know how crazy El Pescador gets on the weekends. We need to leave now so we can get our table before the restaurant gets too packed."

"Okay, Mijo. But your mother left early to go shopping, so they're going to get there before us. We don't have to be in such a rush," my father blurted out.

Knowing that my father was one of the most impatient people I knew, I pretended I didn't hear that last comment, because he would have been the last person to want to wait to go eat, let alone be late to a party.

Sensing that I might have found out about my surprise birthday party, my father then said, "Let me call your mother to make sure she knows that we're on our way."

Before he could say anything else, I interrupted him and said, "I just talked to her on the phone, Papá, and she just got there. She said that the table is almost ready and that we should go now. That's why Claudia and Mayela are already in the car waiting for us, so we don't have to waste any more time."

Defeated, my father finally said, "Okay. Let me lock up the house."

As we drove down the 126 Freeway to Fillmore, my father started laughing with Mayela as they reminisced about the time he gave her a Rolo chocolate bar before she went to sleep. Knowing that he shouldn't be giving a child a chocolate bar at such a late hour, my father told her to hide it in her pocket for the next day.

Unfortunately, that plan didn't work out too well, and Mayela fell asleep with the chocolate bar in her hand. The next morning when I went to wake her up, I asked her, "Mayela, do you want to tell me anything?"

"No, Michael. Why?"

"Are you sure? You don't want to tell me anything?"

"Like what?" she tried to say innocently.

"Like did you have a chocolate bar last night before you went to sleep?"

"No," she exclaimed in her big five-year-old voice.

"Are you sure?" I asked one more time.

"I'm sure, Michael," she said. I then told her to go to the bathroom and take a look in the mirror.

The jig was up once Mayela saw the chocolate all over her face, and I proceeded to emphasize the importance of her always telling the truth. As we collectively retold the story of Mayela's adventures with chocolate, my father and my little girl couldn't stop laughing. As we passed the orchards of Santa Paula and the agricultural fields of Fillmore, I was getting more and more nervous as we got closer to the restaurant.

Even though I was the one rushing to leave the house, I was now starting to feel like we'd left too early. I wondered whether everyone had arrived on time or whether we would see someone we knew in the parking lot. I was now thinking that maybe we should have stopped at Salzer's before making our way to the restaurant.

Despite my concerns, there was no going back now, and we had finally arrived at El Pescador. As I slowly drove into the parking lot, I was able to find the last parking spot between two large trucks that thankfully blocked any view of the restaurant. We got out of my car and walked inside the main entrance, where the waiter told us that our party was next door in the patio area. As we thanked him and started to walk to the outside

SACRED LESSONS

section of the restaurant, I couldn't see anything. The entire area was surrounded by a thick tarp-like material.

"Are you ready to go inside, Papá?" I asked as I was about to move a flap that served as the entrance to the back patio.

With a big grin on his face, my father said, "You go first, Mijo."

"Are you sure, Papá?"

"Yes. You go first."

"Okay then," I said as I slowly opened the tarp.

Suddenly, the patio erupted, and everyone yelled, "SURPRISE!!!!"

"Surprise, Mijo, we planned a surprise birthday party for you!" my father said with a level of excitement that almost made me cry.

Giving him the biggest hug I could, I responded, "No, Papá, the party's for you."

Uncertain about what was happening, I gently pushed my father inside ahead of me, as the singer of my father's favorite band from East LA, the one and only Thee Midniters, screamed into the microphone, "Mayo, happy birthday from Thee Midniters!"

My father was in complete and total disbelief. He couldn't believe it. He couldn't grasp what was happening, and he just kept looking at me with this look of utter shock and awe.

As people started to come up to him and congratulate him, I saw a look on my father's face that I had rarely seen. My father was genuinely happy. He was beaming from ear to ear, and my heart was completely filled with an immense amount of love and gratitude.

As I stood there watching my dad interact with people from every part of his life, from the person who had first hired him at Ventura College almost forty years earlier; to Michelle Serros, one of my favorite writers and poets from Oxnard, whom my dad had mentored since she was a teenager; to his best friends Cliff, Antonio, Peter, and the rest of his running crew; to almost everyone from both sides of my family; my dad was surrounded by people who absolutely loved and adored him.

It made me feel so good to see my father getting the love and appreciation he deserved. As the night went on, we had a moment when people came up and shared heartfelt stories about my father. It was an emotional time as my father got to hear what he meant to so many people. That portion of the evening ended with my brother and me sharing a few words and then my father being presented with an official proclamation signed by the Los Angeles City Council and mayor in honor of his birthday.

My father's surprise sixtieth birthday party was one of the most memorable moments of not only his life but of our lives. Next to marrying Claudia and the birth of my son, it was one of the greatest days of my life. My father and I had everything we had ever wanted or needed in one place. We had our family, and we had each other. In fact, we partied at the restaurant until they kicked us out, and then continued partying at my parents' house.

The next day, my mother told me that she found my father at the corner of the bed, lost in his thoughts before he went to sleep. Given that I wanted to know as much as possible, I asked my mom to recount their conversation to me.

Smiling, she said that my father had asked her, "Hon, how long have you been planning the party for me?"

With a mischievous look on her face, my mother replied, "At least for the past two months. The boys wanted to do something special for you. Albert and Michael planned the entire thing."

"Really?" my father said, still in shock about everything that had happened. "But—" he continued before my mother interrupted him.

"The boys did it all. They were so proud and happy for you."

"And Thee Midniters! How did you get them to play?"

SACRED LESSONS

"Michael."

"Michael? How?"

"He was a judge of some music competition alongside one of the original members of the band. So he asked him to perform at your party."

"And the restaurant? How did they get El Pescador?" my father asked, even more confused.

"That was your brother's friend talking to the owner who loves you."

"And all the people? Gary and Michelle, Mason, your family from up north?"

"That was your boys once again."

As my father stared at my mother with an empty gaze, overwhelmed with a sense of appreciation, he said, "I'm so grateful for you, hon. I'm so grateful for my boys. I truly am. I'm the luckiest man in the world. Thank you for giving me my boys. Thank you for all that you did to make today happen. Thank you for my life."

Knowing how my father had difficulty expressing himself, my mother simply hugged him and said, "You are loved, hon. You are loved."

A few weeks later, unbeknownst to my father, I contacted the *Ventura County Star*, the local newspaper, who wrote an article about his surprise birthday party and his many contributions to the community.

The article, entitled professor shares what he's learned about effort, pride, was published on Monday, September 28, 2009, and had quotes from his students and friends and an interview that my father had done with the writer a few months before.

In the article, the writer said, "Family, friends and colleagues recently celebrated de la Rocha's life at a surprise sixtieth birthday party, where he received a resolution from the mayor and City Council of Los Angeles."

The article even featured a quote from Cliff Rodrigues, my dad's best friend, who said, "De la Rocha encourages Latino students to be proud of their heritage and to make the most of their opportunities."

"He's been dedicated to the Latino/Chicano Movement, to the betterment of not just Latinos but of everybody," Rodrigues continued. "He wants these kids as they're coming up to have every opportunity to participate in the American experience."

Reading the article made me feel proud once again to be the son of Ismael "Mayo" de la Rocha. It capped off an incredible month of celebrating my father. A month in which we did everything to make sure that he felt special. A month in which we did everything to make sure that he felt appreciated. A month in which we did everything to make sure that he felt loved.

Two days after the article came out, I received an email that my father had sent to both me and my brother Albert.

> From: Papa de la Rocha
> Sent: Wednesday, September 30, 2009, at 11:23 AM
> To: Michael de la Rocha, Albert de la Rocha
> Subject: article
>
> Mijos —
>
> Here is the article from the Star. Thanks for the party and all the fuss about being sixty. I greatly appreciate it. I have two very wonderful sons and it makes my life worthy.
>
> Love you both,

SACRED LESSONS

Mayo de la Rocha
Department Chair
Social and Behavioral Science
Professor of History

"Be the change that you want to see in the world."

M. K. Gandhi

Almost immediately after receiving the email, my brother Albert replied with words that I know that my father will cherish forever.

Pops,

You deserve it all!

I must have read this email at least one hundred times, because within it lies the essence of my father's relationship with me and my brother. Within it lies his desire to always run home to his family. Within those four short lines, he's not only sharing what makes his life "worthy," but he wrote the words that he still has a hard time saying out loud to me and my brother: "[I] love you both."

Chapter 8

The "Saint" and the "Wildman"

The subject of patriarchy is rarely spoken of in my family. In fact, most of the men in my family wouldn't even know what the word means. As I've been reflecting on my life, I've realized that I learned to abide by a toxic definition of manhood that I've had to consciously learn how to identify and unlearn. This can be seen in so many aspects of my daily life, including the fact that the men in my family rarely show each other any kind of physical affection, and when we do, it's often an awkward partial hug, not a full-on hug, and sometimes just a pat on the back. This way of being has resulted in my own discomfort with showing affection to the men, and the women, in my family.

As I've said so many times before, the only time when the men in my family are able to share our emotions is when we drink beer and tequila until we can't drink beer and tequila anymore. That's been the right of passage with me and my father,

SACRED LESSONS

and with me and my brother, since I could remember. Alcohol provides us with the liquid courage to be truthful with one another. And through the years, this has become our unspoken ritual, our unhealthy tradition, and our silent way of telling each other "te amo" without having to be vulnerable enough to say the actual words.

As I've gotten older, I've begun to see how much my brother and I have subscribed to the pressures of how a man is supposed to act. We may want to share our feelings with each other, but the pressure of looking too "weak" often prevents us from just being ourselves. This results in us being vulnerable with each other only when we're drunk.

Drinking has become our escape and a kind of medication that helps us soothe our pain. It provides us with a safe space to cry and to be affectionate. And just like I did with my father when I drunkenly asked him why it was so hard for him to tell me that he loved me, I found myself once again drinking as a way to get closer to my younger brother.

"I love you, bro," Albert yelled as we both lay flat on our backs staring up at the night sky.

"I love you too. You know, we should probably get out of here before the cops come," I responded.

"Nah. We're fine. Let's just chill out here for a little bit. The cops aren't gonna come."

We had just finished wrestling each other for God knows how long on some stranger's lawn. It was 2:30 in the morning, and my brother and I were completely belligerent. We were celebrating my birthday at Skinny's, a friend's bar down the street from my old condo in North Hollywood, and rather than ride home with my wife after the bar closed, we decided to walk across a busy intersection to try and find our way home.

As we lay on the ground laughing and giggling hysterically, it was a classic picture of two brothers enjoying each other's company. We didn't care if anyone saw us. We didn't care if the cops came. We were just happy to be with one another. Of course, we may not have remembered anything that happened in the morning, but at that moment, it didn't matter because we were finally free and able to say the words "I love you."

My entire life I've wanted to tell my brother what he means to me, not just when we're drunk but when we're sober. We were never really that close growing up because we had two very different lives and two very different circles of friends. And while we were close in age, we weren't close enough for it to be cool for an older brother to have his baby brother around. Regardless, I guess the false expectation of what a man can and can't say to another man has prevented me from ever telling my brother how much I truly love and appreciate having him as my one and only sibling.

Recently, as I was helping my mom get rid of old boxes of papers, I found the following assignment that I wrote when I was in the sixth grade, entitled "Two Brothers." During middle school, my teacher gave us a homework assignment to write about two people in our family. And while most students wrote about their moms and dads, I decided to write about my younger brother Albert.

Two Brothers

Once upon a time, there were two brothers who lived in Ventura who had some wild adventures. One brother was "Saint" Michael who is eleven years old and loves to skateboard,

SACRED LESSONS

follow sports, and listen to good music…his favorite personalities include Mike Tyson and Jose Canseco. His favorite musical groups are U2 and INXS. He says that his favorite sport is soccer but would one day like to play football. Michael enjoys doing artistic work but does not get inspired too often…his last works were spontaneous caricatures of Tio Javier and of Dennis the Menace.

The other brother is "Wildman" Albert. He is nine years old and enjoys remote control cars. He likes to race his BMX bike, ride his ATC, cruise on his mountain bike, and read about fast racing cars. He isn't too sure if he would like a Ferrari or a Porsche. He doesn't really have any favorite personalities but enjoys rad music on his headphones. Albert enjoys sports and would like to run a marathon real soon. He says that he likes to write stories but hasn't had any inspiring revelations…his last stories were about a dragon that he kept in his garage, and most recently about a mouse that helped Santa Claus.

Reading "Two Brothers" makes me laugh because, despite my brother no longer writing stories about dragons and mice helping Santa Claus and me loving to skateboard, watch sports, and listen to music, our hobbies and interests are still exactly the same. Thirty years later, my brother and I are still battling the interchanging roles of the "Saint" and the "Wildman." And although we're now both married with children, we are still those innocent and rambunctious eleven- and nine-year-old kids trying to figure it all out.

Big and burly, if you met my brother Albert you would think that he's the older of the two of us. Even though I may look younger, Albert was actually born two years after me. He is charming, funny, and the life of any party, and I absolutely love and adore him. More than any other person in my family, Albert is the one person I've been intentionally working on letting my guard down with so we can develop a deeper relationship. All our lives, our parents reminded us of the importance of developing a close bond because, as they consistently told us, "When we're gone, all you will have is each other."

I've come to appreciate that comment more and more, but growing up, well, let's just say that I was mean to my brother. "Mean" doesn't even come close to describing what I did to him. "Vicious" might be the more appropriate word. Being an instigator who relied on my bigger size to get him to do whatever I wanted, I would tease my little brother with reckless abandon and blame him for everything. To this day, I feel horrible for the constant torture that I put him through. I regret what I did to him and know that my bullying may have pushed him to be more tough and hardened than maybe he would have been. I know that I took out a lot of my anger on him, and for that I am still trying to make amends.

Once we started going to school, my bullying settled down a little because we weren't spending as much time together. As I shared before, given that my mom was determined for her boys to get a Catholic education, she worked multiple jobs to pay for us to go to private Catholic school. Since my dad was a teachers union president and a staunch public school advocate, he refused to contribute to our private school expenses. So he and my mom

SACRED LESSONS

agreed that she would pay our monthly private school tuition all by herself. However, once my father found out that Albert was having a hard time adjusting to the private school environment, he immediately took my brother out of the school and enrolled him in the nearest public school he could find. And from that moment on, my brother and I began to live two very separate and different lives.

For most of my life, as my "Two Brothers" homework assignment made clear, I've been seen as the "angel" of the family. I was the one who attended private school from pre-K all the way through high school. I was the one with better grades. I was the one working at thirteen years old at the Majestic Ventura Theater. And while I may have been seen as the responsible one, my brother is far from being just the crazy and wild sibling. Yes, I was the son my parents could rely on growing up, when we all lived in Ventura, but as we've gotten older, and I moved to Los Angeles, my brother became the son my parents could call on whenever they needed anything.

There's a common belief that the second child gets away with everything because they don't get the same amount of attention as the first child. Psychologists even have a name for it, Second Child Syndrome, where parents pamper the younger child and give the elder child more responsibility. And while my near-death experience at birth definitely contributed to my close relationship with my mamá, and probably played a role in how much attention I got from both my mom and dad, I would definitely say that my parents tended to go easier on my younger brother. And even though my parents recognized that we had two different personalities, they were definitely stricter with me. Call it the elder child curse or whatever you want, but

I have felt that my parents have always expected more from me than my brother.

Reflecting on our childhood, my parents did spend equal amounts of time with both of us, but in the end, my brother is just more mischievous and fearless than I am. He's the type of person who doesn't always think about the consequences of his actions. Whether that's drinking too much alcohol and then lighting a match to spit out a flame like a makeshift flamethrower, or motorcycle racing at extremely dangerous speeds on any city street or steep mountain he can find, my brother isn't scared of anything. And this is a quality that I wish I had. He pushes the limits and has absolutely no fear. And while we couldn't be more different, we've learned how to complement and support each other.

While it was far from easy growing up as two brown boys in a small, predominantly white town, my brother and I made it work. With little to do, we found our own niches and communities. I was saved by skateboarding and punk rock music, and my brother was saved by motorcycles and his love of football. My brother's speed, talent, and fearlessness made him the best player on any field. He would literally run over anybody, and I mean anybody, that got in his way. Given how violent our culture is, and the fact that men are often rewarded for their brutality, especially in sports, my brother became very popular in school.

Being pretty good at football myself, so much so that I even made the varsity team during my sophomore year, I remember how proud I was watching my brother play. I bragged about him to all of my friends when he won Ventura County Defensive Player of the Year and got a full scholarship to play in college. To this day, I am still proud when I'm introduced as Albert de la Rocha's older brother.

SACRED LESSONS

That's why I was extremely excited and honored the day he asked me to be the best man at his wedding. I had secretly wanted him to ask me because I knew how momentous that occasion was for him, and for my family. After six long years of dating Quenby, his college sweetheart, my brother had finally decided to tie the knot in an intimate ceremony in Hawaii. Someway and somehow, Quenby had not only said yes, but she had figured out how to deal with all of my brother's madness. And despite being complete opposites, they knew how to balance each other out. They knew how to make each other laugh. And ultimately, they knew how to make it all work.

The night before boarding a plane to one of the most beautiful places on earth, my brother did what he loves to do—he went to a bar with a couple of his closest friends to memorialize one of his last nights as an unmarried man. They went to their customary watering hole in Camarillo and then proceeded to talk shit and drink as much beer as they could.

After about an hour, my brother's friend noticed that a table of three men kept looking at them and said, "Hey Albert, those guys keep looking over here."

"Whatever, they aren't going to do anything. Let's get another round of drinks," my brother said.

"No, for real. They're coming over here right now."

Just then the three men came over and started heckling my brother and his friends.

"Hey, we don't want any trouble. We're just drinking some beers," my brother's friend said.

"You're being too loud," the youngest one said sternly.

And with that comment, my brother stood up and got right in front of the youngest one's face.

"Hey, hey, hey. We're just drinking and having some fun. Chill out. Just go back to your table. You don't want to start any trouble here."

Without taking his eyes off my brother, the youngest man stepped back and got into a fighting position.

Seeing that the man wanted to fight, my brother once again said, "You don't want to do this. Come on. Go back to your table and chill. Trust me. You don't want to do this."

And before you knew it, the kid swung at my brother, who instinctively moved to the side before the punch struck his face.

"Come on. I told you that you don't want to do this," Albert said one last time.

The man threw another punch, but this time, he missed my brother's face completely.

"Okay then," Albert said as he clocked the kid right in the temple and laid him out flat on the floor.

Right away, the second gentleman, who happened to be the young man's father, came straight up to my brother.

"Hey, what are you doing? That's my son you just knocked out!"

"I don't want any trouble. I told your son to back off, but he kept wanting to fight. I told him to sit down, but he didn't listen."

Sensing that the father was about to throw a punch, my brother continued, "Grab your son and leave us alone. We just want to drink our beers. You don't want to do this."

"You just knocked out my son!" the father yelled as he took a swing at my brother, who by this time was ready to fight and landed yet another hard punch that knocked the father down.

Finally, the third and eldest gentleman, the young one's grandfather, stood up and approached my brother.

Seeing a man in his late sixties, my brother said, "Come on! I don't want to hurt you, old man."

SACRED LESSONS

And like his grandson, and his son, the old man swung, missed, and my brother landed a solid punch on the old man's face, dazing him and forcing him to grab a stool to break his fall.

"I told you not to swing, old man," my brother said.

By this point, the bartenders had called the police, who had quickly shown up and started questioning everyone in the bar.

As the police spoke to my brother, who by this time was sitting outside on the curb, his knuckles bruised and bloody, a fire truck pulled up right beside them.

As two firefighters ran inside to tend to the young man, who had hit his head pretty hard on the concrete floor and was still unconscious and bleeding, a second firefighter jumped off the truck and screamed, "Albert?!"

"You know this person?" the police officer who was writing up the incident report asked.

"Ya. That's my best friend, who's on his way to get married tomorrow."

And with that, and the fact that the folks in the bar corroborated his story about how the three other men had started the confrontation, my brother was let go.

Even now, every time Albert walks into that bar, the bartenders line up three shots of Tres Generaciones tequila for him in honor of his knocking out three generations of men.

I can recite countless stories of the nine lives of Albert de la Rocha. But this one seems to encapsulate so much. It defines him perfectly. His enjoying the company of his boys. His being the loud and funny one. His getting into a fight. Actually, no, his getting into *three* fights. And his getting away with all of it. That's my brother. My one and only sibling. The person who holds a special place in my heart, and the person I would do anything for.

85

No matter what happens, I will never stop loving my younger brother Albert. He is my other half, and I want nothing more than to have a deeper relationship with him. And while spending time with him is a rewarding experience within itself, opening up to my brother is hard. It takes an active effort on my part to talk to him about our past, and about our father. I'm making a conscious effort to spend more quality time with him, because I know this is what's required, this is what's needed for us to build a truly lasting and healthy relationship with one another.

While I can laugh in hindsight at all of our crazy stories, I often wonder how much I contributed to my brother being the way he is. I wonder how much my terrorizing him when we were younger led him to think that fighting is the way to solve everything. Did my getting praise from school or from our parents contribute to his having to be the funny and daring one to get attention?

I've never really been taught how to confront and deal with my emotional pain and trauma. I've only been taught to suppress how I'm feeling and to pretend as if everything's okay. But sharing my most private experiences with my brother has become a part of my own healing journey. Being completely honest and vulnerable with him has helped us foster a deeper understanding of one another and has allowed us to acknowledge the scars of our past.

Not too long ago I stayed over at my brother's house, and we spent hours talking about our childhood. Once I drank every bottle of alcohol I could find, I took a big leap of faith and shared my feelings about how I had acted when we were kids. I shared my thoughts about our relationship and about our family. And in doing so, I not only created the sacred space for Albert to share his own thoughts and feelings with me, but

SACRED LESSONS

I was redefining how two men, two brothers, two people could develop a stronger bond with one another.

It was a night that I'd waited for and wanted my entire life. A night where I was completely exposed. Where we laughed and we cried. That night brought us closer than we'd ever been, because we were finally able to be ourselves and just let go.

I know that creating a more intimate relationship with my brother will take time. I know that I have to learn how to let go of my expectations. I have to keep showing up. And while I'm committed to doing the hard but necessary internal work, I'm also committed to making sure that we, and our kids, spend more time together, making sure that our children get to see and learn how brothers, cousins, and men can connect with each other in healthier ways than what they typically see all around them.

The night after staying over at my brother's house, I got the following unexpected text from him: I know that I didn't tell you last night, but I love you bro.

Smiling from ear to ear, I simply replied, I love you more.

After texting each other a few more times, my brother sent his last text before going to bed: Life is funny, but I got you so I'm good…

As I smile at the thought of my brother, I take solace in the fact that we and our children will grow old together. I take comfort in knowing that I have someone who understands me better than anyone else because he has known me his entire life. I take pride in the fact that we are learning from the pain of our past so we can chart a different course forward for ourselves, and for our children.

The truth is that we don't live in a world of binaries, we live in a world of color and complexities. On the outside, my brother and I may seem to be complete opposites, but we're more alike than we like to admit. We both have attributes of the "Saint" and the "Wildman." We both are prioritizing our relationship so that our parents' desire for us to center and value family can live on through us. And we both know, whether or not we say it, that we are mirror reflections of each other. So, as I end this important chapter, I just want to make it abundantly clear that "Saint" Michael will never stop loving the "Wildman."

Lesson III
Love

Chapter 9
My Green Deen

It was a Tuesday evening around 5:30 p.m., the day before my fifteenth wedding anniversary, and my family and I were busy packing our clothes to spend a few days in Santa Barbara. Since I was taking the next few days off, I was frantically trying to make as many phone calls as possible before I disconnected from work.

Before I left, I wanted to make sure to invite a couple of people to an intimate conversation around mutual aid called "The Liminal Space: Let's Help Each Other." Given the divisive state of our country, and the world, two dear friends and I wanted to gather some of our closest acquaintances to have a private conversation about how we could support each other through these increasingly uncertain times.

In thinking of whom to invite, I immediately thought of three friends that I was determined to call before I left for vacation. So I grabbed my phone and made my first call.

"Hello," he said in his deep and soothing voice as he immediately picked up.

"What's up, my brother? How are you doing?" I asked.

"I'm well. I'm here at the house taking care of Yousef and Mustafa. Fatima is out of town with Ismael, and they're coming back tomorrow."

"What are you doing for the next couple of days?" I asked, and he then started to tell me about his full schedule of sports, packing, and then more sports.

Hoping he'd be available to attend the small gathering I was co-hosting, I began to talk to him about the purpose of the event, when all of a sudden, even before I had a chance to invite him, he interrupted and said, "I'll be there."

But as quickly as he responded, he caught himself and said, "You know what, let me first check in with Fatima to make sure that we don't have anything going on. I'll get back to you tomorrow after she gets back."

"No worries. Take your time," I responded. "I'm gone tomorrow anyways because Claudia and I are taking the kids to Santa Barbara to celebrate our fifteenth wedding anniversary."

"Fifteen years! Wow, it's been that long," my friend said with a sense of excitement in his voice.

"I know. I can't believe it either," I responded, laughing.

As we both reminisced on that day, he continued, "I remember it being the hottest day of the year…oh, and I almost forgot that you got married on summer solstice."

"I sure did. Time's flying by way too fast," I said as we both laughed at the memory of Claudia and I saying "I do" in front of our closest friends and family on the warmest day of the year.

"It sure does. Either way, congratulations, Mike. That's a huge milestone."

I don't remember exactly how the conversation ended, but I do know that we both left the call looking forward to seeing

SACRED LESSONS

each other in one week's time. As I said goodbye I felt a sense of relief, because I had called my three friends whom I really wanted to attend and was now ready to disconnect from work and celebrate my anniversary with my wife and kids.

There are certain people you meet who you instantaneously know are going to be a part of your life forever. For me, ibrahim abdul-matin is one of those people. From the first moment we met, there was an immediate connection. We became fast friends and made it a point to stay in each other's lives. It was almost like we were destined to meet, because we are kindred spirits or, as we like to say, cosmic brothers from some other lifetime.

I met ibrahim during my last year at UCLA, and from that moment on we developed a special bond. He is one of only a small handful of male friends whom I can count on for anything. He's someone I can be completely vulnerable and honest with. Someone I feel comfortable sharing my deepest secrets and my wildest dreams with. And, lately, we've been getting excited because we've been planning our future lives together. One where our families will be able to spend more time together, and where we can make a sustainable living through our art and writing.

From our love of books to our love of the most depressing acoustic love songs we could find, ibrahim and I are inseparable when we're together. We love the exact same things and are literally "brothers from another mother." But more than anything else, our desire to learn from our own childhood experiences and become the best fathers we can possibly be has brought us even closer together as we've gotten older.

A devout Muslim and an absolute lover of life, ibrahim is one of the most studious and inquisitive people I know. He even decided to lower case his name because he said only the Creator's name should be capitalized. A giant of a person who makes everyone around him feel seen and heard, ibrahim is the kind of person who makes you believe in yourself. A person who makes you instantaneously fall in love with him and feel as if you've known him your entire life. No matter what race, what ethnicity, what gender, ibrahim has that gift of bringing people together from all backgrounds and all cultures.

And I would be completely remiss if I didn't mention the fact that ibrahim continues to play an absolutely critical role in the environmental justice movement. More than a decade ago, he wrote *Green Deen: What Islam Teaches About Protecting the Planet* (Berrett-Kohler, 2010), a groundbreaking book that shows the direct correlation between Islam and environmentalism. A book that has taken ibrahim all around the world to talk to hundreds of audiences and given him his third favorite title behind that of husband and father: writer.

To me, and to so many others, ibrahim has always been ahead of his time, and he's one of the most remarkable people I've ever met. That's why he was the first person I thought of inviting to the salon. I knew that he, more than anyone else, needed to be there because he would light up the room with his contagious smile and make everyone feel comfortable and open to share in front of complete strangers.

So, before I forgot, I made sure to text him all the details for the salon as I made my final preparations for my trip. And within seconds of him getting my text, he immediately wrote back: Got it. Thanks for the love, hermano.

The next day, the family and I got into my Jeep and traveled north to spend a few days along the Santa Barbara coast. After spending the day celebrating our wedding anniversary and having arguably the greatest dinner of our lives, my wife and I drove

SACRED LESSONS

back to our Airbnb to watch a new Marvel series with the kids before going to bed.

The next morning, I woke up early to get some work done before everyone got up. I quietly put on my hoodie, shorts, and running shoes so I could sneak out of the house and take a long walk along the beach. After grabbing a cup of coffee from a local café, I started to make some work calls as the cold morning temperature started to rise.

As I walked along the sand, I decided to make a phone call to Mark Gonzales, another close friend whose family moved from LA to the ancient city of Sousse in Tunisia a few years ago. He and his wife purchased a 1,200-year-old building and converted it into a global residency center, and since then I have been trying to make my way there. Located in the northern part of Africa, their home is literally walking distance to the Mediterranean Sea and has some of the best cuisine in the world. In a word, their place is as close to "paradise" as you could imagine.

Knowing that I was desperate to visit him, Mark had texted me earlier that morning with some dates to come, or at least that's what my mind thought he texted. So, as I looked out into the vastness of the sea and sipped on the last of my vanilla latte, I decided to call him.

"Good morning, Marky!" I said with a burst of excitement. "How are you?"

"I'm good, my friend. It's great to hear your voice. Did you read my text this morning?" he said with a little bit of hesitancy in his voice.

"I sure did. What are those dates again? I'm going to try really hard to make it to Tunisia this time because I really need a break. I can't wait to go because we'll have plenty of time to catch up, and I could get a lot of writing done for my book."

MIKE DE LA ROCHA

Interrupting me before I was done speaking, Mark said, "Mike, read my text again."

It's not like him to interrupt me, or anyone else for that matter, so I sat down on a rock a few yards from the water and reread his text: Mike! We had a mutual friend pass. Do you have time to talk today? Wanted to make sure you knew.

When I realized what his text had actually said, I finally got the courage to ask him, "Who? Mark, who passed away?"

"ibrahim."

"ibrahim!" I said, unable to comprehend the magnitude of what he was saying.

"I'm so sorry, Mike."

"No, that can't be. I just talked to him the day before yesterday. I'm going to see him in a few days. We had plans to see each other on Tuesday. This can't be true, Mark, this can't be true!"

"It is. He passed away yesterday. I texted you as soon as I found out. I'm sorry."

"No, no, no!" I said, still in a state of complete and utter disbelief.

As the tears started to fall from my eyes, I said, "Marky, this can't be true."

I don't know how many times I said this, but I do know that I didn't want to believe the news. I didn't want to believe this was happening. I didn't want to believe that my dear friend ibrahim had passed away.

Still grappling with this new reality, I said, "Mark, he was literally packing to go back to New York and then planning to come back to LA. He wanted to stay here. His heart wanted to stay here. I was even planning to hire him or find him a good job somewhere in LA."

SACRED LESSONS

I don't know how long I stayed on the phone, crying and telling Mark about ibrahim and our plans for the future. But I do know that as soon as I hung up, I just stared intently into the ocean and spoke to my dear brother ibrahim. All I could think about doing at that exact moment was telling ibrahim how proud I was of him. All I wanted to do was to make sure to tell him how much I admired him, and how much he inspired me. More than anything, I wanted to make sure to tell ibrahim that I loved him dearly.

ibrahim was my twin. The person who, like I said before, loved all the things that I did. In fact, out of all my closest friends, ibrahim was my biggest cheerleader. He supported me wholeheartedly in everything I did. He kept me grounded, he kept me honest, and he always wanted the best for me and my family. To this day, there are no words that can describe the immense light that is ibrahim abdul-matin. No words. He was, and is, the blueprint and model for how I can strive to be a better father, husband, and friend. He was, and is, complex, beautiful, and humanly flawed and perfect, just like all of us.

As I sat there crying, I saw a seal sitting a few feet away and immediately googled what a seal represents in indigenous cosmology. I learned that seals are spirit guides who remind us of the importance of finding happiness in every moment of our lives. They are animals who are known to be happy, and therefore their contagious energy is one of lightheartedness and love, just like my dear brother ibrahim.

Stuck in a scene that reminded me of the movie *The Notebook*, I FaceTimed Mark because I didn't think he, or anyone else for that matter, would believe me when I told them the story of how I was sitting next to a seal when I learned the news of ibrahim's passing. As we laughed over the phone, I suddenly looked about twenty feet down the sand and saw another seal, only this time the seal was making its way back home, back into the ocean.

Walking back to our Airbnb, I read an article about how toxic algae was killing seals by the hundreds along the California coast. As I learned more about the reasons for this tragedy, I was reminded of ibrahim's drive to protect the planet, of his decades of work in the environmental justice movement. He, more than anyone else I knew, lived his life in service to teaching all of us how interconnected we are to each other, and to the earth.

The next day we buried one of my best friends. It was a somber day, but also a day of celebration. And, as his father mentioned, ibrahim couldn't have written a more perfect ending. Not only did he pass away on the brightest and longest day of the year, he passed away on the third day of Dhul Hijjah, the twelfth month of the Islamic calendar, and the month in which the Hajj, the sacred pilgrimage to Mecca, takes place.

I vividly remember ibrahim completing the Hajj in 2018 and sharing how that experience completely transformed him. He described with immense gratitude how the requirements of Hajj—to renounce worldliness, to accept the promise of forgiveness by God, and to get one's affairs in order—were an absolute gift that allowed him to grow, expand, and forgive himself. Incidentally, the rituals that are performed at Hajj celebrate the life of the Prophet Ibrahim and his son Prophet Ismael. As such, it's no coincidence that ibrahim's final Hajj, back to his Creator, happened on the day that it did. It's also very ibrahim to leave me, to leave all of us, with yet another sacred lesson about faith.

Minutes before we lowered ibrahim's coffin into the ground, I walked up to his wife, Fatima. No words were exchanged as we simply held each other. After a few minutes of silence, she looked

SACRED LESSONS

up at me and said in a way that only Fatima could, "Mike, I brought him here for you, and now I leave him here with you."

As I smiled and walked back to where I was standing with a dear friend, I cried nonstop under my glasses. I knew that I had to try and keep it together, but I was a mess. I didn't want to accept what was happening, and it was all too much for me to handle at that exact moment in time. I was broken. And even now, I still feel as if I lost a piece of me.

Though some time has passed, I'm still trying to make sense of something that doesn't make sense. I'm so devastated that I'm even finding myself crying in my dreams. And even though I know it's impossible, I can't help but try to control something that can't be controlled, to bring back a friend that can't come back. And that's the thing about death: It forever changes you. It forces you to reflect on your life and to really think about what matters most to you. It forces you to confront your own mortality and the legacy that you will leave behind. It forces you to accept the fact that change and transformation are the only constants in life.

That Sunday, the family and I attended a private memorial at ibrahim's children's school. As we made our way to the entrance, we saw Fatima and gave her our condolences. As she was sharing about the outpouring of love and support that she and her family were getting, she invited us to a public memorial that her sons' Little League baseball team was having for ibrahim that same evening.

And just like ibrahim did a few days earlier when I had invited him to the private salon, I immediately told her that we'd be there. As we got ready to go inside, Fatima suddenly grabbed my arm and asked, "As his oldest and longest friend here in LA, can you please say a few words or sing a song at his memorial tonight?"

And without even thinking, I said, "Absolutely. I'll play something. I have no choice."

With a smile, she simply said, "Thank you."

Before ibrahim's eldest son and family shared several stories about his remarkable life, I struggled to decide what song I would play. I hadn't performed by myself in years because of the COVID-19 pandemic, and I wanted to play something special for my dear brother ibrahim. I knew that I would have a few hours to practice before I had to leave for the memorial, but I didn't know what I was going to do.

When I got home, I had a few hours to put something together. I tried practicing the Beatles' song "In My Life," but my mind was too preoccupied with getting the chords wrong. I tried remembering one of my old solo songs, but it didn't feel right playing something that wasn't necessarily about ibrahim. Trying not to get frustrated, I started strumming some random chords, and before I knew it, I was humming a new melody and creating some new lyrics.

"Dear brother, why'd you go? Dear brother, why'd you leave? Someday, I will know. Why did you have to go?"

In minutes, I had written an entirely new song for my brother ibrahim that I would perform in a few hours. And although I felt as if the song was a gift from the Creator, I was still unsure whether I should play it. Feeling insecure about whether the song was good enough to perform, I walked down the hallway and knocked on my daughter's bedroom door.

"Mayela, can I come in?"

"Sure, Michael," she said as I opened her door. "Did you decide on what song you're going to play at ibrahim's memorial?"

SACRED LESSONS

"I think so," I replied. "I just wrote this song and I wanted to play it for you to see what you thought about it."

I sat on the side of her bed and poured my heart out, and when I finished strumming the last chord, Mayela stared at me with a look of bewilderment and said, "You wrote that right now? That's such a beautiful melody, Michael."

"Ya. I just literally wrote it a few minutes ago. Should I play it?"

"Yes. It's perfect."

With the reassurance of my daughter, Claudia and I made our way to Arcadia. When we arrived at the baseball field, I was struck by the sheer number and makeup of the hundreds of people in attendance. As we walked in, I was in awe of the different kinds of people that this beautiful black Muslim man had brought together. There were white people, Asians, Mexicans, and black people from all walks of life.

As Fatima introduced me to the baseball coach who had put together the entire memorial in just a few days, I smiled at the thought that ibrahim was still bringing people together from beyond the grave. ibrahim, in death, was reaffirming my belief that we could still heal the divides in our country despite what the pundits and the mainstream media were saying.

As I witnessed all those people from different backgrounds crying and expressing their shared grief and sorrow, I knew that there was still hope, that there was still a way forward. ibrahim had done that. ibrahim had always done that. He had reminded us all of our interconnected humanity and was sharing his final lesson with us on that fateful day at the Santa Ana Little League baseball stadium.

As the MC welcomed everyone and asked us to take our seats, the coach came up to the microphone behind home plate and said some very beautiful and heartfelt words about ibrahim. When he was finished, he said that ibrahim had spoken to the team and parents at a barbecue at the stadium the previous Monday, commenting on what a blessing it was for him and his family to have found such a wonderful and embracing community.

The coach then surprised us all by playing ibrahim's speech, which they had recorded less than a week earlier at that same field where we were now celebrating his legacy. As I clutched my wife's hand, ibrahim's voice came through the loudspeakers:

"When European colonists came here, the Tongva people couldn't even understand war the way that we understand war because there was so much bounty in these hills and in these mountains. And the way that you guys are existing right now, as we're sitting here together, my wife came over to me and said, 'This is not real life. This is kind of a fantasy.'

"There are so many people in the world that don't experience this sense of community and this sense of connection, so that sense of bounty still exists today. It's not just us coming here together, it's actually every single thing. It's in the land, it's in the soil, it's in the wind, it's in the trees, so let's just acknowledge that for a moment. That we are in a place that is very blessed, and we are honored to be here, and we should always sit with that reality.

"I also want us to remember that today is Juneteenth. Juneteenth is not a day of celebration. It should be a somber day, to think about the legacy of this country and where we come from. We all have to make a decision about what kind of place, what kind of country, what kind of people do we want to be a part of.

"All of us come here from different parts of the globe. All of our ancestors came from different places, but we choose to

SACRED LESSONS

be here, and we choose to be in community, and we choose to create family where we are.

"So, I want us to sit with that for a moment and for us to acknowledge that. Think about our history, think about our relationship to that history, and our commitment to what's coming in the future, and our commitment to the kind of community that we want to create.

"I think that all of you have decided that you want to be around people from all parts of the globe, and that you want to acknowledge their humanity, so I want you to give each other a big round of applause right now.

"And finally, I want to say that our family came here, and we literally just pointed to a spot on a map. We had no idea, we had no clue. This is truly the grace of God, to put us in a place where our children go to a Muslim school that's been an incredibly nurturing environment for them, and that we live around the corner from here, which has been an incredible space for our children's growth and development.

"So be thankful for what you have, and use these fields, use them. When your kids are sitting around on their gadgets, get them out here and play soccer, get them out here and play baseball, get them out here and play basketball. Don't sit around and wait for things to happen. Join all of the organizations and be a part of them and push them forward so you can make them better, and make them reflect the vision that you want to see.

"I also want to acknowledge that my wife is one of the most amazing people. She rarely gets all of the accolades, but she's the engine that makes all of this hum for our family, so can you please give her a round of applause?

"In Islamic tradition, we always end by saying that anything that I have said that is good comes from the Creator of the universe, and anything that I've said that's offensive comes from me, so please forgive me.

"Thank you very much."

As ibrahim's speech concluded, there was a collective sigh. People couldn't stop crying. His speech epitomized who he was: A person who showed up with his full and authentic self. A person who made people think differently about their views of religion, of people, and of issues. A person who absolutely adored his wife and loved his family. ibrahim was truly an angel sent from the Creator, whose life purpose was on full display in that Little League baseball stadium.

A few days later, out of nowhere, my son's stomach began to hurt. Still on edge from the sudden loss of my dear friend, I knew this was not a typical kid's bellyache but a deep pain that I could see was becoming unbearable for him. Afraid that he would throw up, my son would stop eating after a few bites and just grab his stomach. Thinking that maybe he was becoming lactose intolerant, my wife and I stopped feeding him dairy, hoping that the pain would go away. We meticulously watched everything he ate, but nothing worked. It was getting so bad that my son didn't even go outside to play at his own cousin's birthday party. Afraid that something was terribly wrong, we frantically called his pediatrician, trying to make an appointment as soon as possible.

After more than two weeks of my son's condition getting worse, my wife and I couldn't wait for his doctor's appointment any longer. Being the research ninja that she is, Claudia immediately found a doctor in Santa Monica who could see Mio the next day. Not wanting to take any chances, and anxious to know what was happening, we booked the appointment and prayed

SACRED LESSONS

that we would find out what was wrong with our precious little boy.

One of the things I've been reflecting on since ibrahim's passing is his unwavering devotion to his faith. Being a part of numerous Muslim traditions during his transition to the spirit world made me dive deeper into my own spiritual practices. During the past couple of years, I've been learning the practices of my ancestors and consciously reclaiming ancient Mesoamerican traditions that have guided my family for generations.

More recently, I started to learn more about how to perform *limpias*, Mexican rituals used to cleanse the body of negative energy and imbalances. I've been reading everything I could find on the subject and learning from experienced *curanderas*, traditional native healers, on various indigenous-based remedies to help me, and my loved ones, heal.

Curanderos or curanderas are part of a larger indigenous healing system known as *curanderismo* that has been practiced for hundreds of thousands of years throughout México and Latin America. The root of these words comes from the Spanish word *curar*, which means "to heal," and many of these practices combine elements of Catholicism and traditional indigenous practices. Recognizing that we can only be fully healed by addressing our physical, mental, emotional, and spiritual blockages and needs, the purpose of curanderismo is not just to treat a person's symptoms but to heal the whole person, to contribute to the healing of whole communities.

And that's why I knew that my son's stomach problems were being exacerbated by his anxiety and his overall emotional state. I knew that I had to do something more than just take him to a Western medical doctor. And still mourning the loss of my dear friend ibrahim, I knew that I had to teach Mio about our traditional healing practices so he could feel more confident and have faith that his doctor's appointment would be fine.

"Mio, come here, I want to show you something," I said as he was in the living room watching TV.

As Mio entered my office, already accustomed to me sagging (i.e., cleansing) him and asking him to pull his oracle cards, he asked, "What is it?"

"See this picture of my friend ibrahim?"

"Yes."

"You know how bisabuelo is always looking after us?"

"*Yes.*"

"Well, now ibrahim is doing the exact same thing. He's now your guardian angel."

As Mio looked up at me, and at the picture of ibrahim, I continued, "Come with me outside. I'm going to teach you something."

As we walked outside, I gave Mio my pouch of tobacco and told him to grab a small bundle as we stood in front of some red flowers in our backyard.

"Before we do what I'm going to show you, we have to make an offering to our ancestors. Do you know what an offering is?"

When he just shook his head no, I proceeded to tell him. "When we ask for something from the spirit world, we always have to give our ancestors a gift or something in return. That's why we place tobacco on the ground, as an offering of thanks for their love and support."

Watching Mio to make sure he was interested and paying attention, I then said, "Now before you place your tobacco on the ground, say a prayer for what you need help with."

SACRED LESSONS

I smiled as my baby boy closed his eyes tight, made a wish, and proceeded to lay the tobacco next to the flowers.

We then walked to the side of the house, where I had set up a small altar and asked him, "Do you know what the four elements are?"

After he nodded yes, I asked, "What are they?"

"Air, earth, fire, and water."

"That's absolutely right, Mio!" I said enthusiastically. "Where did you learn that? In school?"

Beaming, he said, "I don't remember, but I didn't learn that in school."

"That's okay. I'm just so amazed that you know what the four elements are. Now, take a look at the altar and tell me if the four elements are present there."

Looking at the makeshift altar that I had placed on the ground, he said, "Yup."

"Where?"

Mio pointed to the flame of the candles for the fire, the dirt where he laid the tobacco for the earth, the air that we were breathing for the air, and the water in a cup that I'd placed inside the circle of candles for the water.

"Correct."

I then handed him a piece of paper and a pencil and asked him to write down his request for help. When he finished, he put it underneath the cup of water, and I handed him the picture of ibrahim that I had shown him in my office.

"You know who this is, right?" I said jokingly.

"Yes."

"Who?"

"ibrahim," he said playfully.

"That's right. What's his new job?"

"He's my guardian angel."

"That's right. Now take his picture and place it wherever you want so he can make sure that your prayers are answered."

As Mio placed ibrahim's picture next to the candles, I told him to make one last prayer to ibrahim, bisabuelo, and all of our ancestors. I told him to thank them for helping him one last time.

When he was finally finished praying, I asked him, "How do you feel, Mio?"

Seeming a lot less stressed, he quickly responded, "I feel good, Papá."

"Do you feel better?" I asked with a slight sense of nervousness.

And with a big smile, he immediately said, "Yes."

"Now when we go to the doctor's appointment today, know that you'll have ibrahim watching over you. No matter what happens, you're going to be okay."

I again paused so my words could sink in and then asked him, "Do you understand?"

After he nodded yes, my son and I closed the ritual as I hugged him and gave him a kiss on the cheek. Thirty minutes later, we were on our way to Santa Monica to see the pediatrician. Since Mio hadn't eaten breakfast, my wife and I decided to stop and get him a plain chicken sandwich to try and calm his nerves and to act as if everything was normal.

Mio took a small bite of his sandwich and then immediately put it down, noticeably not feeling well.

"Mio, do you feel sick?" I asked.

When he nodded yes, my wife and I parked the car so Mio could get out and breathe some fresh air. As he slowly walked

SACRED LESSONS

around the parking lot, he suddenly stopped and came back to me. Without saying anything, Mio simply laid his head on my shoulder, needing some fatherly love and attention.

Holding him, I whispered, "Remember your guardian angels. You're going to feel better soon, I promise. That is why we drove out here, so we could see the doctor right away and find out what's happening with your stomach."

After a few minutes, Mio started to feel better, and we drove down the street to the doctor's office. After asking him, and us, a series of questions, the doctor checked Mio's heartbeat and stomach and performed some other tests.

Looking upbeat, she said with an air of reassurance, "Everything looks fine. His heartbeat is good, his temperature is fine. Everything looks great."

Seeing everyone's relief, the doctor then said, "I'm going to schedule you to take him to get some blood work done so we can be absolutely certain that nothing's wrong."

Looking at Mio, the doctor asked him, "Mio, can you describe how you feel when you eat?"

And in his big boy voice, he responded, "I get full quickly, and sometimes I feel like I want to throw up."

Looking intently at him, the doctor continued, "Are you eating less because you're afraid that you might throw up and you hate how that makes you feel?"

Looking at me and then at the doctor, Mio said, "Yes."

The doctor proceeded to tell us that it's common for children to stop themselves from eating because of their fear of throwing up or because they don't know how to process something that has recently happened. Many kids start to feel anxious and then their emotions start to impact the way they act. She told us that

Mio's fear of getting sick might actually be the reason why he was feeling nauseous.

Turning to Mio, I asked him, "Do you have any questions for the doctor, Mio?"

"No, I don't have any questions. I'm fine."

"Do you feel better now?"

He nodded yes as I asked, "Are you sure?"

"Yes."

"Then what do you say to the doctor?"

"Thank you."

As we left the doctor's office, I stopped my wife and my baby boy and asked if we could say a prayer of thanks since Mio was feeling better. Having packed our swimsuits in the hope that everything would turn out fine, we decided to spend the rest of the afternoon at the beach, the place that had comforted me when I learned of ibrahim's passing and the place that would now provide that same kind of comfort to my son.

Wanting to be absolutely certain that Mio was feeling better, we stopped at Subway to pick up some turkey sandwiches to see if he could hold down his food. Seeing him devour his sandwich assured me that our prayers had indeed been answered.

As we made our way down the Pacific Coast Highway, I felt an enormous amount of gratitude. I felt grateful that my son was finally feeling better. I felt blessed that I got to teach him about our ancient ways and traditions. I felt humbled that I was a part of ibrahim's life and knew without a shadow of a doubt that he was still very much in mine.

After about thirty minutes of playing football on the sand, Mio went out into the water. As I stood there watching him having the time of his life, Claudia ran up to me and said, "Michael, look!"

SACRED LESSONS

Just then, I saw my wife pointing toward the ocean where a seal was bobbing its head in and out of the water.

"Mio, Mio, look! Look, Mio!" I yelled.

When he turned around and saw the seal, my son looked back at me and confidently said, "It's ibrahim, Papá. It's ibrahim."

Chapter 10
Surrendering to the Ocean

I've always had a special connection to the water. From an early age, I always wanted to go to the beach. I've always gravitated toward the cool ocean breeze and soothing sound of the waves hitting the shore. From as early as I can remember, the one place where I felt completely safe and welcome was when I was in the water.

Growing up in Ventura, California, my proximity to the beach made it easy for me to spend countless hours in or beside the water. In middle school, and later in high school, I learned to bodyboard, then skateboard, then surf. It became almost like a religion for me. I would try to go to the ocean as much as I could. And although I've never really been that good at surfing, it gave me a reason to go to the beach.

From that first moment on, the ocean has been my place of comfort and refuge. A place that I go to when I need clarity, or just a place for me to go to breathe and to get centered. A place where I can be my full and authentic self. And a place where I

SACRED LESSONS

can go to heal and reflect on myself and my relationship with the world.

Surfing has taught me more about life than almost any other relationship I have. It's more than just a metaphor for life, it's a way of living. Through surfing, I have learned how to endure hardship and keep going forward no matter how tired or frustrated I am. Through surfing, I've been forced to get back up even when I've been knocked down. Through surfing, I've learned how to forgive, and how to let go.

While I try to go to the beach as much as I can by myself, I mostly go surfing with Ron, one of my closest colleagues and friends. And that's the thing about life, about surfing, about healing—it doesn't happen in a vacuum. Healing happens in community.

Surfing, and being in nature, is a very intimate and personal endeavor. Water is the great equalizer because when you're out in the water, you're figuratively naked and have to learn how to swim by yourself, but also with the help of others. It's not about how you look or even how much money you have. It's a dance between a person and the waves. And the only way that you can survive a huge swell, the only way that you can endure the ups and downs of life, is by learning how to surrender.

The act of surrendering is a process of becoming vulnerable enough to trust in the unknown, the unseen, and the sacred energy that connects us to everything. No matter what culture, what spirituality, or what tradition one is born into, surrendering is paramount to our personal and collective healing, restoration, and strengthening of our connection to the cosmos, to ourselves, and to each other.

This is a challenge for me, and for many of us, because we live in a society that wants to control us and push us to pretend that we need to know everything. But the truth is that the more that I let go, the more I surrender, the more I trust that the medicine I need lies within me, the more I will be able to receive the blessings that are inherent within every lesson, every person, and every challenge in my life.

And that is the secret I've been learning for the past couple of years. That in order for me to develop a deeper understanding of and relationship with myself, I have to heal alongside others. Despite society telling me that healing is a solo journey, my personal experiences have shown me that the more I can be honest with myself, and the more I can share with those I trust, the more I can make sense of my wounds and the ways I can begin to remember and recover my sacredness.

That's the reason why, even though I can meditate, do yoga, and surf all by myself, it's not the same as when I'm with a group of friends. The truth is that my healing and sense of connection are magnified when I'm around others. When I do any of these practices outside in nature, it becomes even more magical and life-altering. And that's because healing has always been a communal practice. Healing has always been done within the sacredness of the outdoors, with the assistance of our ancestors and the earth's sacred plants, animals, and nature itself.

That's why I'm so in love with surfing. Because through the act of paddling out into the ocean and becoming one with the water, I have no other option but to be completely present. I can't be stuck in the past or thinking about the future. I must be completely in the moment or I risk getting pounded by the waves. That's why so many of my mentors and elders consistently remind me to let go of my thoughts. They teach me how to quiet my mind so that I can temper my ego and be here, now.

SACRED LESSONS

That's the sacred lesson that nature teaches all of us: that all we have, all we ever have, is this moment.

On a recent camping trip to spend time with myself and to have the space to write, I was confronted by my fear of being alone. I was confronted by my anxiousness of not knowing where I was going or what I was going to do. And in that moment, I had to put into practice what I "believe." You see, my beliefs cannot just be ideas or something that I talk about, they must be integrated into my daily life. I have to live my values and trust that there's a reason why my inner voice was telling me to leave and spend time alone in nature.

On that first evening, I walked by myself to the beach to watch the sunset and give thanks to the Great Spirit for the opportunity, the privilege, that I had to go camping. As I walked along the shore, I saw an eagle in the sky. Eagles are very sacred creatures who represent courage, wisdom, and cleverness. In Mesoamerican mythology, and in many other cultural stories, eagles symbolize listening to your intuition and having the fearlessness to believe that you can accomplish your sacred purpose in life.

As I watched the eagle soar, I texted a video of the bird flying to my beloved friend Juan, someone I admire for his ability to teach our sacred practices to those who have been negatively impacted by mass incarceration and the criminal legal system. A few minutes after sharing the video with him, he texted me back: Good one brotha...enjoying nature and creation! Walk barefooted homie! Feel life cause you know like folks said we ain't from the left or the right. We coming from the bottom to the top.

Smiling, I immediately stopped and took off my shoes. For the next couple of minutes, I just stood there underneath the sun with my bare feet touching the ground. In that moment, Juan had reminded me of the importance of being directly connected to the earth. He had reminded me of the importance of never forgetting to keep myself rooted and grounded in the wisdom that I could only gain from being outside in nature.

As I stood there with my bare feet touching the warm dirt, I felt alive. I felt I was a part of something bigger than myself, connected to the past, to the present, and to the future. I felt blessed that I didn't have to pay anything for this healing. All I had to do was simply go outside, take off my shoes, and feel the healing power of Mother Earth.

As I made my way back to my campsite, I began to think about my father. In that precise moment, whether it was because I'd taken off my shoes to let my feet touch the ground, or because I'd gotten to spend time with the ocean, I realized that my father is the reason why I love the water so much. My father is the reason why every time I feel down, every time I feel alone, I go back to the beach.

You see, some of my fondest memories as a child are of me riding my bike alongside my dad on the beaches of Ventura. I vividly remember him throwing our bikes in the back of his pickup truck and driving along the coast. I was absolutely mesmerized by the waves and the way the sun hit the sand and reflected off our bikes. We would ride our bikes for miles upon miles, and I wouldn't once complain because I was not only at the beach, I was at the beach spending time with my father.

One moment that I will always remember is riding my bike along the water with my father when I was seven years old. We were on the bike path by the Ventura County Fairgrounds and had stopped to listen to the loud music coming from the grandstand speakers.

SACRED LESSONS

As I looked up, I noticed a huge cloud of smoke and pointed to the sky. "Papá," I said, "what's that?"

"It's nothing, Mijo. Let's keep going," he replied.

Confused, I asked, "But Papá, what's that horrible smell?"

Trying not to laugh because I'd used such a big word at such a young age, my father repeated, "It's nothing, Mijo. Come on, let's keep going."

Not wanting to leave, I persisted, "But why does it smell so bad?"

My father couldn't stop himself from laughing as he started pedaling away. "Let's go!" he said.

Years later, I found out that I was smelling the stench of cannabis as I rode through my first ever live concert, listening to the music of the greatest jam band of all time, the Grateful Dead.

It's this and so many other memories that have cemented my love of the beach. You see, my father isn't the typical beach guy. In fact, he doesn't even like going into the water. But nature has always been the place that my father goes to when he needs to get away from the pain of life.

Even before I learned how to ride my bike, my father would take me and my brother camping at least three or four times a year. And this wasn't glamping. Oh no. This wasn't camping with bathrooms and showers down the road. This was real camping complete with us having to pack everything that we needed in our own backpacks and then carrying them up the mountain all by ourselves. We would spend the entire day walking with these heavy backpacks until we finally stopped and put up our tents.

My father absolutely loved to go camping, because it's one of the few places where he could just let go and not worry about work or life or anything else. He didn't have to stress about whether he was going to be judged or ridiculed for how he looked or for who he was. He could be transported back to that feeling of abundance and acceptance that he'd felt as a child playing among the apple trees and orchards in Atascaderos. He could put himself back into a situation where he could relive that undeniable feeling of being loved.

Looking back at it now, camping was a sort of ritual for my father to escape the bustle of everyday life every couple of months. Like running, it provided him with a space to disconnect from the monotony of work and reconnect with his core, his own inner being. And through these experiences, he taught me that being in nature was a powerful way for me to rejuvenate myself for the weeks, the months, and sometimes even the years ahead.

I remember being six or maybe seven years old, camping for the weekend with my papá and my brother in Santa Paula. I remember packing my small backpack and then looking over at my father and saying, "Papá, why are you packing so many things?"

"Because once we're camping up in the mountains, we can't come back home to get anything. We have to pack everything that we need right now."

"Everything? Even my toys?" I asked as only a young, naive little boy would do.

"Michael, you can only take one toy with you because we have to take a lot of stuff with us. We have to take our sleeping bags, our tent, our food, and our clothes for the entire weekend. And Mijo, remember that we have to put everything in our own backpacks."

"Our own backpacks? But Papá, mine's too small to take everything that I need."

SACRED LESSONS

And with a smile, my father simply said, "I know, Mijo. Just pack one toy to take with you and we'll figure out the rest."

During those precious moments, my father was teaching me about what mattered most in life. He was teaching me that the material items were secondary to having the space and the time to just be with myself and my family. When we went camping, he was adamant about us bringing only the bare necessities, the essentials. No more, no less. And this was an important lesson that he wanted me to learn: that I didn't need any of the material "things" that I thought I needed to be happy and content.

As I contemplate this lesson that my father was trying to instill in me at such an early age, I think about my relationship with material possessions and overconsumption in general. I think about how I buy things that I really don't need because for most of my life I've struggled to accept my inherent value. I've struggled with feelings of inadequacy and of not feeling worthy.

A direct by-product of this way of thinking is that I buy unnecessary things that bring no tangible benefit to my life. Worse, I know that I have become addicted to shopping, which I now realize is a result of my childhood trauma and my not thinking or feeling that I was good enough. Shopping has, unfortunately, become a way to fill a void within myself.

Looking back on it now, I see that my father took me camping because he wanted me to learn that I had everything I needed within myself. That I didn't need material goods to make me feel whole or bring me a sense of value and happiness. In fact, the opposite is true, and my love of surfing, an activity that anyone can do for very little money except for the cost of a surfboard and wetsuit, is proof of that.

As I reminisce on that childhood memory of feeling that we were never going to make it to the top of the mountain, I remember my father taking my brother and me to the punch bowls to swim and to play in the water.

"Mijo, jump into the water," my father would say.

I remember timidly looking at the water and saying, "But it's too cold, Papá," as I stood on the edge of the lake with my arms crossed.

"Jump into the water," he would say in an even sterner voice.

And when he said it that way, with that tone, I knew he wasn't asking me to do it, he was telling me I had no choice but to jump into the water.

Sucking up whatever courage I could muster, and giving my brother a side eye that said he'd better do it too, I jumped into the water without thinking about it. Was I cold? You bet. Was I scared? Absolutely. Did I want to immediately get out of the water? You know it!

And every time I tried to get out, my father would say in an even sterner voice, "Mijo, you better stay in the water. Your body will get used to the temperature and you won't be cold anymore."

"But it's too cold, Papá," I pleaded.

It was no use because my father would say, "Stay in the water. Don't come out. Put your head under the water. Michael, you're going to be fine. Stay in the water."

My father was definitely hard on me, but I know that he wanted me to learn the value of not giving up, of not taking the easy way out, of sticking through the discomfort of it all. He wanted me to get over the initial shock of the icy-cold water so I could find the joy on the other side. And he was always right, because afterward my brother and I would stay in the water for hours upon hours until the sun started to finally go down.

My father always intuitively knew that the lessons my brother and I needed to learn could only be found in nature. He

SACRED LESSONS

always knew that children, and people in general, learn through experience and watching others. That's why he was so adamant about taking me camping before I could even walk. He wanted me to know that the outdoors provided not only the greatest lessons in life but also the greatest medicine. He wanted me to know intimately the healing power of the land and that anything was possible when we stuck together as a family, and as a community.

When my father's back problems started to get worse, I did the one thing he taught me to do: I took him outdoors, or to be more specific, I took him to the beach. I made an appointment with a chiropractor whose office was next to the Santa Barbara beaches. Knowing that I had to do something drastic, I took my father to a chiropractor who was more like a shaman and who I hoped could help heal my father's increasing back pain.

As I sat in the room next door waiting for my father's appointment to end, I imagined him feeling better. I envisioned his health and vitality coming back stronger than ever. I even drew a picture in my mind's eye of us camping together once again, only this time we'd be camping alongside the beach rather than on some steep mountaintop.

Afterward, I took my dad to the grocery store to buy some herbs and other items the chiropractor had told us to purchase. And as much as I wanted my father to feel better, or for him to believe that changing his lifestyle and eating habits would improve his health, it was his choice to make. But no matter what I said to convince him, no matter what I did to make him consider that taking these small steps would help him feel better, my father was unfortunately too stuck in his old ways.

As we drove down the 101 Highway looking out into the Pacific Ocean, I instinctively rolled down my father's window so the healing powers of the sun and the ocean breeze could bring him some semblance of comfort.

Trusting my intuition, I slowly turned down the radio and hesitantly asked him, "How are you feeling, Papá?"

"I'm fine, Mijo. Thank you for asking, and thank you for taking me to the chiropractor. I really needed that, and the massage part felt great."

Sensing an opening for me to continue the conversation, I asked him, "Are you going to do what the chiropractor told you and try to walk more and watch what you eat?"

Knowing that he didn't want to let me down, or maybe not even wanting to answer my question, my father simply replied, "I'll try," even though I knew in my heart of hearts that he was lying.

As we got closer to the beaches of Ventura, I knew I needed to stop at the beach for my own sanity. I knew I needed to be as close as possible to the waves. So, this time without hesitating, I asked my father, "Papá, do you want to stop at the beach?"

"No, Mijo, let's just go home. I'm tired."

"Are you sure? How about we just stop for a quick minute?"

And without waiting for him to respond, I got off on the next exit and went straight to the spot where I had learned to surf decades ago.

As we pulled into the parking lot, I found a spot where we could watch the waves hit the rocks. Knowing that my father was tired, and likely in too much pain to get out of the car, I sat there with him in complete silence as we both looked out into the nothingness.

I've always felt a little uncomfortable with silence, but for some reason on that day, I ignored the discomfort and didn't

SACRED LESSONS

say a word. I knew that the medicine that he and I both needed would come to us in that moment of quiet.

As I said before, I stopped at the beach that day because I needed to heal. I needed to let go of any expectations. I needed to surrender.

After a few awkward moments of us not saying a word to each other, I looked at my father and said, "Okay, Papá, we can go home now."

As I left that corner of the world that had provided me with so many moments of comfort, I looked in the rearview mirror and surrendered to a higher power. And without knowing what to do, and without wanting to leave my father's side, I silently said a prayer as the waves of the ocean crashed behind us.

Dear Lord, please take care of my father. Please make him feel better. Please take his pain away. He needs you now more than ever.

Chapter 11
Confronting Whiteness

Growing up, I was acutely aware of my brown skin. It wasn't that I was as dark as my father or the majority of the people in my family, but I always knew I was different.

Living in a predominantly white community and attending predominantly white schools, people would always ask me, "Mike, you're not Mexican, right?"

As a child, I would always hesitantly reply, with my head down, "Yes." And under my breath, I would add, "I'm Mexican," with my voice so low they could barely hear me.

Without fail, and without being able to hear what I mumbled, their follow-up question would invariably be, "You're Mexican and what?"

I was asked this question so many times that I knew they were expecting me to respond by saying "Italian" or "French" or better yet, just plain ol' "white."

The concept of whiteness was so prevalent during my childhood, and even today as an adult, that I developed an inferiority

SACRED LESSONS

complex and began to hate myself. I hated my body. I hated my skin. I hated absolutely everything about me.

I felt terrible about who I was, and who I would always be. As such, it's no surprise that for many years I began to do everything I could to hide any semblance of my brownness.

I remember going to a summer camp and hearing a story that completely changed my life. One of the chaperones, Mrs. Hernandez, my classmate's mother and one of the few adults of color on the trip, recounted a story of her growing up in Ventura. As she shared what was clearly a painful memory, she looked right at me and said, "I was so ashamed of the color of my skin that I would always wear long-sleeve shirts no matter how hot it was."

With her voice cracking, she continued, "I remember hating my hands as a child because every time I would look down at them, I would be reminded that I was a dark-skinned girl. I would wash my hands nonstop thinking that somehow the color would fade away. When that didn't work, I did anything I could to hide my brown skin, even wearing gloves in the daytime."

Up until then, no words had ever pierced my soul as much as the words of Mrs. Hernandez. As a young boy, I resonated with everything that she was saying. As a young brown boy, I felt the anguish behind her words. And I wondered if I would ever feel comfortable in my own brown skin.

It's extremely difficult growing up in a society that compares everything to whiteness. It's hard to love myself when the standard of beauty, the standard of greatness, the standard of what's considered "normal" is white. When everything around me is pressuring me to be as white as possible, then it's an everyday act of resistance to simply ignore the social pressures and accept the beauty of who I am.

I sometimes still catch myself struggling not to compare myself to this dominant white narrative. Looking back on my life, it makes perfect sense why I dyed my hair blond, it makes perfect sense why my first real girlfriends were white, and it makes perfect sense why I did everything I could to hide the fact that I'm of Mexican descent.

The white gaze, and the striving to attain the razor-thin bodies of the actors and rock stars I saw on TV or in the magazines, even led me to starve myself throughout middle school. From the sixth to the eighth grade, I literally would not eat. My mother would make me lunch for school, and I would either give it away or throw it in the trash. I became so thin that I couldn't even recognize myself anymore.

I hated the fact that I was too big to fit into regular jeans, so the only places where my mom and I would go shopping to find pants that would fit me were JCPenney and Mervyn's.

"Michael, what about these?" my mother would say as she held up a brand-new pair of black trousers.

"They're okay."

"They're on sale, so we could get two of them for almost the price of one. What colors do you want? They have navy blue and black," she'd reply.

Defeated, I'd say, "It doesn't matter. Whichever ones you want."

It wasn't that I didn't need or want the pants. It was the fact that they were a size "husky" that made me uninterested. You see, I was so big that none of the regular-size youth pants fit me. We had to go to a special clothing section, which made me feel fat and ugly. In fact, I got my first pair of jeans when I entered high school, after two years of starving myself.

And while I'm still coming to terms with the way that whiteness has impacted my life, and with accepting the beauty

SACRED LESSONS

of all body types, including my own, I'm also acutely aware that despite my heaviness as a child, my proximity to whiteness allowed me to survive and navigate a world that benefits and centers on those with lighter skin. I know that I was, and still am, invited into privileged spaces and given access to opportunities simply because people think that I'm white.

In college, I began to take my first Chicana and Chicano Studies classes, which gave me the vocabulary to understand not only my privileges but also my cultural and ethnic identity. It gave me the context as to why I am the way I am. It gave me an understanding of the dynamics of a society that still maintains a power structure and belief system that prioritizes and benefits those of us who are lighter skinned.

My parents unconsciously, and probably consciously, knew about my struggles with my racial identity and made sure that I spent almost every weekend at my grandparents' house in East Los Angeles. No matter how often I went, it was always culture shock. In Boyle Heights, I would rarely see any white people. In fact, all I ever saw was Mexicans, and the only language that I ever heard was Spanish. It was as if my parents had dropped me off in another country, in a completely different and foreign land.

And even though I was staying in a Mexican neighborhood in probably the brownest part of the country, I still couldn't outrun the pervasiveness of whiteness. I still saw images of light-skinned people as the news anchors and game-show hosts on TV. Everywhere I went were billboards with light-skinned, possibly "brown" people, just like me. I still saw my naná desperately doing everything she could to be as lily white as she wanted to be.

Every morning, my grandmother would pile tons of white makeup on her face to make herself look as light as possible. She had learned implicitly and explicitly that white was right and that dark was dangerous. She knew that lighter-skinned people were always portrayed as the most "attractive" on her telenovelas and in the dominant society. She knew that lighter-skinned people were afforded more opportunities and more access. She knew all of this and had internalized racism so deeply that it just became automatic.

As a young boy, I would curiously ask her in my broken Spanglish, "Naná, ¿Por qué usas tanto makeup?"

Without looking up from her daily ritual of trying to erase her skin color, my abuela would always reply, "Mijo, porque quiero parecer más bonita."

Hearing my grandmother tell me that she looked prettier when she whitened her skin left an indelible imprint on my spirit. It made me more confused and validated the false belief that I was somehow better than others because I was lighter-skinned. Here I was thirsty to find acceptance in my natural brown skin, but instead, my grandmother's words and actions unfortunately made me feel uglier and more ashamed.

It's something rarely talked about, not only in Latino circles but in society in general, that we give preferential treatment to lighter-skinned people because society makes us believe they are somehow more "intelligent," more "attractive," and more "normal" than everybody else. How "senora" culture is one in which too many grandmothers, like my own, would never go outside without their umbrellas to hide their skin from the sun in the hope that they won't get any darker. How all of us are victims of a false narrative that centers and focuses predominantly on whiteness.

As I've gotten older, I've come to realize that I can't blame my grandmother or anyone else for this way of thinking. We all live

SACRED LESSONS

in a society where race and racism are embedded in every single thing around us. Racism is a part of the very fabric and foundation of our country and our culture. Racism, along with sexism and all the other isms, are intentionally designed to take us as far away as possible from our spirits, our cultures, and ourselves in order to maintain a system of manipulation and control.

I know this all too well because like my Naná Cuca, I too tried to downplay my Mexicanness. Like Mrs. Hernandez, I too wore long-sleeve shirts and hoodies to hide the color of my skin. Like my father, who as a child changed his name from "Ismael" to "Ishi," I too changed my name, from "Michael" to "Mike." Like so many other people of color, I too am still decolonizing my mind and raising my consciousness so I can fully love and accept myself.

The irony about this way of thinking is that no matter how much I tried to assimilate, no matter how much I tried to embellish my background, no matter how much I tried to run away from myself, I was still rejected, I was still ridiculed, and I was still not able to fully fit in. No matter how hard I tried, I could never, and I will never, be "white."

Even now, when I think about it, I get embarrassed. It was sad, really, really sad that I was so confused. But, as I've said before, I've realized that it wasn't my doing. It's the way I was treated, it's the way that I'm still treated, that forced me to feel ashamed of my culture. It's the way society is structured that made me feel uncomfortable and ultimately made me lose myself for way too long. And although my father tried to instill in me a sense of pride in my culture, race, and identity, it was not enough for me, as a child, to counter the insidiousness of white supremacy on my mind and my body.

MIKE DE LA ROCHA

In those moments when my mind wants to trick me into thinking that darkness is not beautiful, I always think about my grandmother's struggle to survive in America. You see, my Naná Cuca did her best to raise a family all by herself. And the bottom line is that she had a very rough life. Not only was she a Mexican, she was a woman. Not only was she a Mexican woman, she was a Spanish-speaking Mexican woman. Not only was she a Spanish-speaking Mexican woman, she was also raising a family in a completely foreign country that didn't appreciate or value her or her dark-skinned children.

Even though I would visit my grandparents in East LA almost every weekend, the truth is that I would spend most of my time with my grandmother. My abuelo was always gone either working, drinking, or partying somewhere. As such, my grandmother was doing what society, and my grandfather, expected of her: She was working nonstop and taking care of the children. She was cooking and she was cleaning. She was sacrificing her own dreams so my abuelo could do whatever *he* wanted to do.

When my grandmother first immigrated with my family to Boyle Heights, they lived in a one-bedroom house in the back of my Tia Griselda and Tio Benito's home on Eighth Street and Mott. There, she divided their one-bedroom home in half with a curtain so she and my abuelo could have their privacy. The other half was where the children slept, while also serving as a makeshift living room. A few years later, my family moved a couple of blocks away when my abuelo bought their first "real" home on Camulos Street.

Even though my family's first home was moderately sized, there were always nieces, nephews, cousins, and other family members coming from México to stay with them. In our culture, it's customary to have relatives stay with you for months

130

SACRED LESSONS

and sometimes even years at a time. It's a value that my father instilled in me, and it is why even when I lived in a small condo, I would always have friends or family live with me when they needed a place to stay.

With the purchase of their first home, my family had a lot more bills to pay. My Naná Cuca immediately started looking for a job. Fortunately, both she and my Tia Consuelo were able to find employment in the garment industry working as skilled seamstresses in a broken-down building in downtown Los Angeles. Or to be more specific, they both began working in a sweatshop on Broadway Boulevard.

Alongside countless other poor, predominantly Mexican women, my grandmother worked nonstop for very little pay. Unlike my abuelo, who enjoyed the privilege of going to work and then coming home to fully cooked meals, my grandmother's reality was completely different. Despite her exhaustion from a long day of work, she still had to cook dinner, help the children with their homework, prepare the kids for bed, and meticulously arrange my grandfather's clothes and lunch for the following day—all before he arrived home from work.

Nevertheless, amidst it all, my grandmother never once complained. I always wondered how she was able to do this all by herself. Despite working late into the night hemming a brand-new pair of pants or some fancy new dress on her antique Singer sewing machine, my grandmother was able to find some semblance of joy within all the turbulence of her life. And I will always remember my grandmother singing along at the top of her lungs to her favorite Julio Iglesias songs on the radio, or talking with her beloved parakeets that she adored as much as her children.

131

But the memory that I will always love the most is seeing my abuela laugh out loud as she watched her favorite telenovelas on her small portable TV in the kitchen. No matter how late it was, this would be the only time when I would see my grandmother completely free. She didn't care who was watching or what was happening in the house because this was her time, this was her escape, this was her moment to not have to worry about anything.

Like most households in America, and I would argue across the globe, women like my Naná Cuca are the backbone and the center of our families. My Naná Cuca took on the majority of the family responsibilities. My Naná Cuca was the one who my father and all his siblings went to when they needed a safe haven. It's the women, it's always been the women, who made sure that we have everything we need emotionally, physically, and spiritually.

My Naná Cuca was no different. It was my grandmother who single-handedly traveled with my father, my niño, and my Tia Guadalupe when they left Atascaderos and took a small single-propeller plane to Culiacán before taking a freight train to Ensenada, where they would stay with relatives for over a year. It was my grandmother who took care of the children while they waited for my abuelo to pick them up to travel to the United States. It was my grandmother who defied my grandfather's wishes and encouraged and ultimately pushed my father to apply to and eventually attend college—the first in his immediate family to do so in America. It was my grandmother who did all of this and so much more.

I remember my father telling me the story of when he got the courage to finally ask my abuelo for permission to attend UC Santa Barbara. As the story goes, my father hesitantly asked my grandfather, "Papá, ¿qué pensarías si me fuera a estudiar en la universidad?"

Translation: "Papá, what would you think if I went to study at college?"

Without flinching, my grandfather immediately responded, "¡No! Tienes que trabajar para ayudar a la familia."

My father knew that my abuelo would say no, that he would tell him he needed to start working immediately to support the family. It was a foregone conclusion that my grandfather would be adamantly against him going to college. As such, my father did what he always did: he approached my Naná Cuca for help.

"Mamá, ¿y tú qué piensas si me fuera a estudiar en la universidad?"

As expected, my Naná Cuca immediately said, "Hijo, tienes que ir a estudiar!"

My grandmother's reply was more of a command, more of a statement, than a response. She knew all too well that going to college would transform my father's life for the better. She knew this would be his way to escape the Vietnam War and to have a fighting chance at achieving the elusive "American Dream." She knew that going to college would provide my father with the experiences she had always wanted for herself but had had a hard time achieving in the United States because of her gender and the way society viewed her.

One day, while in high school, my Uncle Albert asked my grandmother, "Mamá, what are you doing working in a sweatshop?"

Replying in Spanish, my grandmother said, "I could never grasp the language. English has always been so difficult for me to learn, so I had no choice but to work there."

Stunned, my uncle continued, "But Mom, you're one of the smartest people I know."

"Si, Mijo, pero…" she said as she proceeded to tell my uncle that she had attended one of the most prestigious universities in all of México. She let him know that she even got a teaching credential and taught fifth- and sixth-grade students before immigrating to the United States. Despite what society thought of her, my grandmother had always loved teaching and was hopeful that she would be able to teach in America.

When my uncle shared this story with me, it made complete sense why my grandmother was the driving force behind my father's decision to go to college. She was his constant motivation because she knew the inherent challenges that race, gender, and income had on one's future. She knew that my father could succeed despite what his racist teachers had told him throughout his schooling. Because of her own experiences, and because of her love of education, she knew that my father could go further than anyone else in our family ever did, and so she pushed him to do so.

My grandmother was brilliant. She loved math and took pleasure in helping me with my homework. Despite her difficulty speaking English, she always took the time to ask me about my grades and if I needed help with my studies. She was a natural-born teacher, which probably explains why my father also fell in love with teaching. She was humble, but she was proud of her children attending college, and she always pushed them to do more.

Who knows what would have happened to my father, or if I ever would have been born, without my Naná Cuca's insistence that he go to college. Who knows what would have been the trajectory of my family if my father hadn't gone to Santa Barbara

SACRED LESSONS

and met my mother. Who knows what would've happened without the constant push of my dear Naná Cuca.

And while I could dream up different scenarios of what would have happened, what I do know for sure is this was my Naná Cuca's way of confronting whiteness. This was her way of silently disrupting an educational system that didn't want brown people like her, or my father, to advance economically in life. This was her way of rebelling against a belief system that till the day she died wanted her to always be "white."

Chapter 12

Wishing on a Star

Work. I've always had a complicated relationship with work, especially since I was raised by two overachieving workaholics. Growing up, and even till this day, my parents don't know how to stop working. They still wake up before the sun rises to be the first person at work, and they're always the last person to leave.

On top of their regular nine-to-five work schedule, my parents have always volunteered in the community, and my father coached practically every sports team my brother and I played on. Through watching them as a child, and now as an adult, I've learned that work, or to be more specific productivity, was how they and society defined their worth.

One day during a conversation with my mother, I asked, "Mamá, you and Papá really don't know how to rest, do you?"

Laughing, my mother replied, "I don't like to rest. The only time that I sit down is when I need to eat, and even that I don't do often."

SACRED LESSONS

Hearing my mother basically describe my everyday workday, I proceeded to ask her, "Why are you and Papá like this?"

Smiling, she continued, "Because we're workers. When you like what you're doing, then you don't even think of it as work. We don't even think about the time. But boy, are we both exhausted at the end of the day."

She went on, "It's hard to rest. I know that I'm tired, but I don't know how to slow down. I just can't do it."

Before I had a chance to ask a follow-up question, my mother changed the subject. Hearing her explain the difficulty that she and my father have always had slowing down made me realize that I too don't know how to rest.

My relationship to work, and to rest, is definitely inherited from my parents and my grandparents. Throwing myself completely into my career is a de la Rocha trait passed down from generation to generation of family members from México to the United States.

But now, as I think about my father's time in the hospital, I can't help but wonder how much of this unhealthy relationship to work contributed to his recurring health problems. How much not setting work boundaries led to his increasing back pain. And in the end, I know the debilitating effect that grind culture had on my father and my mother, who sacrificed their bodies and other parts of themselves in order to be valued as "workers."

As I sat there thinking about all of this, I remember my father lying on his hospital bed and grabbing his phone to make a work call two days after his back surgery.

"Hello, Mason...how are you?" my father asked his colleague from Ventura College who was covering for my dad in his absence.

137

Trying my best to listen in, I heard Mason respond, "How am I! How are you? You're the one that just got out of a major surgery!"

And with his big, husky laugh, the kind that seemed to come from the core of his soul, my father replied, "Everything's fine. The doctors say that I should be going home soon. How did the departmental faculty meeting go?"

Even though my dad had just had a major surgery, here he was once again working. I couldn't believe it. In his freaking hospital bed, my dad was chit chatting with his colleague about administrative politics, proctoring his final exams, and miscellaneous shenanigans happening on campus for about ten minutes.

Finally, my father said, "Mason, why don't you come over to the house when I get out of the hospital so we can have some breakfast and catch up on everything in person?"

And before I could tell my father to hang up the phone, I heard Mason reply, "Sounds good, Mayo. Please take good care of yourself. And don't hesitate to call me if you need anything."

After my father hung up the phone, I told him, "Papá, you shouldn't be working right now. You need to just rest."

"I know, Mijo, but I have final exams at the end of the week, and I just need to make sure that Mason has everything he needs to cover for me."

Irritated, I said, "I get it, but I can do that for you. Don't worry about it. Just give me his email and I'll make sure that everything is taken care of."

Since my father retired from teaching full time a year before his third back surgery, he had been trying to keep himself busy. He never wanted to retire in the first place, because teaching was what kept him alive. Teaching gave him a sense of purpose.

SACRED LESSONS

Teaching was his destiny, his calling. Next to his family, teaching meant absolutely everything to him.

Ventura College, a community college, had become my father's home away from home. It was the place where he made lifelong friends and helped build a campus that was more accessible and welcoming to all students. It was the place where he could look outside his office window and remember that his father had picked fruit at this exact same location decades ago as a farmworker. It was the one place that defined him and made him into the person he is today.

Fortunately, after almost a year of not being able to do what he loved the most, my father had finally gotten a part-time job teaching a couple of classes at his beloved Ventura College. And like my dad always did, he couldn't just teach one or two classes; he once again threw himself completely into all of the campus politics and drama. Since he wasn't the chair of the Social Sciences Department anymore, he did the next best thing, which was to mentor and give advice, often unsolicited, to his friend and colleague Mason, who was now in Dad's previous leadership position.

I remember coming home to check up on him on the weekends and finding out that my father had spent the past few days preparing for a departmental meeting with the college president. The best part about all of this was that he wasn't even going to attend the meeting, but here he was providing strategy on how to make sure their budget or faculty positions were safeguarded in case they were forced to downsize the department.

My father and Ventura College have had a long-lasting love affair, and their history is intimately intertwined. My father started working at the college in 1974. At that time, there were no Chicano professors. None. He was the first Chicano professor

MIKE DE LA ROCHA

hired at the college, even though it had opened its doors in 1925. Besides my father, Ventura College had one other Chicano counselor and another Chicano who worked in the Equal Opportunity Program. Other than the janitorial staff, that was it. It was just the three of them.

In the late 1970s, Ventura depicted itself as an almost exclusively all-white community even though people of color had been a part of the city since its inception. In fact, in the 1880s, the west side of Ventura was called "Tortilla Flats" because it was known as a "Spanish" and "Indian" town. A mural down the street from where I learned to surf says, *This mural is a narrative depicting historically significant or interesting buildings and pictures of the varied cultural backgrounds of the population—"Chumash, Mexican, Spanish, Asian, African-American, and European" which evolved into Ventura, as we know it today.*

Despite the multiracial history of Ventura, and the fact that the Chumash have been on this land for at least the last ten thousand years, Ventura College, like the powers that be in Ventura, was predominately white. However, as a direct result of the civil rights movement, my father was hired alongside Ola Washington, the first African American professor hired at the college, and Dr. Joyce Evens, one of the first women professors on campus. Together, they affectionately became known as the "Big Three."

Being the first of anything is always hard, but being the first Chicano, the first African American, and one of the first women ever hired was extremely difficult. They were confronted with constant racist and sexist attacks. For many years the three of them had to fight like hell to directly challenge the institutional racism and the overt racism of the campus staff and the Ventura College leadership.

SACRED LESSONS

Together they made a pact that whenever any of them needed anything, they would all show up, no questions asked. They always had each other's backs, and they were my first examples of the power of multiracial solidarity and organizing.

The three of them—Ola, Joyce, and my dad—constantly fought with the college administration and faculty. They would go to meetings, which often became all-out wars. They fought many battles and eventually succeeded in bringing ethnic and women's studies to the college's curriculum. My father once told me that a white professor tried to hit him in the head with a chair because he didn't think that he or any of the other Big Three were "qualified" to be teaching at Ventura College.

Knowing this history gave me an understanding and a context as to why my father was still working from his hospital bed. Now, I don't agree with it, but I can see why calling Mason was so important to my father. He absolutely adores Ventura College, and despite my telling him to stop working, he can't seem to let go. Even in his current physical condition, he's still doing everything he can to ensure that the hard-fought wins of the Big Three are institutionalized and never scaled back or, worse, forgotten.

As I contemplated all of this, I began to think about how much I worked, despite my body, and my wife, telling me to slow down. I started to ponder whether this was a direct result of my ego or some sort of savior complex that made me, and my father, believe that if we didn't keep working, then no one else would.

A couple of days later, I emailed my father's colleague about grading his blue books, since it was clear that my father wasn't coming home from the hospital anytime soon.

MIKE DE LA ROCHA

From: Mike de la Rocha
Sent: Saturday, August 01, 2015, at 8:58 AM
To: Mason Court
Cc: Albert de la Rocha
Subject: Mayo's Health + Grades

Mason –

This is Mayo's son Michael reaching out to see if you or someone else could grade my dad's final blue books?

My brother Albert (who's cc-ed on this email) could drop off his grade books so you could determine the final grades so please reach out to him to arrange him dropping it off.

My dad has been in-and-out of intensive care since Tuesday and is not doing very good. As such, he will not be able to teach in the fall semester as of now.

As you know, he's at Ventura Community Memorial Hospital if you'd like to stop by, and please let us know if we could do anything for you.

Thanks,

Michael

After sending that email, I tried to stop myself from getting too emotional. As optimistic as I am, it was the first time that I had ever written the words "not doing very good." I didn't even want to consider anything other than my father getting

SACRED LESSONS

better and going back to teach once again at his beloved Ventura College. But, as I sat there, I began to realize just how depressed my father really was. Not being able to teach had affected his mental health, and not being able to run with his friends had led to his declining physical strength. In fact, not being able to work was contributing to him believing that he no longer had any worth, or value.

And right when I was about to jump into a dark rabbit hole, right when I was about to let horrible thoughts flood my mind about whether my father would ever be able to walk out of the hospital, I saw that I had gotten a response from Mason.

> From: Mason Court
> Sent: Saturday, August 01, 2015, at 9:40 AM
> To: Michael de la Rocha
> Cc: Albert de la Rocha
> Subject: Mayo's Health + Grades
>
> Thank you, Michael, and Albert,
>
> I just spoke with Albert, and we'll connect sometime over the next few days regarding your Dad's gradebooks, etc. I'll take care of his final exams over the weekend.
>
> Take good care of your Dad; from what Albert told me, it's going to take some time for the anesthesia to work its way out of his system (your Dad told me on the phone on Thursday that he had a seven-hour surgery). It's difficult for him right now, but he will be doing really

well very soon. I am glad to know you're there with him—he is so very proud of you both.

My wife Ann and I are available to help in any way, so please don't hesitate to call me; let your mom know, too.

Take care,

Mason

After reading his reply, and especially the words "It's difficult for him right now, but he will be doing really well very soon," I felt like I could finally breathe a little better. Unfortunately, like my father, I too only slow down when my body completely shuts down. Like both of my parents, I go hard. It's almost as if I'm trying to do as much as humanly possible because I know that time is not promised to anyone. And trust me when I say that my father's latest hospital visit is not making me want to slow down any more than I have to.

But I'm also starting to realize that I overwork myself to overcompensate for what I'm lacking inside. I work myself to the bone because that's the one thing I can control. I work myself to the brink of exhaustion because I'm postponing the difficult work that I must do on myself. And I work too much because work has always been the one place where I could get the external validation that I can't seem to give myself.

Like my parents, I only know how to give of myself. All I know, all I've ever been taught, is how to serve. I feel an immense amount of guilt if I focus too much on myself and not on others. And despite knowing this is a false and harmful way of thinking, deprogramming myself and my mind is a slow process. I know

SACRED LESSONS

that I have to prioritize self-care. I know that I have to learn how to receive as much as I give. I know that I have to learn how to let go and be okay with other people helping me.

And like so many times before, knowing and acting are two very different things. So the Creator did what the Creator always does: She forced me to stop and reflect. She forced me to reconsider why I only know how to give, and why it's so hard for me to be open to receive. She forced me to stop and focus on me.

A couple of days before the conversation I had with my mother, I contracted COVID-19 for the second time. Getting sick forced me to slow down, stop working, reflect on my unhealthy work habits, and finally rest.

This is why my early morning routine, early morning ritual really, of prayer and meditation has saved my life. In the silence of the morning, and within the silence of myself, I find the courage to do the necessary healing work. I feel the presence of my abuelo, ibrahim, and all of my ancestors guiding me. I know that through these ancient traditions and practices, I'm able to return to my full and authentic self each and every morning.

But I also know this inward journey is the one place where I can get the courage to shed the layers of indoctrination that have made me think that I have to take on the work and responsibilities of others. This inward journey is the one place where I can love my inner child and tell him that he's indeed safe and beautiful. The one place where I can begin to recognize that I'm not the same person, but rather someone who's constantly growing and changing every single day.

I guess this is the secret that's been intentionally hidden from me, from us: That the magic I need, the courage I seek, can rarely, if ever, be found outside of myself. That the validation I seek can never be found externally through my "work" or my career. That the medicine I need has always been, and will always be, within me.

That's why I'm committed to doing the necessary shadow work and confronting those aspects of myself that have been broken and scarred. For the past twenty-plus years, I have dived deep into African and indigenous spiritual practices to learn how to heal and love myself. I have read a ton of books, participated in various rituals and ceremonies, and have learned that healing is not linear, healing is not easy, but healing is sacred.

As I lay in my bed after a night of intense night sweats caused by the COVID-19 virus, I received a text message from my dear friend, my dear colleague, my dear angel, Carola: Brother, remember our bodies take a beating through cell mutations to prompt us to stop and reflect on something.

As I read those words, my heart skipped a beat, as the truth of her words could not mask the "work" that I still needed to do. I needed to stop and reflect on where I was, where I was going, and whether it really was what I wanted for myself, and for my life. Was I really, genuinely happy? And if not, what needed to change and what course of action did I need to take?

I know I have inherited my unhealthy work habits from my parents, but there's something much deeper at play here. I know that I mask my fear of failure by working too much. I know that I blame the fact I'm a Virgo for my unending drive and desire to be perfect. And although I know that perfectionism is a lie, I still have a hard time shedding the layers of societal indoctrination that tell me I'm not worthy if I'm not perfect, if I'm not productive, if I'm not overworking myself to the bone.

I know that my thirst for perfection, my thirst to excel in everything, my innate competitiveness is rooted not only in my desire to be loved but in my desire to make my father proud.

SACRED LESSONS

And although I know deep down that my father is proud of me, I guess I overwork myself because I want him to know that I'm doing as much as I can to make sure his devotion to our family, and to the community, will live on through me. That I acknowledge his sacrifice, and that all of his hard work was not done in vain, but was indeed all worth it.

As I lay there thinking about my father, and our relationship to work, I proceeded to read the rest of Carola's text: You're strong-bodied, heart, and spirit, so I know that you're going to be okay. I invite you to go within and see what your Highest Self or your ancestors want you to pay attention to? To reflect on? to try?

Carola, like life itself, was pushing me, inviting me, asking me to pay attention. She was asking me to reflect, and just as importantly, to try. As I smiled at the fact that I had such a beautiful friend in my life, I continued reading her text.

This is my offering of being an Action Warrior for you, inspired by this excerpt from our last book club reading of Mariame Kaba's "We Do This 'Til We Free US," ...self-care is really tricky for me because I don't believe in the self in the way that people determine it here in this capitalist society that we live in. I don't believe in self-care: I believe in collective care, collectivizing our care, and thinking more about how we can help each other.

In that moment, Carola's text redefined my understanding of "care" and broadened it to include more than just myself, but also my loved ones and my communities. She had not just invited me to slow down, she had given me a clear reminder that our society may once again try to force me to think that healing is an individual journey, when in fact it is both an individual and collective experience. She was modeling for me, in real time, how my healing was connected to her healing, and in that recognition, we would both be more than okay, we would be healed.

I know that I am stepping into a new version of myself. I can feel it. A version that knows when and why to slow down. A version that's calmer and more aware of my triggers and my bad habits. A version that's unafraid to verbally express my love for myself and for others.

I don't believe that wishing on a star is naive anymore, because I've witnessed the power of ritual, of prayer, of belief. I believe, in fact I know, that my father will get better because we are connected in ways beyond just the physical. I believe, in fact I know, that we are creating a new world that prioritizes self-love and community care because we are creating this world together in our everyday actions.

As I've said before, I am healing not just for myself, but for my father and for my family. Yes, I am on an inward healing journey that requires me to do a lot of work by myself underneath the early morning rays of the sun or the late-night light of the moon, but it's always magnified in the presence of others.

Carola's text continued with Mariame Kaba's call to action: How do we collectivize care so that when we're sick and we're not feeling ourselves, we've got a crew of people who are not just our prayer warriors, but our action warriors who are thinking through with us?

This is indeed the work ahead for not only me but for all of us. This is our collective test. This is the work that my father and the Big Three started decades ago at Ventura College. A deconstructing and rebuilding of what care, of what work, means for all of us. An acknowledgment of the role of society, systems, and structures on the welfare of our minds and our bodies. Of the need to prioritize self- and community care once and for all.

148

SACRED LESSONS

My spirit guides are telling me that it's my time, it's mi tiempo. This is a new phase in my life, a new moon, a new time to dream, a new time to fall in love with me once again. And that's why Carola's text was another sign, another reminder that I was indeed on the right path. As I sat there alone in my room recovering from my body forcing me to slow down, I simply smiled as Carola's text concluded with her saying the three most important words in my life:

"I love you."

Lesson IV
Compassion

Chapter 13
The Willingness to Let Go

"Sleep with the angels," my mother says as I'm about to hang up the phone.

"I will, Mamá. Good night."

For as long as I could remember, my mom has always ended her evening phone calls this way. It's her way of telling me to never lose faith, and to know that I'll always be protected.

My mom is by far the most religious person I know. Hands down. There's no competition except for maybe Jesus Christ himself. My Auntie Rose even calls her "my angel" because of her almost saintly demeanor and willingness to give of herself to the church, and to anyone else in need. To this day, I still joke around with my mom and tell her that someday I'll become the Catholic priest that she always wanted in the family.

All jokes aside, my mom is the epitome of compassion, forgiveness, and above all else, love. She has shown me the power of spirituality and prayer through her daily actions. Every Sunday, she's at church giving the Eucharist. Every morning and every evening, she reads her Bible. Every night before going to bed, she says her evening prayers. And every week, she visits a friend who has no family around so they can feel less alone.

When I asked my mother where she got her thirst for Catholicism, she immediately replied, "Your Naná Daria."

My maternal grandmother, my Naná Daria, was the strongest and most independent person I've ever known. A woman who was named after her grandfather Dario, she worked in the fields of California while raising eleven children almost all by herself. A woman who would give a random stranger the clothes off her back so that no one would be without. A woman who taught me what unconditional love not only looked like but felt like.

Born on October 25, 1915, in Westminster, California, to Tiburcia Padilla from Chihuahua, México, and Mercede Padilla from Aguascalientes, México, my working-class grandmother did all she could to provide for her family. With a high school education, and sleeping on a wooden floor for most of her childhood, my Naná Daria traveled with her farmworker parents up and down California looking for work. As a child, she picked cotton, lemons, and whatever fruit or vegetable was in season. After her first husband purchased a home on San Jose's east side, my Naná Daria stopped traveling from labor camp to labor camp, and started working full time in a dangerous packing house.

It was against this backdrop that my mother learned her hard work ethic and unflinching belief that we always have to help our family. At eight years old, my mother began working alongside my naná and her brothers Jess and Paul in the fields. My mother worked all day underneath the hot sun picking prunes, despite tarantulas running all around and buzzards trying to attack her and her family. For years, my mom and grandmother would fill

SACRED LESSONS

huge wooden crates with prunes so they could make just enough money to survive.

From that point on, my mother never stopped working. When my grandmother's third husband demanded that my Naná Daria stay home, my mother got a second job during the summer at the same packing house where my grandmother worked sorting out fruits and vegetables. After working as a cashier at a local pharmacy, my mother would then work from four in the afternoon to four in the morning to help provide for the family, enduring extremely harsh working conditions and unwanted sexual advances from an older white male foreman, who also happened to be a teacher at her high school.

Unfortunately, my mother was the main child who worked to support the family because everyone else was too busy running the streets and getting into trouble. When my mom's father left, my naná had a very difficult time raising her children by herself. She relied on Emagene, a close family friend, who would take care of the kids when she was at work, but that proved too difficult and she left soon afterward.

Despite my Naná Daria trying her best to keep the family together, there was little to no money, so she had few options. Under the weight of poverty, and with an utterly broken heart, my Naná Daria made the difficult decision to put my aunties into foster care. To this day, my mom tells me how she used to drive with my grandmother to visit her sisters on the weekends and sit quietly as my Naná Daria cried nonstop during the entire trip.

This is the context that helps explain the difficult dynamics within my family. This is the reason why my aunts ended up in juvenile prison and got pregnant at the ages of fourteen and fifteen. This is why some of my cousins numb their pain with drugs and alcohol. This is why some of my family are houseless and can't find jobs. It is a textbook example of how structural racism works and how trauma gets passed down from generation to generation.

But it is also a textbook example of how patriarchy destroys people and families. You see, my grandmother's husbands were absolutely terrible to her. "Horrific" might be a better word. From being physically beaten and left to die, to being cheated on multiple times, to being verbally abused and constantly yelled at, my grandmother endured a level of pain that no person should ever have to go through.

This is why my family is the way we are. This explains the pain and the hardship. However, my family's situation is not unique; unfortunately, we've lived a universal experience that can be found in so many other families. We all hide certain family secrets because of societal expectations or fear of judgment. But my family's struggles are what makes them real. My family's struggles are what makes me love them even more.

I've always felt closer to my mom's family because they've always been more truthful, more authentic, and more giving than my father's immediate side of the family. As the side of the family that has the least to give, they, like so many other poor people, always give the most. It's so humbling to witness my cousin who literally lives off of $800 a month be the first person to offer money or a place to sleep anytime somebody needs it. And while it's true that their hard life may have forced them to be more guarded and suspicious of others, with me and my family, they've always been nothing but pure love and support.

My mom's family doesn't try to hide their hardships. Oh no, they lay everything out on the table for full display. If someone's beefing with someone, trust me when I tell you that you're going

SACRED LESSONS

to know about it. There's no hiding any drama in my mother's family. Nope. None. Personally, I identify with this attitude and am drawn to their willingness to be who they are no matter what others, especially other family members, think of them.

Despite their struggles, my mother's family has persevered and overcome incredible odds. And truthfully, more than anything else, my Naná Daria and my mother's family have shown me that in spite of not having material wealth, they have survived because they have each other. Despite having certain strained relationships, they still show up for each other when anyone is in need. And despite what the outside world may think of them, they have always been there for me and my family. Always.

Writing about my mom's family, and my Naná Daria in particular, is hard, really hard. It brings up issues of poverty and inequality, sexism and violence, and completely complicates my idealized perception of my father. You see, writing about my mom's family has forced me to confront some hard truths about the ways that I've inherited my father's trauma, and the need to always be in control.

As a child, I remember looking forward to my Naná Daria spending the entire summer with us. When she visited, we would go on mini excursions to the mall or the zoo or even go camping by the beach. It became a yearly tradition and was something that brought me and my grandmother closer together. I looked forward to her staying with us every year, and it became my favorite part of the summer.

Regardless of what we did, I absolutely loved being around my Naná Daria. I would spend countless hours going on long walks with her, playing rummy, or watching her favorite Oakland A's play baseball. I never left her side and developed an almost inseparable bond with my grandmother.

However, being so young and naive, I never really picked up on all the tension between my father and my grandmother. As I got older and became more aware of what was happening, I noticed my father's hostility toward my Naná Daria, and without getting into too many details, let's just say that my father was completely jealous when it came to my grandmother. In fact, he was outright hurtful and disrespectful to her.

A case in point: Every morning during these summer visits, my grandmother would offer my father some coffee and say, "Good morning, Mayo," and without fail, he would pretend that he didn't hear her. It was awful. I would get out of bed and run downstairs to spend time with my Naná Daria and find the two of them sitting there in silence. It was not until my mother would come downstairs and demand, "Mayo, my mother's talking to you. You better answer her!" that my father would finally say, "Good morning."

At the time, I couldn't comprehend what was happening, but the situation got bad, really bad, really fast. Speaking with my mother years after my Naná Daria passed away, I gained a bit more insight into why my father didn't speak to my grandmother, and why they had such a strained relationship in the first place. And like most relationships, the truth is a lot more complicated than it seems.

As I slowly tiptoed into a conversation that I hoped wouldn't trigger my mother, I softly said, "Mamá, why didn't Papá have a good relationship with Naná Daria?"

Looking at me with an expression that said "So you really want to do this?" my mom subtly asked, "Why do you want to know?"

"I'm just curious. I know that they sometimes didn't see eye to eye on things, so I was just wondering what happened."

SACRED LESSONS

And without wasting any time, my mother got straight to the point and matter-of-factly said, "Your father was mean to my mother. He was really, really mean to her."

Somewhat surprised, because I vaguely remembered the arguments my parents had about my grandmother staying with us every summer, I responded, "But why? Why do you think that Papá was so mean to Naná?"

Without acknowledging my reaction, my mom simply responded, "Do you remember when Naná got sick, and I had to go to San Jose almost every weekend to take care of her?"

"Yes, I remember that, Mamá," I said hesitantly.

With tears starting to form in her eyes, my mother then said, "Nobody helped me. Not my sisters, not my brothers, not your father. Nobody. I was all alone."

Not knowing how to respond, I kept quiet as my mother continued, "I had no choice but to go visit Naná as much as I could because I couldn't depend on anyone else. She needed nonstop attention, so I became the only person that would take care of her."

And right when I was about to ask a question, my mother said, "Your father would get so mad at me for going to take care of my mother. He would tell me that I needed to stay home. He would try to make me feel bad for leaving so often."

Finally able to get a word in, I asked, "And what did you say?"

Raising her voice, my mother said, "I told him that he didn't have a say. If he didn't like me going to visit my mother, then it was just too bad."

"Too bad?"

Aggravated as the memories seemed to be as vivid as ever, my mother immediately said, "Yes, too bad! Nothing mattered more to me than being with my mother."

"What did Naná say about all this? Did she know that Papá didn't want you to visit her?"

"Naná used to ask me, 'Mija, why doesn't your husband like me?'"

As I sat there quietly as the gravity of the situation began to sink in for both of us, my mother continued, "She used to say that I needed to stay home more with Papá. She said that that was what I needed to do. She said that that was my duty as a wife."

"And what did you tell her?"

"I would tell her that I wanted to be with her. I would tell her that she was my priority. It would make me cry because Papá was so jealous of my relationship with Naná."

After trying to compose herself a little more, my mother finally said, "After Naná passed, your father had the nerve to tell me, 'I'm sorry that your mother passed away, but at least I have you all to myself now.'"

Not knowing what to say, I stayed completely quiet, like a schoolboy who just overheard something that he wasn't supposed to hear. Then my mother said, with a level of contempt in her voice that I had rarely heard before, "Can you believe that your father would tell me that? Can you believe that your father would be so selfish?"

Wanting to redirect her anger toward anything besides my father, I quickly said, "He probably meant to say that he missed you and wanted to spend more time with you. It probably just came out the wrong way."

At this point, my mother wasn't paying attention to anything I was saying. "That was so selfish of your father," she said. "It was horrible. To tell me that he was happy because he had me all to himself was just plain wrong."

SACRED LESSONS

With utter sadness in her voice, she continued. "Every time your father and I would argue about Naná, I would cry and tell him, 'If you don't change, I'm leaving you. I don't know where I'll go, but I'm not going to stay with you. If you're not going to support me, then I will leave. Even if I have to live out on the streets on my own.'"

Not knowing how to respond, and wishing that I had never brought up the subject in the first place, I didn't say a word as my mother said, "He would tell me that he felt like he wasn't even married to me anymore because I was never around, I was never home. He would tell me that I spent more time with my mother than I did with him. That was so wrong, Mijo, so wrong of your father to do that."

By this point, my mother was crying. It felt as if she was not only releasing but also teaching me an important lesson about life, about love, about marriage.

With tears streaming down her cheeks, she said, "Your father hurt me, he really did. I told him that I'd have the rest of my life to spend with him, but I'm not going to have my mother for that much longer, so I needed to be with her."

Reaching for her hand, I gently said, "I'm so sorry, Mamá. I'm so sorry that Papá acted that way."

Hoping to change the subject because I didn't want my "perfect" image of my parents to be ruined even more, I contemplated talking about something superficial, like whether she was hungry or whether she wanted to go shopping at the mall. But I couldn't do it. Although I didn't want to know the whole story, something inside me needed to know the truth, the whole truth.

As I sat there wondering what to say next, I could hear the underlying resentment in my mother's voice. I could feel the pain in her body. I could sense the overwhelming hurt of it all.

And before I knew it, my mother was letting everything out. Absolutely everything. There were no more secrets, there was no more hiding, there was just the truth.

"Years later, after your Naná Daria passed away, your Naná Cuca got really sick. So your father and I would go to Fresno every weekend to check up on her. And before you knew it—"

"Before you knew it, what, Mamá? What? What happened?" I asked.

"And before you knew it, I was doing the exact same thing for Naná Cuca that I did for Naná Daria. Your father didn't know how to process the pain of losing his mother, so there I was once again at the hospital, the only one taking care of her. There I was dropping everything in my life once again because no one else wanted to be inconvenienced to take care of Naná Cuca."

"So you did the exact same thing for Naná Cuca that you did for Naná Daria?" I asked, bewildered.

"Yes. I did the exact same thing. I would cry in the corner of the hospital all by myself because it was too hard for me to take care of Naná Cuca. It reminded me too much of Naná Daria."

As I gently held my mother's hand, she said, "I would tell your Aunt Guadalupe to help, but she never did. I would get Naná Cuca up in the morning and put her on her wheelchair so I could dress her. Seeing her decline and decline, it was so hard. It was just so hard."

As the tears rushed back, she continued, "I didn't want to do it, but no one else did. So there I was driving up north to take care of Naná Cuca every weekend like I did with my own mother."

My mother changed her whole life around to take care of my Naná Cuca. Eventually, my Naná Cuca even moved into my family's home in Ventura so they could take care of her 24/7. My

SACRED LESSONS

parents reorganized their home, changed their work schedules, and made sure she had the best care and medical attention possible. They even rearranged their entire kitchen nook and made it into a makeshift bedroom for my grandmother.

Despite being triggered by the memories of taking care of her own mother, every night my mother would make dinner for my grandmother. Every night, my mother would feed and bathe my Naná Cuca. Every night, my mother would stay up with her until she fell asleep, and then sleep downstairs so she could be close by in case she needed anything.

It was my mom, not my aunts or my uncles, not even my own father, who took care of my Naná Cuca every night and every day. And in doing so, she taught me another important lesson, a sacred lesson that my grandmother had instilled in her: that family, both biological and chosen, matters, and that our relationships with our parents, no matter how strained or complicated, also matter.

As the heaviness of the entire situation sank in, I waited some time so my mother could finally gather herself and then asked, "What did Papá say about you doing all of this?"

Before answering, my mother must have picked up on how I was feeling, as her body language shifted. It had been a tense conversation, and I wasn't trying to dig up even more hurt or resentment toward my father.

As we sat there holding hands, my mother looked at me and said, "It took your Naná Cuca to get sick and pass away for your father to understand why I had to be with my mamá so much."

"So did Papá finally apologize?"

Without directly answering my question, my mother brought up the issue of jealousy once again as a way for me, or for both of us, to make sense of it all. "Your poor father was jealous of my relationship with Naná because he never received that kind of love as a child. That was why he acted the way he did when both of your nanás got sick."

Stunned at her response after such a roller-coaster ride of emotions, I said, "But Naná Daria loved him so much. Why would he be so jealous of her?"

"Naná always loved Papá. But it was too hard for your father to accept her love because he didn't know what love from a parent should look like. That's why he didn't know what to do when his own mother passed away."

With her head down, almost as if she felt ashamed for telling me the truth, my mother then said, "When you don't get love, you get jealous when other people do because you wish that you had that kind of love for yourself. I don't agree with how your father treated Naná Daria, or me, for that matter, but I do understand why it was so hard for him to accept my relationship with her."

After saying this, my mother got quiet, very quiet. After a few seconds passed, I got the nerve to ask, "How did that make you feel? How did all of this make you feel?"

Anticipating that I would ask that question, my mother blurted out, "Your father just wanted us. He didn't need anybody else. He just wanted us all to himself. He didn't even want to be with his own family. I used to tell him, 'I'm sorry, hon, but I need other people in my life. I love my family, I really do. You and the boys mean everything to me, but I need to be around other people.'"

Stopping for a second, as if considering what she was going to say next, my mother then said, "That's how your father kept acting when he retired and I was still working."

"What do you mean kept acting?" I asked.

"After work I like to go to the store, and he always calls me and asks, 'Where are you? What are you doing?'"

"I'm shopping," my mother said, almost with an air of defiance.

In a deeper voice, imitating my father, she said, "Are you almost done? When are you coming home?"

Switching back to her normal voice, she said, "I'll be home when I'm done."

This sums up the complicated dance between compassion and control. This sums up how two of the most important women in my life, my mother and my Naná Daria, raised me and why writing about my grandmother is so important to my life story.

To this day, my mother never makes excuses for my father's behavior, but she did, and still does, have a deep understanding of the difficulty that he had expressing himself. She has a deep compassion for the lack of love he received as a child. And like my Naná Daria, her concern for my father, for everyone, is limitless and allows her not only to hold my father accountable but never to give up on him.

My mother and my grandmother, more than anyone else, have always taught me the importance of giving people a second chance. They have shown me time and time again how I lose a piece of myself when I lose hope in another person's ability to change. They have taught me how multiple truths can exist at the same time, and how it's critically important for me to see and understand different perspectives and points of views. And in doing so, they have taught me not only how to truly love but how to be loved.

This is what makes my mother and my Naná Daria so special. This is the essence of who they are. That's why my father fell in love with my mother in the first place. It was her heart, it's always been her heart. I can't tell you how many times I've wanted to write off someone for being disrespectful or selfish, but then my mother reminds me about the importance of understanding context. She always pushes me to get a better perspective on a situation so I can develop a deeper sense of empathy for why a person acted the way they did. She always reminds me that I must center compassion in everything I do and in everything I believe.

This is the reason why it's been so hard for me to write this chapter. I can't understand why my Naná Daria's first husband physically beat her. I get angry knowing that her second husband stayed around just to get his citizenship papers before going back to México, where he had a whole other family waiting for him. Yes, I can point to the lack of love that my father received as a child for his inconsiderate behavior toward my grandmother. Yes, I can do all of this, but this still doesn't justify any of it or account for the underlying truth. And that truth is that my father and so many of us men try to control women because this is what we've been indoctrinated to do for our entire lives. We have been taught that women, and everything else for that matter, are there for our benefit and for our taking.

Writing about my Naná Daria forces me to consider the aspects of control that I've inherited from my father and from the broader society in general. Writing about my grandmother forces me to reflect on my own behavior and question whether I act the same way with Claudia. Do I try to control her? Do I get jealous of her relationships? Am I acting like my father still does with my mother?

Unfortunately, if I'm being honest with myself, then the answer is probably yes. Yes, I do try to control my wife and dictate what she does. Yes, I have inherited my father's bad habits and behavior. And yes, I recognize that I have a lot more work to do in order to stop these harmful patterns so I can model and teach my son a different way.

I would like to say that I'm getting better, I would like to say that I'm improving, but only Claudia and God know the answer. What I do know for sure is that I constantly have to check myself. I have to remain aware of my thoughts and my actions. I have to check in regularly with Claudia about not only our marriage but about how I can better improve as a partner and a friend.

My Naná Daria never really had that companion she could grow old with and trust. All three of her marriages were toxic at best, and abusive at worst. That's one of the main reasons why she poured so much love into me and my family. Unlike my father, who carried the shame of not knowing how to show his love, my Naná Daria freely gave her love to me and to everyone else she encountered.

To this day, I think about my grandmother often. I even have her picture tattooed on my left arm, the arm closest to my heart. She taught me how to give and how to receive love. She taught me how to forgive and how to understand. And although we're not supposed to have favorites, in my heart of hearts, I knew that I was her favorite, as she was mine.

"I love you more than you'll ever know, Naná," I said during the last year of her life.

As I sat beside her, playing with her gray silky hair as I was accustomed to always doing, I was acutely aware of how special those remaining moments were for both of us. I wanted her to know that whatever happened in the next few months, she had positively impacted my life. That she was my inspiration and my motivation. That she had succeeded in planting seeds in me, and in all of her family, that would water the earth and our families for generations to come.

"You know that, right, Naná? You know that I love you more than anything else?"

And like she responded every time I said that, and like I teach my son to respond when I or anyone else shares their love for him, my grandmother simply replied, "I know."

Chapter 14
Seeing My Father Cry

As much as I love the summer because I get to spend more time with my kids, go to the beach more regularly, and even sneak out for one or two family vacations, I must say that I absolutely love the Christmas holiday season.

In Latino households, many of us don't celebrate Christmas on December 25; instead, we get together on Christmas Eve. For as long as I can remember, we have always alternated between celebrating Christmas at my parents' home or at my Tia Guadalupe's house. Every year, every family brings something to dinner—whether that be tamales, turkey, salad, dessert; you name it, someone brings it, and we all feast together.

My father absolutely loves this time of year, not so much because he gets to see his brothers and sisters, but because he gets to spend quality time with his boys. It's become a yearly tradition that my brother and I try to get to our parents' house a little earlier on Christmas Eve so we can go with my father to pick up some booze and cigars before we help him and my mom with any last-minute preparations.

Without fail, every year is like a well-choreographed dance. My mom spends days making the house immaculately clean, and then we help my father clean up the backyard. We put up all the chairs and tables, test the makeshift sound system, bring out the chips and salsa, and then wait for the arrival of all the other family members.

My niño is often the first one over, often with his daughter as his designated driver. He says his customary hellos, asks my mother, whom he affectionately calls "Big G," if she needs any help in the kitchen, and then immediately goes to the backyard, where we start drinking beer before the dreaded tequila makes its way out.

This is usually followed by my Tio Albert, who shows up with my abuelo, since he's been taking care of him for the past fifteen years. After driving from Clovis all the way down to Ventura, my uncle is happy to be able to just sit down and rest. The second youngest of the family, my Tio Albert is not only godfather to my brother but someone I've gotten closer to in the past couple of years.

"Hola, pops," my father says as my grandfather sits next to him, both of them opening their Coronas and proceeding to partake in the male bonding ritual of getting drunk.

My grandfather, like my father, loves to be around his family. So, beaming from ear to ear, my abuelo proceeds to sing the lyrics to the ranchera music blasting from the speakers. As I sit outside next to my grandfather, I too bask in the warmth of being around the men in my family, and love seeing my father so happy.

SACRED LESSONS

By this time, my youngest uncle, Uncle Javier, and his family arrive, bringing tamales and some soda, followed by my aunt. The last person, without a doubt, is always my second aunt, Tia Guadalupe. It doesn't matter if we tell her we're starting four hours earlier, because she's always going to be no less than one or two hours late.

Once she arrives with her family, and people have had a chance to settle in, the festivities begin with all of us getting our own food and sitting at our designated "kids" or "adults" table. I can't seem to relate too much to the adults, so I often find myself at the kids' table or outside eating with my niño, who's often drinking all alone.

But before anyone starts eating, it's customary that my abuelo says his annual prayer and blesses the food. It's a sweet tradition that I adore where everyone gathers around my abuelo as his love, tenderness, and warmth are on full display.

After drinks have been drunk and the food has been eaten, without fail, my father and I get into some heated argument with Guadalupe and Uncle Javier's wife about politics or religion. Of course nothing's ever resolved, and I end up completely stunned at their conservative views and wonder how we could even be related. Regardless, before it gets too out of control, we silently agree to disagree and begin to open presents.

I don't know how this tradition started, but in my family, Tia Guadalupe hands out presents to everyone one by one. After receiving their gift, the person gets up, hugs the person who gave them the present, and then opens it in front of everyone. And while this is a very heartwarming custom, it's exhausting watching hours and hours of people opening gifts.

For me, I prefer not to wait for my Tia Guadalupe, as I find joy in personally giving my gifts to my parents and then sitting next to them as they open them. Apart from birthdays and other special occasions, this is a chance for me to show them how much I love and appreciate them. And while I understand that love cannot be measured by gifts and material possessions, I still try my very best to make sure that I give my parents the most thoughtful Christmas gifts possible.

I will never forget one Christmas that took place during a year that was particularly difficult for my father. He had been having a hard time at work with his peers and the college administration. On top of all the campus dynamics, the politics of the community was starting to really wear on him.

That year, while Tia Guadalupe was handing out gifts, and knowing that my father didn't like to be the center of attention, I went around my aunt and grabbed my father's gift while someone else was opening their present.

"Here you go, Papá," I said, breaking the order of the gift giving.

"Thank you, Mijo," my dad said as he set the present aside.

Wanting him to open it while everyone else was distracted, I said, "No, Papá. Open it. You don't have to wait. You can open it now."

As he ripped off the red Christmas wrapping paper, I stood next to him in anticipation.

"Thank you so much, Mijo," my father said enthusiastically as he held a box set of Neil Diamond's greatest hits on CD and some Cuban cigars that I'd thrown into the box. Looking at him, he seemed genuinely excited and happy about his gift.

After I leaned down to give him a kiss on the cheek, I slowly walked away, making sure not to let my eyes leave my father. It was in those milliseconds that I could tell whether my father really liked his gift. If he set it down right away, he was somewhat indifferent, but if he held it a little longer or showed it to my mom, then it meant he genuinely liked it.

As I walked toward the kitchen, I saw my father show the CDs to my mom, and I knew that I had succeeded in my Christmas gift giving. Later that night, after all the festivities were done and I was helping wash the dishes and clean up the house so my mom wouldn't have to do it all by herself in the morning, I made my way upstairs to get ready for bed. My family was sleeping in my old bedroom, with our children on an air mattress and Claudia and me on the bed. Once everyone was in their pajamas and ready to call it a night, I decided to go around the house one last time to make sure all the lights were turned off.

As I walked down the stairs, I noticed that the living room light was on. Not only that, I heard some music faintly playing. Slowly, I tiptoed from the stairs to the kitchen so as not to disturb whatever was happening downstairs.

As I quietly turned the corner, I noticed my father all by himself in his recliner and recognized the lyrics to one of his favorite Neil Diamond songs.

"But I got an emptiness deep inside / And I've tried / but it won't let me go / And I'm not a man who likes to swear / but I never cared / for the sound of being alone."

Hearing Neil Diamond's voice didn't shock me, but I witnessed something I never thought I would see. Here was my father, all by himself in the dead of night, thinking that no one else was awake. Here was a man who gave so much of himself for others, who defied societal expectations and judgment, only able to express himself because he thought he was all alone. Here was the most important man in my life, my father—who I saw crying for the first time.

Suddenly, I heard him sing the chorus of the song with utter pain in his voice, and my heart sank even further as he began to cry harder: *"'I am'…I said / To no one there / And no one heard at all / Not even the chair."*

Seeing my father in such a vulnerable state brought me an immense amount of joy as well as heartache. Now crying softly in the distance myself, I heard my father utter the last lines of the song: *"'I am'…I said / 'I am'…I cried / 'I am.'"*

Just a few years earlier, my Nana Cuca passed away in the same room where I was now watching my father break down. The day that my grandmother died, I did see some tears in my father's eyes, but he wouldn't let me see him cry outright. However, in that moment, alone, not knowing that I was there, my father could finally let his emotions out. My father was finally able to be free. My father was finally able to release his pent-up pain and simply cry.

I didn't know what to do. I just froze. I remember thinking, *Should I say something and disrupt the moment? Or do I quietly go back upstairs?* I was truly lost and didn't know what to do. In hindsight, I wish that I could turn back time because I would have done things completely differently.

As the song ended and I saw my father try to compose himself, I waited in the shadows so he wouldn't know that I was watching him. After a couple of minutes, I slowly walked into the kitchen, turned on the rest of the lights, and said, "Papá, are you okay?"

Caught off guard, my father quickly wiped his eyes and said, "I'm fine, Mijo. I was just listening to the CDs that you gave me."

Wanting to make small talk so my father wouldn't feel embarrassed, I responded, "They're pretty good CDs, huh? You now have all of your favorite Neil Diamond songs."

SACRED LESSONS

"Yes, I do, Mijo, thank you. Listening to Neil Diamond makes me really emotional."

I was shocked because this was one of the few times my father admitted how he was feeling, so I took a chance and asked, "Why does listening to Neil Diamond make you feel so emotional, Papá?"

Clearing his throat, he replied, "I guess I can really relate to his lyrics. I feel like he's writing for all of us who are immigrants, all of us who don't feel welcome, all of us who just want a better life for our families."

And after a short pause, he said, "I just feel like he's talking to me."

Jokingly, I said, "Who would have ever thought that a Jewish boy from Brooklyn, New York, would have penetrated the heart of a puro Mexicano from Chihuahua, México?"

Wanting to laugh, but still too emotionally moved by the song, my father couldn't control himself any longer, and he started to cry once again, but only this time in front of me.

In unfamiliar territory, I went up to my father and put my hand on his shoulder. He just sat there with his face in his hands crying and trembling ever so softly.

"It's all right, Papá. You don't need to cry," I said almost automatically.

Even though I didn't want to say those words, they just came out of my mouth. Given that that was the immediate response I got anytime my father saw me crying, I guess it must have been instinctual for me to do the same.

Despite me wanting to tell my father that it was okay to cry. Despite me wanting to tell him that it was okay to show his emotions. Despite me wanting to tell him that he didn't have to feel ashamed or embarrassed, I just stood there quietly without saying another word.

"Thank you, Mijo, I'm okay. I was just thinking about México and life—"

"I know, Papá," I interrupted.

It wasn't that I didn't want my father to share more, but I was caught off guard. I was unprepared, and felt unequipped to handle such a deeply personal and intimate moment with my father. So I ended the conversation. And I did what I was trained to do: I ran away from a beautiful moment that was deeply personal and vulnerable for both of us.

Sensing what I was doing, my father slowly tried to get up and said, "Mijo, thank you for the CDs. It's late. Let's go upstairs so we can both go to bed."

Feeling as if I'd made a drastic mistake and let a rare moment slip by, I said, "Are you sure? We can keep listening to music if you want."

"No, it's okay. I'm tired. We can listen to Neil Diamond tomorrow morning."

"I'm…I'm…" I stuttered, then forced the words to come out. "I'm sorry, Papá. I didn't mean to ruin the moment."

And just when I was about to say more, my father got up and said, "It's okay. Go to bed. It's late already."

"What about you? I thought you said that you were tired. You're not going to go upstairs and go to bed?"

Sitting back down in his recliner, my father replied, "I'll be right up, Mijo. Don't wait for me. Go to bed. I'll be okay. I just want to be alone for a little bit longer."

As I was about to walk upstairs, I paused and looked at my father. I wanted so badly to walk back and hug him. I wanted so badly to tell him what he truly meant to me. I wanted so badly

SACRED LESSONS

for him to know how proud I was to be his son and to know that I truly loved him with all my heart.

Torn, I turned around and said, "Okay, Papá. Have a good night."

My father and I have never spoken about that night. It was a moment that I'm sure we'll both always remember. A moment I know that I will always cherish. Two scared little boys who just wanted to be themselves. Two scared little boys who just wanted to express themselves. Two scared little boys who just wanted to cry.

Years after that Christmas, my father's health started to decline. First, the doctors told him that he wouldn't be able to run anymore, essentially taking away his one form of self-care. The one thing that saved him as a child when he felt so alone. The one thing that helped him create a sense of community and companionship with his running partners and close friends. The one thing that he so desperately needed to survive.

Knowing how much running meant to my dad, Cliff, my father's best friend, told him to buy a bike so that he could still be a part of their weekly runs. Even though it wasn't ideal or what my dad wanted to do, he complied and started riding his bike alongside his friends on their weekly runs. It was such a beautiful gesture that Cliff and his friends made to accommodate my dad and make sure that he felt included in their weekly ritual. They made sure that he still felt needed, and just as importantly, that he still felt wanted.

My dad did this for a few years, but the pain got increasingly worse and the doctor finally told him the dreaded news.

"Mayo, you're going to have to stop riding your bike. You're going to have to concentrate on changing your eating habits. You're going to have to get another back surgery."

MIKE DE LA ROCHA

Knowing there was nothing left to say, my father remained quiet. On top of being forced to retire, now two of the main loves of his life had been taken away from him. Without running and teaching, my father lost a sense of who he was. He was a sailor without a ship, a person wandering without purpose.

My father was devastated. He was lost. He was lonely. He just wanted his old life back. This is when I started to notice that his bouts with depression were becoming more and more prevalent. His temper got shorter, and he would lash out more. I saw him fighting more with my mother, and he just seemed genuinely unhappy.

I tried to come home more often. I tried to call him a couple more times a week. I even confided in Claudia that I was worried about his mental health because he was doing the opposite of what his doctors were telling him to do. Rather than watching what he was eating, my father was eating more to cope with his depression. Rather than seeing a chiropractor or massage therapist, he was spending more time in his recliner watching *Law & Order* reruns. Rather than trying to be more optimistic, he was starting to lose hope.

This is when I started to grasp the real meaning behind his tears that fateful Christmas Eve. This was why he could only utter the words "I am...I cried," but he couldn't cry in real life. This was why his body was starting to rapidly break down. My father was slowly giving up.

But we de la Rochas, we Mexicanos, don't know how to give up. There's always a fighting spirit as long as there's a fighting chance. There's always a way if there is a will. My father's crossing of borders, both physically and mentally, proved that. And I was still holding on to the hope that the de la Rocha magic would appear once again.

SACRED LESSONS

I didn't give up on my dad, and I never will. I couldn't even come close to understanding the pain he was feeling. I couldn't even come close to understanding what it would feel like not to be able to do what I loved, or to not be able to fully live my life's purpose. So I made it a priority to come home more and show my father that he was still loved, and that he was still needed.

I wanted him to know, and to start to believe, that he could in fact heal himself. That he could get better. That he could teach and run again. As I slowly started to become the father and my father slowly started to become the son, we embraced this new relationship.

My father and I didn't have to say that things were different, because we both knew they were. We didn't have to doubt our love for each other because that was never in question. We didn't have to make up any excuses for our actions because we both knew this was the defining moment of both of our lives.

A few weeks after coming home to spend the weekend with my mom and dad, I received a longer-than-usual email from my father.

> From: Ismael de la Rocha
> Sent: Thursday, June 11, 2015, at 10:43 AM
> To: Michael
> Subject: thanks
>
> Mijo,
>
> I want to thank you for coming this past weekend. It was nice having you and your family sharing a day with us. I am very grateful that you worry about me. I am in a bad situation with my health…the worst I have ever had. I

am trapped…I do not know what to do. I pride myself on always being in control and resolving family issues…I have no control…It infuriates me that I cannot do anything. I am crippled and it is suffocating me. I am not being difficult with you or your mom. I have so much pain and I do not know where to put it. My boys are the only thing that calm me. I will not take drugs or alcohol. There has to be a way out. I'm terribly disappointed in the doctors.

I look forward to Father's Day. I will be with my boys.

Love you.

Papa

When I read that email, I couldn't help but cry. It was the most honest expression of my father's emotions that I had ever encountered outside of that Christmas Eve. Here he was completely vulnerable and expressive. Here he was admitting to me the severity of his pain. Here he was not only asking for help but also telling me that he loved me.

After I composed myself, I wrote the following response to my father.

From: Michael de la Rocha
Sent: Friday, June 12, 2015, at 3:58 PM
To: Ismael de la Rocha
Subject: thanks

SACRED LESSONS

Papa,

Thank you for your message and I love you more than words could ever say.

I know that you're in pain and it kills me that I can't do anything. At the end of the day, your mindset is of the utmost importance, so I hope that you don't give up, and know that there's always something that we could do.

I just want you to know that there's not an easy or overnight solution but that this will take some time to heal. What I do know is that you told me that going to a chiropractor three times a week did help and so we're looking for someone to come to the house to do that. I know that it's not ideal, but at least it will make you feel better until we figure out how to heal your body. Just don't give up Papá cuz we'll find something and please let me know what you need.

Love you always,

Michael

My father never responded to my email. He knew what needed to happen. He knew that he had to find the will to change. He knew, and I hope that he felt, that he wasn't alone. And like my father, it was killing me that I couldn't do anything to help him. It was killing me that I had no control. It was killing me that I didn't know what to do.

Chapter 15

Becoming Cesar Chavez

Given the important role that my father played in the Chicano Movement, I always tell people that I'm a "movement baby." Even now, whenever I introduce myself, I make a point to say that I'm a proud son of a former teachers union president who grew up attending marches and rallies before I could even speak.

For as long as I can remember, my father would take me with him to organizing meetings and community events. I was surrounded by a multigenerational, multiracial group of people who were working to create a more just and equitable world for everyone. My father instilled in me the importance of working with people from all backgrounds to improve the systemic and structural conditions that disproportionately impact the poor and people of color everywhere.

As an infant, my father would take me in my car seat to his college classes, set me on top of his desk, and lecture for hours. I was like a sponge, absorbing everything he was teaching and everything going on around me. He was determined to make

SACRED LESSONS

sure that I knew my history and that I was equipped with a deep understanding and love of my cultural roots and identity.

I'll never forget when I was in the second grade and we were given an assignment to dress up and share facts about an important historical figure. Part of the assignment was that each student had to write a report on that person and then share a five-minute presentation on their life. From the obvious choices, like George Washington and Abraham Lincoln to Martin Luther King Jr. and Rosa Parks, my classmates were excited about the chance to dress up as famous historical figures.

The day I found out about the assignment, I remember coming home and asking my father who he thought I should be. He was grading a stack of blue books, and not wanting to interrupt, I quietly said, "Papá? Papá?"

Putting down his red pen, my father looked up at me and said, "What is it, Mijo?"

No longer needing to speak in a lowered voice, I replied, "I have an assignment for class, and the teacher wants us to choose a historical figure to dress up as. I was thinking that maybe I could be George Washington or another president."

My father immediately replied, "I have the perfect person for you! Wait here."

With a level of excitement that I sort of anticipated, given the fact that my father was a history professor, I waited while he ran upstairs to his study and grabbed some clothes and a hat.

"What is that, Papá?" I asked in my seven-year-old voice.

"Try these clothes on."

As my father handed me a pair of brown slacks that were too big for me, a colorful serape, leather *chanclas*, and a wide-brimmed rancher's hat, I asked him with a confused look on my face, "What is this?"

183

"This is your outfit for your presentation."

Even more confused, I asked, "What do you mean? Who am I supposed to be?"

"Mijo, you're going to be Cesar Chavez!"

Embarrassed by the clothes that he was asking me to wear, I replied, "Who's Cesar Chavez?"

With an air of pride, and standing a little taller, my father declared, "Cesar Chavez is one of our greatest civil rights leaders. Like Martin Luther King Jr., Cesar Chavez fought for the rights and dignity of all of us, especially farmworkers and the poor."

Not really knowing why Cesar Chavez was so important to my father, I said, "Farmworkers? But...I want to be George Washington."

"No, no. You're going to be Cesar Chavez, Mijo."

"But..." I exclaimed in a louder voice.

"No buts! You have to teach your class about Cesar Chavez. People need to know that without Cesar Chavez, we wouldn't have a lot of the rights that we have today."

As if he were giving a lecture in one of his college classes, my father proceeded to say, "Along with Dolores Huerta and Philip Vera Cruz, Cesar Chavez was responsible for creating the United Farm Workers, the first successful farmworkers union in American history."

Without me being able to get a word in, my father continued, "Cesar Chavez fought for and won better wages and medical care and benefits for all farmworkers. Without him and the union, hundreds of thousands of farmworkers, like your abuelo, wouldn't have the rights and protections that they have today."

Knowing there was nothing I could do or say to change my father's mind, we spent the next hour or so writing down facts about the life of Cesar Chavez on small lined note cards.

SACRED LESSONS

Afterward, my father had me stand in front of him for an hour practicing so he could make sure that I memorized my presentation.

Finally, the dreaded day of the assignment arrived, and despite my last-minute objections, I went to school dressed as the one and only Cesar Chavez. To say that I was mortified would be a massive understatement, especially in light of the fact that I was one of only a few students of color in my class, and in the entire school. Trust me when I say that I knew without a shadow of a doubt that no one else would know who Cesar Chavez was.

As I walked into school, I could feel the stares and the fingers being pointed at me. And with my head down, I quickly walked to my classroom and took my seat. One by one, my classmates got up and shared facts about the characters they had chosen. As my turn was coming up, I kept thinking about my father and how adamant he was that I be Cesar Chavez. I kept thinking about how excited he was that I was going to be an iconic Chicano who had made poor brown people visible to the world. I kept hearing his words ring in my ears, and knew that I had to find the strength to get up and make my presentation.

Finally, it was my turn to present. As I stood up and walked to the front of the class, I tried my best to not look nervous. When I said the lines I had practiced all week with my father, I tried my best to remember the proud look on his face. And I tried my best to become the great Cesar Chavez.

"Hello, my name is Cesar Chavez. I am one of America's greatest historical figures who played an instrumental role in the establishment of the United Farm Workers union, the first and largest farmworkers union in the United States."

As I tried to not go through my speech too fast, I noticed that some of the students were actually paying attention. I was shocked that anyone would be curious about what I was saying. Given that everyone else had chosen mostly the same historical figures, I was actually sharing something new and interesting with the class.

After I finished my presentation, the teacher thanked me for a job well done, and the rest of the class started clapping. I went back to my seat, relieved that it was finally over. I took off my hat, and with sweat running down my back, I sat quietly as the next student began his presentation.

That evening when my father got back from work, he ran straight to the kitchen. "So, how did it go?!"

"It went fine," I said rather nonchalantly.

"And...?" my father prompted.

"It went fine," I said again. "Nobody asked any questions, so I think that I did a good job."

"So, the other students liked it! Did your teacher say anything?"

Hearing the excitement in my father's voice, I knew I should share a little bit more than usual. "It seemed like most people were listening. Everyone else presented mostly on the same historical figures, so I think that most kids were listening because they didn't know anything about Cesar Chavez."

"That's great, Mijo!" my father said enthusiastically. "And did the teacher say anything?"

With an air of confidence, I replied, "She just said, 'Great job, Michael.'"

I'll never forget that afterward, my father came up to me and gave me the biggest hug. He held me longer than usual, and I could tell that he was really proud of me. He knew that I didn't want to do that presentation. He knew that I was embarrassed. But he still pushed me, or rather forced me, to be Cesar Chavez

SACRED LESSONS

because it was important to him that I develop a sense of cultural pride in being Mexican. It was important for him to teach me that we come from proud and dignified people who have contributed and who continue to contribute to US and global history. It was important for him to teach me to never forget where I come from.

In his teens and twenties, my father was actively involved in the social movements of the 1960s and '70s. He was obsessed with the United Farm Workers because he had met Cesar Chavez on multiple occasions and learned a great deal from his philosophy and activism. From marching on the frontlines of the Chicano Moratorium, the largest Chicano-led antiwar rally in the history of the United States, to co-establishing M.E.Ch.A., the largest Latinx college student group in the country, my father was proud to call himself a Chicano activist and organizer.

After completing his degree, my father took that same passion and energy with him when he started teaching at Ventura College. There, he started the first M.E.Ch.A. chapter and played an instrumental role in the development of the college's Chicano Studies and Ethnic Studies Departments. He became the dean of social sciences and a department chair advocating for teacher and student rights, and found his home away from home.

But his activism wasn't just relegated to the campus. Whenever there was a need or a cause in the community, my father was present. As a child, I remember watching him spend every weekend during an election season creating makeshift campaign signs for different political candidates or propositions. And when he received the official printed campaign lawn signs, he would take me with him all over Ventura to put them up at busy intersections or drop them off at the homes of volunteers and supporters.

My father would proudly put campaign signs on our front lawn, despite the fact that we lived in a very conservative, predominantly white neighborhood. There was one black family and one Jewish family, who both got pushed out, and we were one of only two Latino families on the entire block. It was so overtly racist and hostile that the only other Mexican family almost moved out after a white supremacist lit a cross on fire on their front porch. Again, just for context, this was not the South during the Jim Crow era, but Ventura, California—or as some of us like to call it, Ventucky—in the late 1990s.

But that or any other act of racial aggression didn't deter my father from putting up progressive campaign signs to make sure that all our neighbors knew who we were and who we were voting for. From putting up Jesse Jackson for President to Cliff Rodrigues for School Board signs, my father wasn't scared of anyone. On top of putting up signs all over the city and all over my street, my father loved to take me with him to campaign kickoffs, fundraisers, and meetings. He would dress me up in an extra-small United Farm Workers shirt, and we would go everywhere together. It was all such a blur, but no matter where he took me or what we did, I was always the youngest person in the room.

I reveled in these experiences because I got to spend time with my father, and I got to be a part of something that he loved to do. No matter where we went or what we did, people would always tell my father, "Oh, that's so sweet! You brought your son with you."

Like clockwork, my father would proudly reply, "I sure did. He's the best little helper I could ever ask for. A natural-born organizer."

SACRED LESSONS

I absolutely loved the fact that my dad made it known that I wasn't just hanging around but that I was helping out and working on the campaign. It didn't matter that maybe a child labor law might have been broken here or there, because my father was instilling in me the importance of giving back to the community. And in the end, I did play an important role, no matter how small, in various campaigns, and alongside my father helped several people win important local school board and county government races.

As I got older and entered college, that same passion to change the world drove me to jump right into campus organizing. I'll never forget how excited I was to attend my first M.E.Ch.A. meeting. Not yet knowing all the social cues or campus politics, I put on my backpack, complete with a Che Guevara patch, and asked my then girlfriend from Ventura to go with me to my first student club meeting for the organization that my father had helped build.

Simply thinking about going to my first M.E.Ch.A. meeting made me feel absolutely excited. As the anticipation built, I walked to the middle of the UCLA campus where the meeting was being held. As I grabbed my girlfriend's hand, we confidently walked into the meeting. But on our way inside, I immediately sensed something was off. Something was wrong, really, really wrong.

When Summer and I walked into the room, everyone seemed to stop what they were doing and look at us. Suddenly, a student with big, curly black hair came up to us and said, "Hi, I'm Alberto. What's your name?"

"I'm Mike," I replied as my girlfriend proceeded to introduce herself.

"Pleasure to meet you two. This is your first meeting, huh?"

"Is it that obvious?" I asked.

Sensing my nervousness, Alberto sat next to me before the meeting started. And that gesture, that small gesture by an upperclassman, not only made me feel welcome but let everyone else in the room know that he was vouching for me.

Since that moment, Alberto Retana has become one of my best friends. I was always enthralled by his ability to condense complex problems into easily digestible sound bites. I followed him around everywhere I could because I wanted to learn how to command a room like he did. I wanted to know how he was able to move people to action. I wanted to know the magic behind the words. But above all else, I was drawn to Alberto's expansive heart that seemed to advocate on behalf of everyone. Black, brown, Asian, LGBTQIA+, women, the poor, you name it, and in Alberto's analysis of the world, none of us were free until all of us were free.

Months after my first M.E.Ch.A. meeting, I asked Alberto why it was so awkward the day that I first met him. Laughing, he said, "You walked into an extremely nationalistic meeting wearing a Che Guevara patch and holding hands with your white girlfriend. What did you expect was going to happen?"

Despite going to countless organizing meetings as a child, I was completely naive about all of the racial politics and dynamics of not only the broader community but definitely of UCLA. It was Alberto, because he was half Mexican and half Costa Rican, who identified with the freshman who had an image of an Argentine Marxist revolutionary on his backpack. It was Alberto who was dating outside his own "race," who sympathized with a seventeen-year-old who didn't know that it was taboo to bring a white girl to a M.E.Ch.A. meeting. It was Alberto who welcomed

SACRED LESSONS

me and instilled in me the confidence to never stop being me, no matter what environment or room I found myself in.

As I began to get more involved in campus organizing efforts, I could sense that my father was pleased with what I was doing. Here he was watching his son get involved in the student organization that he had co-founded three decades prior, watching me be inspired by the Zapatista movement, plan campaigns to protest the end of affirmative action, and spend practically every waking hour working to educate and mobilize the broader campus community. It was all exhilarating and addictive for both me and my father.

My entire student life revolved around me doing everything I could to ensure that future generations of students could have the same opportunities that I did. When I wasn't in class, I was facilitating meetings and planning events and rallies. I then got actively involved in student government and learned how to redirect resources to student organizing groups and how to create campaigns aimed at changing university policy. Eventually, I started taking on leadership positions on campus, which made me feel even more alive, even more needed than I had before.

After my girlfriend Summer and I broke up, I threw myself completely into trying to prove myself to everyone. For the next year, I signed up for every M.E.Ch.A. committee, did any task that was needed, and just tried to make myself as useful as possible. The M.E.Ch.A. leadership recognized my desire to be of service, and I was soon invited into the inner circle and given a board position in the student-led organization.

Life couldn't have been better. I was not only putting into practice the theories that I was learning in my Chicana/o Studies classes, but I was making a difference, a real difference in people's lives. I was advocating for new campus policies and seeing how organizing could improve the lives of all students. If I wasn't sold before, I was now completely convinced, and trusted the power of grassroots organizing.

Believing that we were indeed transforming the world, a few weeks later I arrived at our weekly M.E.Ch.A. meeting and noticed a chair positioned in the center of a circle of chairs in the middle of the room. I remember thinking this was odd, especially since we hadn't discussed it at our weekly planning meeting.

I approached a fellow M.E.Ch.A. member and asked if he knew what was happening.

Looking at me with a blank stare, he simply shook his head no as I took my seat in the circle.

Right as the meeting was about to begin, a M.E.Ch.ista who was part of the leadership came up to me and said, "Mike, um, can you please stand up and sit in that chair?"

When she pointed at the single chair in the middle of the circle, I asked, "What's going on? Why do you want me to sit there?"

Trying not to look at me, she said, "We have some questions that we would like to ask you."

Sensing that I was being set up, I nervously asked, "Questions? What kind of questions?"

"Please just go sit down so we can officially start the meeting."

Grabbing my black JanSport backpack, the same one I'd brought to my first M.E.Ch.A. meeting over two years ago, I sat down in the middle of the circle with everyone staring at me.

For over an hour, I was grilled by the M.E.Ch.A. leadership about my loyalty to the organization. I was asked who I spent my time with and why. And I was asked demoralizing questions about my commitment to el movimiento.

SACRED LESSONS

Defiant, I stood my ground and reminded everyone how much I had done for the organization, and also that my father had helped establish M.E.Ch.A. as a national organization at a historic conference in Santa Barbara in 1969. I reminded everyone that my father had even contributed to the writing of "El Plan de Santa Barbara," the founding document that anchored the vision and purpose of the student organization.

After a series of back-and-forth questions, I was eventually kicked out of M.E.Ch.A. The official line was that I wasn't "loyal enough to my raza." And as much as I tried to pretend it didn't matter, as much as I tried to pretend that I didn't care when I got up to leave, I was completely and utterly devastated.

That evening, I rushed back to my apartment, doing my best to not run into anybody. I threw myself down on my bed and quietly started crying into my pillow so that no one could hear me.

I felt ashamed, disappointed, and more than anything else, heartbroken. The truth of the matter was that I was kicked out of M.E.Ch.A. because I wasn't "brown enough" or nationalist enough for them. I was kicked out of M.E.Ch.A. because I was organizing too much with other students of color. I was kicked out of M.E.Ch.A., ultimately, because a few months prior to that meeting, I began dating a black woman.

Earlier that year, the beginning of my third year, I started dating Cori, a sophomore who, like me, completely threw herself into student organizing. One of the most brilliant people I know, we were together during some of the most formative years of our lives. We grew closer and closer as our shared love of organizing provided us with moments of extreme emotion. From the highs of executing a student takeover of a campus building to the lows of losing an election, we felt it all, and formed an inseparable bond.

Unfortunately, it was this same bond that sowed jealousy in the hearts of the M.E.Ch.A. leadership. It was their anti-black-ness and narrow nationalism that didn't allow them to see the potential for our union to enhance rather than take away from the work we were doing, not just for Chicana/o students but for all students.

As I lay on my bed, distraught over what had just happened, I called Cori to ask her to come over. Not only did I need a sympathetic shoulder to cry on, but I wanted her to be with me when I called my father to tell him what had happened.

Thirty minutes later Cori arrived at my apartment, and I described every detail of the meeting. Shocked and upset, she was about to call the leadership of the Black Student Union and the other people of color orgs to confront the M.E.Ch.A. leadership.

Embarrassed, and not wanting to make an even bigger com-motion, I convinced her not to do anything. Even though I had just turned twenty, I was old enough to believe in the power of karma. In my heart of hearts, I knew that the M.E.Ch.A. lead-ership knew what they had done to me was wrong. I knew that kind of narrow ideology would only lead to their own demise. I knew that their fear of a truly multiracial coalition would not allow them to fulfill the promise of my father and of all the Chi-cana/o students who had founded M.E.Ch.A. on the unwaver-ing belief in our shared struggle for third world liberation.

After some time had passed, I finally got the nerve to call my father.

"Hi, Mamá," I said as my mom picked up the phone.

"Hi, my angel. How are you doing?"

SACRED LESSONS

"I'm fine, Mamá. Is Papá home?"

Knowing that I rarely called to talk to my father, my mother immediately asked, "Is something wrong? Why do you want to talk to Papá?"

Holding back tears, I lied and said, "No, nothing's wrong. I just wanted to ask Papá a question."

Knowing that I was far from okay, my mother hesitantly put down the phone and yelled at my father to pick up the phone from his upstairs study.

"Hello? Mijo? What's going on?"

Before I said anything, I politely asked my mom to hang up the phone since I could hear her breathing on the other end. Once she got off, I proceeded to tell my dad what had happened.

Hearing the anguish in my voice, my father tried his best to console me and reminded me that I didn't need to be around people who thought that way or who would treat me the way they did. He tried to convince me that they didn't know what they were doing. He tried to tell me that everything would be okay.

In typical movement teacher fashion, my father even quoted Che Guevara, the same person whose face was on my now infamous JanSport backpack. "Mijo, don't forget that true revolutionaries are guided by strong feelings of love."

Not in the mood to hear a quote from Che Guevara, I replied, "I know, Papá, but I—"

"What they did to you was driven by jealousy. No matter what happens, or what they do next, you'll be better off. I know it's hard to see that now. But I promise you that everything will be okay."

My father's words comforted me in ways that I was unable to express to him at that moment. However, shortly after I graduated from UCLA, I was able to tell him how I felt.

I was visiting my parents in Ventura when my father asked me, "Mijo, would you like to go to Reno?"

"Sure, Papá. I would love to go. I've never been to Reno, and I heard that it's absolutely beautiful. It's also close to Lake Tahoe, and I've always wanted to go there."

"Okay. I'll book our tickets," my father said, trying his best to hide his enthusiasm.

Personally, I was extremely excited because the last time I had taken a trip with my father was when he took me and my brother to Havana, Cuba, for a week. That trip brought me and my brother closer together and was one of the most memorable times I ever got to spend with just the two of them.

With the memories of Cuba racing through my mind, I asked my dad, "Did you talk to Albert already? Is he able to go?"

Before responding, I could tell that my father was contemplating his response. Finally, after a few seconds, he said, "No. I thought that maybe just you and I could go by ourselves."

Caught off guard by his reply, I said, "Oh, okay. That sounds like fun. Just let me know the date so I can make sure to reschedule anything that I have on my calendar."

A few weeks later, my dad and I arrived in Reno on a hot Friday afternoon. After checking in and putting our luggage in our hotel room, my dad asked if I wanted to go down to the bar and grab something to drink.

I immediately replied, "Sure, let's go!"

After ordering two Captain Morgans and Cokes, we made our way to a small table. As I watched him, I noticed that my father was squirming around in his chair.

Given the difficulty that we de la Rocha men have expressing our emotions, I broke the awkward silence and asked, "So, Papá, why did you want to come to Reno?"

SACRED LESSONS

Sensing that I knew he wanted to talk about something important, my father replied, "I don't know. I've always wanted to come and…" Not wanting to rush him, I stayed quiet as he said, "Since you graduated from college, I've been wanting to take you on vacation so we could spend some time together."

Trying my best to act normal, even though the start of the conversation was far from normal, I simply said, "Thanks so much, Papá. I've been looking forward to spending this time with you too."

For more than three hours, my father and I sat there talking about everything. As he shared stories of being one of the first Chicano students at UC Santa Barbara, meeting my mother at a party at my Tío Cástulo's house, and so much more, I got teary eyed. I wished I'd known these stories when I was still a student at UCLA.

As he shared college experiences that were almost identical to my own, I asked, "Papá, why didn't you ever tell me all of this before?"

Looking down at the table, his hands fidgeting with his napkin, he said, "I guess I just wanted you to learn on your own. I wanted you to make your own mistakes. To learn from your own challenges. I know that I should have done things differently but…"

Frustrated, and definitely under the influence of no fewer than four rum and Cokes, I said, "But couldn't you see that I was making the exact same mistakes as you? I mean, just knowing that you went through something similar in college would have made me feel less alone."

Trying to get a word in between my tirades, my father said, "I just didn't want to bother you."

"Bother me! Are you kidding? Knowing that you'd had such similar experiences would have helped me out so much. We practically had the same experience in college. We both got sick, we both had our hearts broken, and we both gave everything we could to the movement."

Now on a roll and without holding anything back, I said, "I know that I keep saying this, but man, Papá, it would have been great to know these stories, especially when I was getting kicked out of M.E.Ch.A. Your stories would have helped me make sense of everything that was going on at the time."

And suddenly my heart sank as my father, trying his best to hold back his tears, said, "I'm sorry, Mijo. I should have told you about everything during that time."

Grasping the magnitude of the fact that my father had just apologized to me, I calmed down. "It's okay, Papá. We were both just trying to figure it all out. I'm just completely surprised because I didn't know any of this until tonight."

"I didn't want to share too much with you because I thought that you should go through your own trials and tribulations. I didn't want what had happened to me to have an influence on what you did."

At this point, sounding like a broken record, I said once again, "I know, Papá, but like I said before, it would have helped me out so much."

Seeing the desperation in my eyes, my father said, "I know that now, Mijo. But back then, I didn't know what to do. It wasn't until the M.E.Ch.A. situation that I tried my best to share what happened to me while I was a student."

Just when I was about to interrupt my father, he raised his voice to make sure I wouldn't, then told me, "That's why I called you and sent you emails more than usual. I was trying to—"

SACRED LESSONS

At that moment, I couldn't control my emotions any longer and burst out, "I remember those emails and phone calls, Papá. I mean, you hate talking on the phone, and here you were calling me more than usual, so I knew that you were trying your best to be there for me."

Now looking right at me with eyes that said more than words could ever express, my father said, "I tried my best, Mijo, but I could have done better."

Sensing his deep feeling of remorse, I lowered my voice and told him, "It's okay, Papá. It's just so crazy how similar our experiences were in college. I just wish that I would have known earlier, that's all. I just didn't want to disappoint you."

Suddenly, my father's entire demeanor changed as he replied almost immediately, "Disappoint me? Never, Mijo! I was never disappointed in you."

I started in on the rest of my rum and Coke to distract myself from getting even more emotional. As I sat there drinking, my father said, "I was so, so proud of you during that time. You didn't let M.E.Ch.A. bring your spirit down, but instead, you used that experience to motivate you to do more."

As I sat there drinking in the magnitude of the moment, my father said, "You becoming the student body president of UCLA was one of the proudest moments of my life."

With tears starting to swell in our eyes, he added, "You accomplished something that I had only ever dreamed of my son doing."

His voice cracked as he continued, "And when you were student body president and weren't vindictive to M.E.Ch.A., but rather appointed the M.E.Ch.A. chair to a powerful campus committee that paid her yearly tuition. I just…"

Trying his hardest now to fight back his tears, my father said with his voice cracking, "It just made me so proud to be your father."

And right when I was about to get up and embrace my father, right when I was about to tell him how much that moment meant to me, right when I was about to tell him that I loved him, my father suddenly stood up and went to the bar to order another round of drinks.

With the moment now behind us, my father sat back down, and as I looked at him, I said, "Thank you so much, Papá, for sharing all that with me. I'm so grateful that we get to spend this time together this weekend. This means the world to me."

Smiling, my father nodded, and then unfortunately did what too many men do when we are uncomfortable with a situation: he immediately changed the subject. "So where should we go next?"

That weekend in Reno was one of those rare occurrences when my father's guard came down and he just let me in. It was a bittersweet moment when he tried his best to hide his feelings because he didn't want me to see his real self, his real emotions. He didn't want me to see that he, like all of us, was broken, was healing, was human.

That night brought my father and me closer than we had ever been before. We spent the next two days thoroughly enjoying each other's company as we ate at the best restaurants, gambled at too many casinos, and drank way too much alcohol. In fact, we even went to a Mötley Crüe and a Nine Inch Nails concert together. Well, my father didn't go with me to the Nine Inch Nails concert, but he did go with me everywhere else I wanted to go that weekend so we could spend as much time together as possible.

And even though our conversation might have been cut short, I like to believe that it was the opening, the start, the

SACRED LESSONS

beginning of my father attempting to be more open with me. It was the catalyst for him not to feel shy or embarrassed about sharing intimate stories of his childhood, of college, or of life. It was the beginning of my father attempting to be more vulnerable and open with me.

Ten years later, on Father's Day, my brother and I went to Ventura so we could spend the whole day loving up on our father. We took him to his favorite restaurant for lunch and then had our traditional carne asada barbecue for dinner. And even though we wanted to take him to get a much-needed massage, we still smoked Cuban cigars, drank way too many Coronas, and just basked in the beauty of being with each other.

My brother and I wanted my father to know that he was loved, and that we were so grateful to be his boys. We enjoyed a beautiful day together, and it seemed that our slow picking away at the hard armor that my father had acquired over the years had finally started to wear it down.

With the memories of our trip to Reno still present in my mind after all these years, I was pleasantly surprised when I received the following email from my father the day after Father's Day.

> From: Papa de la Rocha
> Sent: Monday, June 21, 2010, at 7:46 PM
> To: Michael de la Rocha
> Subject: nice father's day
>
> Mijo,
>
> Thank you so much for a great Father's Day. This means a lot to me. I have a tough time expressing myself and for that reason I hardly

ever do. I am learning and your mamá is the best teacher in the world.

For the de la Rocha's, expressing love is difficult. We have been taught to be indifferent and tough. Unfortunately, it is also creating problems in my life because I am becoming the Charlie Brown Man and people take advantage of those that are sensitive and caring.

Anyway, thank you for a wonderful day. I love you and your family tremendously! I look forward to next year. We will still enjoy a good massage.

Hope to visit you guys this weekend. I want to see Mayela's last game and go over to UCLA to find some books.

Love you.

Papa

For a puro Mexicano, and a man in general, I know how difficult it was for my father to write those words. I know how much he must have struggled to press send on the computer. I know that he was trying to teach himself, in real time, how to love.

Maybe it was the fact that he sent me that email the day after Father's Day, or maybe it was the fact that he sent the email on my wedding anniversary, which happens to be on the summer solstice. Whatever the reason, my father was showing me how to reflect, how to process, and how to let go.

SACRED LESSONS

In those four paragraphs, my father expressed himself in a way that I knew was possible but had rarely heard him articulate before. His awareness of how hard it was for him to express himself modeled for me the importance of self-reflection. His willingness to admit that he had been taught to be "indifferent" and "tough" was an acknowledgment of a toxic culture that fed off his fear. And his struggle not to be too vulnerable, because he didn't want to be taken "advantage" of for being too "sensitive" and "caring," reminded me how much more work we both had left to do.

As I read and reread his email multiple times, I was aware that I was fortunate to have a father who was willing to admit his struggles with accepting society's prevailing notion of manhood. Even though he was beginning to question the inherent pitfalls of being too hypermasculine, he was also starting to recognize that being "tough" meant learning how to be vulnerable. He was teaching me how we can't confront patriarchy in isolation but must choose to be surrounded by people, like my mother, who keep us honest, accountable, and connected to one another.

That's why I kept coming back to the lines, "I have a tough time expressing myself and for that reason I hardly ever do. I am learning and your mamá is the best teacher in the world." In those two sentences, my father encapsulated the ultimate sacred lesson: We can only heal *if* we choose to listen and learn from those who keep us honest. We can only grow *if* we are willing to let go of society's expectations of how men and women should act. We can only live our full and authentic lives *if* we learn how to truly love and accept our own selves.

Chapter 16

I Never Wanted to Hurt You

"Just please don't hurt me again," my wife said faintly but loud enough for me to hear.

We were lying in our bed after a week of tension, eggshells, and triggers. It was a textbook example of how not to communicate with someone you love. Years of therapy had finally run its course, and we were both exhausted and tired of each other. It was the end of the line for us, and we both knew that something drastic had to happen.

A few months earlier, we both were staring blankly at our therapist through a computer screen. We were at a breaking point. A crossroads. We were uncertain about the future and desperate to find a way out, or at least a way back to the way things used to be. We had developed a routine that had taken the excitement out of our relationship. A routine that was at the

SACRED LESSONS

root of why I was drinking too much and staying out too late as a way to avoid dealing with the uncertainty of it all.

That day, and in subsequent therapy sessions, we went back and forth getting defensive and upset with each other. The therapy sessions were a mix of silence and anger, uncertainty and guilt, love and hate. I knew that it wasn't all about me, but I also knew that it was in fact all about me. About my unwillingness to fully commit to my wife. About my underlying false belief that something better would be around the corner if things didn't work out between us. About my fear that one of us would finally say the dreaded word that neither of us dared say out loud: *divorce*.

I love my wife. I love her in ways that I have never loved anyone else. Claudia has been my partner for almost twenty years and is the mother of my two children and the co-founder of our creative agency. We have spent most of our lives together, and outside of my mother, she has loved me more than any other woman. She has been with me through thick and thin and has been the foundation for all of my personal and professional success. In short, Claudia is the main reason why I have accomplished so much in life. Despite all of this, my upbringing, my societal conditioning, and my weaknesses sometimes get the best of me.

Days after that tense initial therapy session, Claudia walked into our bedroom and said, "This is not fair, Michael."

"What's not fair?" I said with a raised voice.

Trying as hard as she could to maintain her composure, Claudia struggled to say, "I'm always the bad guy. You never discipline the kids. I'm always the one who has to say something. You never help me parent them."

As I was accustomed to doing, I immediately got defensive and tried to steer the conversation in a different direction. Instead of listening to what she was trying to tell me, I did what I had been trained to do: I flipped it on her.

"Claudia, I don't understand what you're trying to say."

In a tone that was beyond upset, and more on the verge of sadness, she responded, "It's just hard always having to be there for everybody. I never have any time for myself because everyone always expects me to do everything for them."

After a slight pause, she added, "I'm just tired, Michael. I'm really, really tired."

When I heard the pain in her voice, I knew that we were at a critical point in our relationship. So rather than simply reacting without listening to her, I took a long, deep breath. And even though I wanted to rebut what she was saying and deflect attention from myself, I stopped. I just stopped and tried to hear what she was trying to tell me.

After checking myself, and my ego, I listened as Claudia finished sharing her thoughts and then said, "I'm sorry, Claudia. I really am. I will try to do better."

With a sigh of relief, Claudia responded, "Thank you," as she walked out of the room.

In the past, I would have either shut down and not said a word, or I would have gotten defensive and denied any sort of responsibility. But as I've been meditating more, and consciously trying to work on myself, I've realized that Claudia and I process things differently. While she's the kind of person who wants to address an issue immediately, I need more time and space to think clearly about what's been said before I can respond.

After many years of marriage, I've finally learned that despite our differences in how we process information, I still must listen deeply, and I must at least try to express my need for space and repeat what she's said so we can be clear as to what we both need. I've learned that we're both trying to heal from past wounds and that our relationship, our marriage, is about us creating a shared space where we can learn to love each other outside the conditioned pattern of always fighting to be right.

At that moment, when Claudia was completely vulnerable with how she was feeling, I realized that I couldn't run away from my partner, I had to run *to* her. I realized that I couldn't act like my father, who, like his father, was taught to be emotionally unavailable, emotionally absent, and emotionally unwilling to take responsibility for his actions. I had to recognize that I was playing an active role in our conflict, and that this tension was actually an opportunity for us to grow.

This was hard for me to admit, because I had been conditioned to be desensitized. I had been indoctrinated to be "tough," and to not listen. I had been forced to believe that conflict in a relationship is never about me, but rather about what the other person is doing "wrong." And despite all of this programming, my experiences have taught me that conflict is inevitable, conflict is a part of life, and conflict is part of any healthy relationship. That's why I forced myself to listen, because the tension, the conflict that was boiling to the surface between Claudia and me, was revealing something deeper within me.

From an early age, I learned to keep everything inside of me, no matter the consequences to my health and well-being. I learned to focus solely on my perspective and to see the world only through my eyes. Society, and literally everything around me, tells me that women and everything else for that matter are for men to benefit from, control, and exploit. This is what clouds and confuses my judgment. This is why I must consciously work on changing my bad habits and beliefs. This is why I am writing this book.

Nights spent crying about my role in the deterioration of my marriage made me realize that my entire life has been about me trying to love that little lost child inside me. That child who was rejected for speaking Spanish, for being overweight, for being too ethnic. All I ever wanted to be was just me. I'm still traumatized by my childhood experiences, and I can't seem to let it go. This is ultimately the driver of my conflict with Claudia, and why I have to be mindful not to sabotage the relationships that bring me the most joy and happiness. This is why I don't know how to talk truthfully about my pain. This is why neither I nor my father know how to ask for help.

Even though I have been with my wife for almost two decades, and even though I have shared some of the most intimate moments of my life with her, I still have a hard time being completely vulnerable and honest with her. I still feel a sense of shame for what I've done or for what I've said in the past. And even to this day, I have a hard time standing naked in front of my wife because I'm too embarrassed and self-conscious about my own body.

It saddens me that I didn't learn how to process my emotions as a child. That I was taught to deal with my feelings on my own and not ask for help. That I didn't learn about therapy or about my cultural traditions that could have helped me process things when I was a kid. This has contributed to my sense of shame and unworthiness, to me looking at my weight, my receding hairline, my wrinkly skin, and wondering if I was ever beautiful or worthy enough to be loved in the first place. This is the dilemma, the constant battle within me. The reason why I fall back on harmful and unhealthy patterns rather than addressing

SACRED LESSONS

how I'm really feeling about my marriage or getting older or the constant battle of not feeling good enough to be loved.

Days after our conversation, I read a social media post from a friend who reposted the following quote from Toi Smith: "Men have built-in self-care…It's called women." After reading this quote several times, I was absolutely floored by the truth of her statement. I was gripped by the reality of her words that described so many of the relationships in my life, including my own relationship with Claudia, and even that of my parents.

As I sat there contemplating her statement, I read the rest of her quote: "Men don't have to worry about finding time for self-care because women care for and tend to so much of their worlds, which allows [men] not to feel like they're neglecting themselves or their dreams."

After reading the entire quote, I took the time to reflect on what Toi Smith was saying and how it described my own life. I began to acknowledge, once again, that I really don't discipline the kids as much as I should. I began to acknowledge that I get defensive with Claudia because she's forcing me to confront some hard truths about my parenting, and about myself. And I began to reflect on the fact that I must do a better job at providing the space and encouragement for Claudia to follow her own career dreams and aspirations.

As I considered Toi Smith's quote, I asked myself how I've contributed to the problems in my marriage. I questioned how my need to protect a false sense of self contributes to my inability to be truthful about how I'm feeling about myself, or anything else. But like so many times before, my ego once again got the best of me, and I regrettably started blaming Claudia for what I perceived as her not supporting my "dreams" enough. I began to justify my actions by telling myself that it's just the way it is, or at least the way it should be. And I began to retreat into a survival mode where I've been conditioned to do everything in my power to control and manipulate the situation.

And while I began to pity myself, while I began to make up false truths, I took a deep breath once again. And in doing so, I recognized that my sense of not receiving enough support from Claudia arose from my inner child needing and wanting validation, encouragement, and support. I realized that I was being triggered and that the conflict we were having was never about her. It was actually never even about us; it was about something deeper within me that needed to be addressed. It was about me relearning how to voice my fears.

As I sat there thinking about my relationship with Claudia, I had no choice but to check myself because she is in fact my "built-in self-care." She has always been my built-in self-care. And although it's true that I wake up earlier than Claudia to focus on my writing and self-growth, the reality is that she is exhausted from her family and work duties that aren't shared equitably. That's why she's always tired and never gets enough sleep, because she literally has no time for herself or even just time to rest.

Claudia is the hardest working person I know. A person who gives of herself, but also the person who will do absolutely anything to protect our family. Because of her hard exterior, and her willingness to speak truth in any situation, the expectation within our family, and within our company, is that Claudia can handle everything. People, including myself, take advantage of her, which is completely unfair. We are allowed to do what we want, and oftentimes what we don't want, because we know that Claudia will always pick up the slack. And while I can point to my childhood trauma as the main driver of this unhealthy

SACRED LESSONS

conflict in our relationship, the truth is that a lot of the tension stems from an unfair division of labor, an unfair expectation of gender roles, and an unfair emotional burden that everyone places on Claudia.

Unlike me, Claudia doesn't have time to stop working. She's the parent the kids go to when they need help with homework or when they're hungry. She's the person her parents go to for practically everything. And she's the person who people at work, and within our family, go to when they need help, regardless of how she's feeling or what she's doing. Her ability to solve almost any problem doesn't justify me or anyone else from relying on her for everything. And while she is the first person to call out unhealthy family and work boundaries, the fact is that no one, including me, takes the time to stop and ask Claudia if she needs help or if she has the time to do more.

This kind of unequal power dynamic doesn't exist in just my marriage but in many marriages. It unfortunately exists in the broader society, which we mimic in our day-to-day dynamics with our partners, colleagues, and friends. I'm not naive enough to think that couples in a healthy relationship don't argue or have conflicts. And that's why I know that the true measure of my marriage will be how we both navigate the hard times that are a part of every relationship. I know that both of us struggle with our insecurities and get frustrated with each other at times, but this is normal. Healthy relationships don't mean perfect relationships, and time has shown me that the true test of our love will be how we choose to show up even when we're tired, even when we're angry, even when we're overwhelmed by something that doesn't even have to do with us.

Despite my being a Virgo, I know that I'm not perfect. I know that I'm a work in progress. I know that I'm a person

MIKE DE LA ROCHA

struggling with addictions and demons, culture and Catholicism, desire and commitment. I don't have all the answers, and I probably never will. The truth is that the older I get, the more questions I have. But what I do know I need to do, and what I am trying to do, is be a better person. That's the commitment I made to myself. That's the sacrifice I made for my children. That's the reason I hope and pray my wife continues to love me in a way no one else ever has, and probably no one else ever will.

The day after our heated argument, I decided to pull my oracle cards on the new moon to gain more insight into my situation and guidance about what steps I needed to take to help repair the harm I had done. With my father's red running sweatband on my head, I lit my copal and began to shuffle my Mesoamerican oracle card set. However, just as I was about to pull my cards, something inside me, call it intuition or call it magic, told me to invite my son into my office to teach him about our ancestral practices and traditions.

At that moment, I realized that if I truly wanted to break the unhealthy patterns I had learned as a child, I had to teach my son another way. I had to teach him once again about the ways and traditions of our ancestors. I had to show him that our sacred rituals serve as a reminder that we are never alone. I had to model for him the importance of being vulnerable and of trusting a higher power. And I had to make sure that he knew how much I loved him, and how much I adored his mother.

As I smudged my son with my father's eagle feather, Claudia walked into my office holding a picture of her pregnant with Mayela. Two years after this photo was taken, I met my wife, and upon seeing the picture, she quickly drew my attention to the fact that she was wearing UCLA sweatpants in it. UCLA is not only my alma mater but, as I shared before, the place that

SACRED LESSONS

completely transformed my life. The timing of seeing that photo just before beginning the ceremony couldn't have been more perfect. The picture served as a reminder that our ancestors had orchestrated our union two decades earlier, and that they were still conspiring to keep us together today.

With huge smiles on our faces, and a sense of reassurance, Claudia and my baby boy left my office as I lit a candle, poured water into a bowl, and focused on the question that I needed to address: *What is blocking me from prioritizing Claudia as the most important relationship in my life?*

As I got ready to pull the first of three cards in a standard oracle card reading, I paused to thank my ancestors and all those angels who had been looking out for me. I took a deep breath and pulled the first card, representing the past. I pulled Coatl, the snake, an animal that continues to pop up in my dreams, daily breathwork, and readings. A symbol of the need for me to release what was holding me back. A symbol of the need to keep moving forward. A symbol of the importance of shedding what no longer served me.

Months of healing work helped me realize that I was being triggered every time my wife wanted to know what I was doing or questioned why I was going out so much. Of course, this was my own projection and my own interpretation of what she was trying to tell me. The truth of the matter was that Claudia was simply asking me to communicate better with her so we could plan our days accordingly. She wasn't trying to control me, she wasn't trying to take my freedom away, she just wanted to know what I was doing.

As I sat there in silence, I began to understand that my lashing out at Claudia was me subconsciously reliving those moments in school, and even in college, when I felt controlled

213

MIKE DE LA ROCHA

and unable to be myself. My actions and reactions were never about Claudia, they were always about me learning how to forgive and love myself. The snake on my first card was the perfect metaphor to remind me to confront and let go of the pain from decades ago so I could be the person I wanted to be for my wife and for myself today.

With a grin on my face, I shuffled the deck, and with the intention to lean into whatever I needed to do to rectify the current situation, I pulled the second oracle card, representing the present moment. I drew Itzcuintli, the dog, symbolizing my responsibility to share these ancient rituals with others. The card was telling me to accept my calling to teach these tools so that others could get through their own challenges and hardships. It was the card I instinctively knew I would pull because I was being drawn to share more of my cultural practices and traditions with others.

As I got ready to pull the third and final card, I paused, as this card would inform me of my future. This was the card that would determine and influence how, and if, I would still be in a relationship with my partner. I know that this may sound overdramatic, but this was the card that had always prevented my wife from taking part in these kinds of readings, because she feared knowing the "outcome." Needless to say, I was shaken and scared to pull this final card.

With my eyes closed, and surrendering to a higher power, I shuffled the deck and, taking another long, deep breath, intuitively drew the final card. I pulled Cauac, representing upcoming beneficial changes if I commit to doing the hard work. The card represents the storm, the dragon, and the bumpy road ahead if I don't let go of the past and change the way I'm acting. It reminded me that I would continue to have blessings in my life

SACRED LESSONS

if, and only if, I consistently *chose* to love and prioritize my wife. It was a painful reminder but one I needed to hear. It was the message my father and my ancestors had wanted me to finally learn. It was the blueprint for how I could repair the harm I had done and create the life that was waiting for me.

With tears in my eyes, and a big sigh of relief, I called my wife back into my office. Knowing her skepticism with this kind of divination, I cautiously proceeded to share my oracle cards with her as a way to get closer to her. I was trying to be a better communicator, and this was one way that I could let my guard down and let her into my weekly spiritual practice. This was one way to share with her how I was feeling and doing, of showing her that I was working on myself and trying to become a better person.

As the smoke from the copal swirled around us, I held her tightly as I shared my reading with her. I began to get emotional and apologized for how I had been acting and clarified some lingering questions that both of us needed answered. It was a moment where our individual commitment to self- and collective care brought us closer together. Our willingness to surrender allowed truth, without judgment or shame, to come forth from our wounds. And our commitment to each other superseded any lingering doubts and allowed us to once again work on improving our relationship.

Ceremony is an important part of my life. Through ceremony, I can converse with my ancestors and the unseen world. Through ceremony, I can consciously make the space where I'm free to let go and trust my intuition. Through ceremony, I instinctively know that I'll never be alone but instead have countless angels and ancestors watching over me.

That's why in moments of uncertainty, I go back to my cultural practices and traditions. I continue to tap into my spirituality because I know that in doing so, I gain further insight and guidance into the events happening in my life.

A few years ago, I did a reading to get some perspective on my relationship with Claudia. And in that reading, I learned that our souls, our spirits, chose to be with each other in this lifetime. That it wasn't predestined or prophesied for us to be together; instead, we *chose* to be with each other. That our relationship, our marriage, our union, would take commitment and sacrifice. But that reading, and my personal experiences, have reminded me that if Claudia and I choose to work through our challenges, then many blessings will indeed come our way. And our life together thus far is absolute proof of that.

I believe in the interpretation of this reading, not just for my marriage but for my life. I now know that the relationships that matter, the relationships that test me, the relationships that inspire me are portals for growth worth fighting for. They're sacred lessons in the flesh. Teachers waiting for me to listen. Mirrors wanting me to be the best version of myself. That's my wife, and that's all the relationships that I choose to continue to have in my life. Not relationships that simply take, but relationships that give. Not relationships that are merely surface-level, but relationships that go deep and are almost cosmic in nature. This is the syllabus, the master plan, the road map that I'm following.

I'm not going to lie—marriage, and any relationship that matters, is hard, and I'm okay admitting that. No Disney movie or romantic comedy can mask the fact that marriage takes work, a lot of work. And I, like my parents and my grandparents before me, have to commit daily to addressing my flaws and my traumas. I have to remember why I chose to marry Claudia

SACRED LESSONS

in the first place. I have to remember the brilliance and beauty of our partnership, and the impact that my choices will have on our relationship and on our children's future. And I have to remember that the best things in life, the things worth living for, the things worth fighting for, take time and sacrifice.

This is why I pull my oracle cards and choose to participate in ceremonies and moon rituals every month. This is why healing work, even the messy internal shadow work, is so important. Because love, like life, is a series of choices that we make. Love, like life, requires a certain level of self-reflection and conflict. Love, like life, is about trusting in the unknown and having faith in the uncertainty, yet certainty, of the universe.

Lesson V
Acceptance

Chapter 17
Chosen Family

"Mikey, this is Tim. Call me," he said in his raspy baritone voice. And with that I introduce you to the one and only Tim Ngubeni, my mentor, my friend, and my second father.

I met Tim when I entered UCLA at the age of seventeen. At the time, I thought I knew everything, when in fact I barely knew anything at all. Although I hid it well, I was a scared teenager searching for a place to belong on a new campus, in a new city, and in an entirely new environment. It's against this backdrop that the Creator brought Tim into my life. A man who would influence me in ways that can't be described merely in words.

With his burly voice, distressed army hat, and dark skin, Tim immediately commands your attention. He has a presence that's magnetic and mysterious. Take him into any room, whether with grassroots organizers or global dignitaries, and Tim will become the center of attention. He just has a charm that's undeniable. And that, along with his grasp of world history and his experiences as an activist and organizer, made me want to know more about Tim from the moment I met him.

Thamsanqa Ngubeni, affectionately known as "Tim," was born January 2, 1949, in South Africa to a Swazi father and Zulu mother. He grew up in the KwaThema township near Johannesburg, where he became a soccer and track star, very similar to my own father. However, his entire life would be upended when his mother suddenly died as a result of not being given proper medical attention at the hospital because she was black.

This experience, more than any other, was the life-altering moment that Rumi brilliantly summed up when he said, "The wound is the place where the light enters you." For Tim, this was the "wound" that completely changed the course of his life. This was the "wound" that would propel him to dedicate his life to ending racism in whatever shape or form it takes, whether that be in policies or in the cloud that hovers over people's minds. This was the "wound" that would drive Tim for as long as he was breathing.

Angered by his mother's sudden death, Tim threw himself completely into organizing and joined the newly formed South African Students' Organisation (SASO) to fight South Africa's racist apartheid government. Soon afterward, the organization evolved into the Black Consciousness Movement, under the leadership of the brilliant activist Bantu Steve Biko, who was killed in police custody on September 12, 1977, one day after I was born.

Because of the tremendous success of the Black Consciousness Movement in changing the hearts and minds of South Africans and people across the world, Tim and many of his peers were forced into exile. Worried about his safety, Tim eventually fled to the United States, where he enrolled in a small college

SACRED LESSONS

in Odessa, Texas. Wanting to get a better education, and leave the harsh realities of life in Texas, he transferred to UCLA after earning a soccer scholarship. In only two seasons, Tim scored forty-two goals, which still ranks eighth on UCLA's all-time career scoring chart. From there he went on to earn his bachelor's and master's degrees at UCLA in African-American Studies, African Studies, and Public Health.

Tim's role in the Black Consciousness Movement cannot be understated. He was one of the main architects of the anti-apartheid movement and played an instrumental role in starting the international boycott of South Africa that eventually contributed to the end of apartheid. Case in point: There's a picture of a young Barack Obama speaking to a crowd of students at an anti-apartheid rally that Tim organized at Occidental College to keep attention and pressure on South Africa. At this rally on February 18, 1981, the future president, just nineteen years old, gave one of his first public speeches.

When I first met Tim, he was serving as the director of the UCLA Community Programs Office (CPO), or as we affectionately call it, the "Conscious People's Office." Tim assumed this position in 1985 and didn't leave it until his retirement in 2007. During this time, the CPO rose from operating in a basement to become one of the most diverse and active departments at UCLA. Under Tim's guidance, the CPO became a nationwide, even worldwide, model for student-initiated, student-run, and student-funded outreach and retention services and programming. Just as importantly, Tim spent the entire time mentoring thousands of student activists, like myself, who were instilled with the philosophy and historical understanding that "young people are, and will always be, the engines of social change."

Meeting Tim completely changed my life. I always joke that when I first met Tim, he grabbed me by my ear and forced me to calm down so I could learn to listen and understand our interconnected history and my role in continuing the legacy of student activism. He invested in me in ways that few had ever done before. He pushed me to have context and perspective, to be conscious, and to have integrity in everything I did. And ultimately, he challenged me, showing me through his actions that he deeply cared for my personal growth and well-being.

Tim became more than just a mentor, he became family. He, more than any other adult on campus, was the person I would go to whenever I needed someone to talk to. He was someone I trusted, someone who was always willing to listen and to give insight into any issue I was facing. We traveled together to South Africa on several occasions, including co-producing a cultural exchange project and me accompanying him when he retired from UCLA and moved back to South Africa. On that last trip, I helped Tim reacclimate to life back home, from changing his light bulbs to visiting family members to just settling back into the beloved country he'd been forced to leave forty-plus years prior.

In my eyes, and in the eyes of so many others, Tim is the epitome of humbleness, goodness, and the positive rewards that come from dedicating your life to being "in service" to others. He has taught me the importance of raising my consciousness and, in doing so, helping to elevate the consciousness and vibration of the world. He has taught me what it feels like to belong, to really belong to a multiracial, multi-identity community. And while Tim, like all of us, has his flaws, he has shown me the importance of constant self-reflection and personal commitment to self-growth and liberation.

SACRED LESSONS

Years after returning home to South Africa, Tim had a stroke that greatly affected his physical ability and movement on his left side. Uncertain of his well-being, many of us were concerned and did all we could to support him as he started a long rehabilitation process. After he got better, Tim would visit annually, but you could tell that his old fervor was starting to dissipate, and he was becoming much more pensive and quiet.

Knowing how special he was, not only to me but so many others, a few of us wanted to plan something really special for Tim during his next trip to Los Angeles. In keeping with the tradition of honoring the father figures in my life, including planning my father's surprise sixtieth birthday party and the surprise seventieth birthday party for my father-in-law, it was only fitting that I would do the same thing for the man I considered my second father. The man who made me feel as if I mattered, and that I belonged.

Weeks before the surprise party, Vusi, a colleague and friend from the CPO office, and I began inviting as many UCLA students and alumni as we could find. But it wasn't just any group of UCLA students; it was those who were actively involved in the student movements of their time. Students who learned how to organize on campus and then took that consciousness and discipline into the workforce, whether as teachers, C-suite executives, or community organizers. Students involved in the establishment of the Student Retention Center, Student Initiated Outreach Committee, and so much more. Students, faculty, and alumni who gave of themselves to causes and issues bigger than any one of us.

When the day finally arrived, it was arguably the most multigenerational, multiracial, multi-identity group of people ever to walk through the doors of the Community Coalition.

MIKE DE LA ROCHA

People waited with great anticipation as Vusi texted me to let me know that he and Tim were walking up to the building. I quickly told everyone to lower their voices so we could surprise Tim as he walked into one of the main organizing hubs in all of Los Angeles.

Running outside to greet him, I yelled, "Tim!"

As I grabbed his arm, he looked at me with a big smile and asked, "How are you, my brother?"

"I'm good, Tim. Thank you for coming."

"For sure."

Just then a CPO alumnus Tim hadn't seen in decades walked through the door. Hoping that he wouldn't ruin the surprise, I immediately said, "Tim, look who's here."

"Who?" he said, startled.

Before he had a second to ponder what was happening, I gently pushed him inside and said, "We're having a meeting with a lot of folks that you might remember from our UCLA days."

Confused about what was going on, Tim asked, "What kind of meeting, Mikey?"

Not wanting to answer his question, I said, "Let's go over here. Alberto wants to show you something."

"Alberto. Where is Alberto?"

Alberto walked out of the Community Coalition's Karen Bass Empowerment Room, the organization's main hall for countless community events and meetings, gave Tim a hug and said, "You've been here before. You remember this place…"

And right as we turned the corner, everyone yelled, "Surprise!"

The look on Tim's face was priceless. As he looked around the room at the seventy-plus people in attendance, my heart was overflowing with joy. This is exactly what I, what we, wanted to accomplish. We wanted to give Tim his flowers. We wanted to

SACRED LESSONS

love up on the person who had radically transformed our lives for the better. We wanted him to know how much he meant to each and every one of us.

In typical CPO, or should I say indigenous people of color fashion, we rearranged all the chairs from a standard classroom style into a circle. We did this because like energy, the circle represents our commitment to each other. The circle, a sacred symbol of unity, represents the infinite nature of the universe. And like our enduring love for Tim, the circle has no beginning and no end.

Once everyone was seated and Tim's eyes were bloodshot from holding back his tears, I began the informal program. With my voice cracking, I began the two-hour-plus celebration by saying, "Thank you all for coming to Tim's surprise celebration. It means the world to him that you were able to make it here today."

With Tim sitting right beside me, I could feel the outpouring of love and emotions in the air. As I looked around the packed room, I made sure to look everyone in the eye so that I could remember this beautiful moment.

As people situated themselves in their chairs, I continued, "One of the best things that I've ever done in my life is to throw my father a surprise birthday party. And the second-best thing is doing the same thing for my father-in-law. So when Fidel asked me what we were going to do for Tim, it was a no-brainer that I would…"

I turned to the side to make sure I was looking right at Tim and continued, "I would throw you, Tim, a surprise party and give you all the flowers that you deserve while we can still share them with you."

As Tim sat next to me trying his best to hold all of his emotions together, I said, "Before going into the program, I just want to say thank you to Alberto and the Community Coalition for opening their doors for us today. I also want to say that there were a lot of people that wanted to be here but couldn't make it. So they sent us messages that we included in a slide-show presentation that we'll watch later. But the real program is for us to just go around the room and have folks share any words that they want to share...but please know that your presence here today is enough."

At this point, I was completely overwhelmed with emotion and once again turned to look directly at Tim. "But really, on a personal and professional level, Tim, my life is so blessed because of you. I would not be who I am today, I would not be in this space, if it wasn't for you. I know how to navigate the world because of my multiracial, multi-identity view and perspective that was developed by you while I was at UCLA.

"And when I look around this room, it gives me hope, because with everything happening around the world, from Gaza to skid row, this is the kind of world that we really need to build, one rooted in solidarity, community, and love."

As both Tim and I fidgeted in our seats, I then mustered up the courage to tell him, "So right now I'm just going to open up the floor so you can know just how much we love you."

As soon as I said those three magical words, "we love you," Tim started shaking his head as the audience of friends and family burst out laughing because it was clear that Tim was uncomfortable and that this setting, one where he was going to be forced to sit through people sharing their love and appreciation for him, was hard, really, really hard for him.

SACRED LESSONS

As the two of us joined the rest of the room in laughter, I started to say, "As strong men, this is oftentimes hard—" when Vusi suddenly yelled, "Hey, Mike, he's already saying you already know!"

After another collective laugh, Tim was able to shake off his nervousness, and Christine, one of the most effective executives on the planet, started speaking. "I'll kick it off. Whenever I hear this deep-rooted 'Christina'—and he's literally the only person in the world that I wouldn't say I allow but would say I love to hear put the 'a' at the end of my name, because of who you are and what you mean to me. Tim, I wouldn't be who I am, I wouldn't have had the opportunities to make an impact, if it wasn't for you. I've told a million people that if it wasn't for what I learned at the CPO and at the Academic Supports Program [ASP, the retention project of the Afrikan Student Union at UCLA], I wouldn't be where I am today."

Sitting next to her son, Christine continued, "This young man next to me wouldn't have the sense of self that he has at such a young age if it wasn't for you. And this is something that you taught me, being biracial, me in my exploratory adventures through the corporate world, and me still trying to be a corporate activist through all the ebbs and flows. To be able to see my son understand who he is and who he wants to be at twelve years old is also because of you."

As tears started to form not only in my eyes but in the eyes of everyone in that room, Christine finished by saying, "And all of this you have instilled in all of us. Not only how to love ourselves, but how to show up for each other...that is going to continue generation after generation. And we are so grateful for you, Tim, and we love you."

For the next two hours, one person after another recounted their personal experiences with Tim and the impact he had on their lives and the lives of their families. People from all walks of life shared heartfelt stories of how Tim had mentored, guided, and loved them through the hardest and most joyful moments of their lives. Everyone gave freely of themselves as they put their full hearts on display to make sure that this beautiful man knew how much he was loved and appreciated.

As I listened to their stories, I couldn't help but think about my biological father and the enormous contributions that both he and Tim had made to the trajectory of the country, and to the lives of thousands upon thousands of students. I couldn't help but think about how history is made up of little, and big, acts, by everyday people just like you and me, just like Tim and my father, who are the backbone of every great and successful social movement in world history.

There were so many profound reminders shared that afternoon. But two lessons that really resonated deeply with me centered around Tim's insistence on the importance of perspective and of us living our values. You see, what made Tim so effective was that he would never tell us what to do. Instead, he would provide us with different perspectives so that we could come to a more holistic conclusion before making our decision. He would push us to make conscious choices based on multiple levels of understanding and awareness. And throughout this process, he would always remind us that the most important thing was for us to be "conscious people in the community."

And while I could quote every single person who spoke that day, I will share a couple of stories that encapsulate the lessons that Tim instilled in all of us. These are sacred lessons that I still hold close to my heart. Lessons for how to be a better person,

SACRED LESSONS

and how to contribute to the betterment of our interdependent and interconnected global community.

One CPO alumnus recounted, "I attended UCLA in the 1990s, my sister attended in the 2000s, my son recently graduated, and I now have another daughter at UCLA who's able to take advantage of the Student Retention Center. We consider ourselves blessed to even have a smidgen of time to be with you. Every memory that I have of any encounter with you is one of pure joy, and one of you just expressing how much love we have. You brought light to us even when we were having a bad day, because you always brought perspective. There was always a story for you to tell us, to educate us. There was always 'but did you know this?' You always had something to say that would bring perspective to our lives. We are so much more enriched because of that. We have, whether consciously or unconsciously, fully adopted that in how we speak to our own children. It's 'Did you know this?' We are very appreciative of that, and this is continuing from generation to generation. It's clearly visible in the steps that my younger siblings have taken, and my daughter has taken. And we appreciate that. We appreciate you, Tim."

Here's another reflection from a dear friend I hadn't seen in almost a decade: "I just want to say that for every person that is here today, there's at least a hundred people or a thousand people that have been influenced by you and just the ripple effects of you alone. It's undeniable, the legacy that you have created on campus, and the history that will live on because of you. Speaking for myself and many others who are now working in the belly of the beast, we're in there not as empty shells but as conscious people. And you taught us that. So when we hear people talk to us, we already have a perspective on the world, we already have a worldview that frames how we think things could

231

be better and how we envision a future for our children. And we're passing that on to our children, and we are so grateful for that. We are raising beautiful families because of you, Tim. We are forever grateful for you. Thank you."

And one more beautiful comment from a former CPO staffer: "Tim, I don't have a particular story, but I just wanted to give thanks. The impact that you have had is obviously phenomenal and doesn't stop. You supported us, loved us, agitated us, encouraged us, pushed us outside of our own comfort zones. You taught us about the importance of the collective. You taught us not to do anything by ourselves. That's not who we are. You showed us how society is forcing us to figure everything out on our own, but you would always remind us of how important it was for us to work together. Those were life lessons, not just for school, or a particular project, but for everything. And that is what we take with us. How are we bringing in more people to the movement, who are we missing from the table, who's not being heard or seen, and what role could we play in making sure that we are inclusive and that things are changing. That's what you taught us, and that's why we are forever grateful to you."

After nearly everyone had shared some beautiful and heart-felt words, Mandla, a man who had also mentored so many of us, and the person I had hoped would succeed Tim as director of the Community Programs Office, began to speak:

> "Tim took my leadership to a transformative level by focusing on my consciousness. Tim mentored me in the ability and the understanding of what it meant to be a conscious person. Which was different from simply being a leader on campus or a community service project

SACRED LESSONS

director. I had taken several ethnic studies courses, but I was not yet a conscious person. I didn't know what it meant to be a conscious person. Tim exposed me to the teachings of Bantu Steve Biko, as I had already been exposed to Malcolm X, Martin Luther King Jr., Marcus Garvey, and Ella Baker. But coming into my consciousness, my conscious awareness, was a game changer. When we talk about honesty, integrity, compassion—these are the qualities of a conscious person. A person who understands the concept of *Ubuntu*, 'we are all one.'"

As everyone in the room hung onto every word that Mandla shared, he continued, "These are teachings, these are conscious ideas that you can manifest in your being. But as it relates to Tim, my peer counselor, what I came away with is that I must manifest in my day-to-day behavior, in my day-to-day practice this idea of the Conscious People's Office. You can call it the Community Programs Office, but the Conscious People's Office determines whether the CPO is actually the CPO that we know and love. The consciousness is what makes it what it is. Something that Tim did for me as my peer adviser is that he planted in my head, like many of you, is that I have to ask myself at times whether or not I am operating as a conscious person, whether I am seeing in every problem my role in the problem. Whether I am recognizing the full understanding of who I am as an African, which Tim has shared with many of you. And part of the reason why people of so many backgrounds are here is that it's just part of being a living being in this world. And please know that I had to consciously not say 'human being' because Tim

233

even questions the idea of being a human being. So I say that we have to be conscious living beings in this world, in this universe, in this cosmos."

Mandla's words resonated with all of us because he, more than anyone else, had spent a considerable amount of time with Tim as a peer, colleague, and friend. He had taken Tim's lessons and created a consulting firm whose main purpose is to educate, empower, and raise the consciousness of the community. He knew that the work was still unfinished, and needed to continue.

As people were leaning out of their seats, Mandla finished his comments by saying, "So when we talk about paying tribute to Tim, the question is, Are we manifesting, building, carrying with us, re-creating the Conscious People's Office everywhere we go? We can sit in the circle and talk about Tim the man, the myth, the legend, and I won't say anything to take away from that mythology. But I will say that the ultimate test about whatever we feel about him is whether or not we are manifesting the Conscious People's Office, the idea of a Conscious People's Office, everywhere we go. Can we look at ourselves in the mirror, can we look at the work that we do, and do we see Tim? Do we see the person that we've described? Do we see the qualities that we have described? Can we look at our work and say that those ideas, those teachings that we are all celebrating here today, are manifesting right now, at this particular moment in time. And if not, then let's in tribute to Tim check ourselves and get back to that space. Where I can say that the Conscious People's Office is in me. Because that's the only real reality at the end of the day in terms of how we feel about Tim. It's about the Conscious People's Office and what it means to express it, to live it, to be it."

Mandla's remarks struck at the core of the celebration. He reminded us that while we were there to celebrate Tim, the real

SACRED LESSONS

work of transforming ourselves, of transforming the world, was not done. And in fact, may never be done in our collective lifetimes. Mandla was lovingly calling us all out. He was pushing us to ask the critical questions that are the foundation of any conscious person. He was asking us to consider whether the teachings that Tim gave us were being manifested in our daily lives. And if not, then we had to ask ourselves why. Because at the end of the day, it's not about what we say, it's not about what we remember, it's about how we put into practice these ideals in our daily lives.

As the celebration was winding down, Fidel Rodriguez, one of my best friends and the person who planted the seed of having the celebration for Tim, closed out the circle. "I want to share a perspective as an observer. I remember sitting at UCLA the last time Tim was here, and we were talking about Tim and I knew that the conversations were already happening, but I said, 'Man, Mike, there needs to be a celebration. Tim needs to be honored. A lot of times our elders leave us and we don't get to celebrate them when they're alive.'

"Since I've known Tim, I remember him talking about the concept of Ubuntu, and he always says, 'A person is a person because of another person.' So look around. It's not knowing the concept of Ubuntu, it's living the consciousness of Ubuntu. I see you, and you see me, and we are one. In Lak'ech, this same concept I have in my own culture, my observations are that I have been blessed to be able to build a relationship with Mike when he was graduating from UCLA, and I had already graduated from USC. I was also mentored by another African man who is the splitting image of Tim. Consciousness. Black Consciousness. Learning about Stephen Biko and the saying, 'The most potent weapon in the hands of the oppressor is...'"

And when everyone automatically responded in unison, "The mind of the oppressed," Fidel smiled and looked at Tim and said, "Look at what you've done!"

"When I first met Mike, I said to myself, 'Look at this other Chicano being mentored by a beautiful black man.' We have been best friends since then, and when I got to meet Tim, I realized that Tim is a living example of the energy that has touched all of us. When you go to Africa, you get to see the consciousness of the continent. So when I got to meet Tim, it was like the continent all in one. All I wanted to do today was to witness the capacity that consciousness has living in the belly of the beast. It ain't easy. We have to live this consciousness every single day for these little ones that are running around here."

Looking right at Tim, Fidel continued, "To see the effects that you have had here, my brother, you are to be commended. And all your ancestors are here, all of our ancestors are here. Believe that. To decolonize, and to be a part of this movement that was launched not only in Africa but obviously here and in other parts of the world, is a testament to your parents and to your own brothers and sisters. And I just want to say thank you for touching the hearts and minds of all of these people. I know that this is not everybody—there are so many more people that wanted to be here today—but I did want to say that I love you, my brother. It's been an honor that I have been able to meet you through your other son Mike."

Fidel pointed at me and smiled. "And I know this man very well, probably too well, but I'm saying that to say that even when Mike's father was going through his health challenges, he knew that he had another dad. I've seen the effects that you have had in his life, the healing that you have helped him to go through

SACRED LESSONS

on his journey. So I thank you, my dear brother. I love you. And continue to decolonize minds."

Getting up from his seat, Fidel walked over and stood directly in front of Tim and said, "I wanted to honor you with some sage. I'm part Chumash, and we did a sacred trip from Oxnard to Santa Cruz Island, and this sage is from that ceremony. It was given to me by my elders, and I am now giving it to you, my dear brother."

As Tim kept repeating, "Thank you, my brother," Fidel got on his knees at Tim's feet, lowered his head to the floor, and said, "We honor you at your feet, my dear brother."

With a humbled heart, Tim continued to say, "Thank you, my brother," as the two of them embraced in a hug that meant so much not only to them but to all of us.

As Fidel concluded with a beautiful Ifa prayer, I looked over to Tim and asked, "Do you want to say anything?"

"No, Mikey, I'm too emotional."

I knew that response all too well because it's the same response my father gives when he's too overwhelmed with emotion. It's the response that too many of us men are taught to give, and that we must break if we truly want to be free.

Looking out into a sea of seventy former UCLA student activists, I concluded the circle by saying, "I just asked Tim if he wanted to say something, but he's so overwhelmed with emotion that all he wants me to say is that he appreciates every single one of you for being here today."

As I looked at Tim to make sure that I wasn't speaking out of turn, I continued, "For many of us cis men, it's hard for us to be vulnerable. It's hard for us to share what we truly feel because society teaches us to do the opposite. So as someone who's actively trying to change gender norms and the ways that I, as a man, show up in the world, I just wanted to say…I just wanted to tell you Tim publicly, in front of everyone, once again how much I, how much we, love you. You have transformed our lives in a way that is incomprehensible, and please know that we are living testaments to the goodness of your heart."

As we closed the celebration with an Umoja Circle, where we all stood in a circle holding hands and shared something we were grateful for, I held Tim's hand. The circle gave us the permission to be vulnerable and to hold hands without ridicule. It gave us, all of us, the opportunity to tell Tim and each other how much we meant to our individual and collective healing. It gave Tim the chance to say "Thank you."

A few days after the surprise celebration, Tim called me. Not being able to pick up my cell phone because I was in a meeting, he ended up texting me the following: My brother, I hope all is good with you and your family. You did surprise me. I did not expect this. You are an amazing young man and you showed me love in a way that no one else has ever done for me. I hope our ancestors always keep your heart open and multiply it a hundredfold. You will always be a part of my family forever and ever. Amen.

After reading his text over and over again, I called him with my heart full.

"Tim, how are you, my brother?"

"I'm good."

Eerily reminiscent of my own father, Tim is a person of few words on the phone. Knowing this, I did the majority of the talking and let him know that everyone who came to the surprise celebration absolutely loved it and had been telling me how grateful they were to have had a chance to spend some quality time with him.

SACRED LESSONS

"That's good, Mikey, that's good," he said, and I could tell that he was more than likely smiling on the other end of the phone.

And as I was about to hang up, Tim showed a level of strength that even I didn't have at that moment.

"Did you get my message?" he asked.

Hesitating because no matter how much self-work I do, I still struggle at times with being intimate with the men, and the women, in my life, and trying hard to not spoil this important moment, I responded, "I did. Thank you so much, Tim. It meant a lot to me, my brother."

"I'm glad, Mikey. You really made my trip memorable."

As I held back my tears yet again, I simply said, "No, Tim. You have made our lives memorable. Thank you."

Chapter 18
The Wisdom of Children

I believe that children come from a sacred source and are born with a divine purpose and a divine reason. They are born innocent and pure. According to ancient teachings, as well as the wisdom of my mentors, there's a special connection between children and elders because of their connection to the spirit world: one just came from the spirit world, and the other one is on their way back. And seeing the way my father interacts with his grandchildren is confirmation that this statement is absolutely true.

My father's relationship with his grandchildren is nothing short of miraculous. He adores his grandchildren in ways that are almost indescribable. Watching him play with my brother's and my kids brings me immense joy because I see my father defying society's expectations of him. I see him being loving and vulnerable. I see him being playful and spontaneous. I see him being a child once again, innocent and free.

SACRED LESSONS

Maybe it's true that the relationship between children and elders is magical because of the wisdom that they're both carrying. Children enter this world with wonder and imagination, while elders leave this world with, hopefully, a more profound and deeper sense of knowledge gained from a life full of beauty, hardship, and love.

Whatever the case may be, I believe that life is a process of remembering who you were when you first entered this world. A process of remembering the gifts and talents innate to each and every one of us, remembering our life's purpose so we can positively impact the world through our unique and special selves.

As the proud son of two teachers, I can honestly say that my children continue to teach me and my parents some of our greatest life lessons. And while I hope that I don't become a grandparent anytime soon, what I will say is that my children have provided my father with a gateway to a time when it didn't matter what anyone thought of him as long as he could freely share his thoughts and feelings. A time when societal expectations and judgments were not yet fully understood, when he was simply a child playing among the apple trees and riverbeds of Atascadero, Chihuahua, México.

I don't know how to explain it, but my children bring out a side of my father that I knew always existed but was too difficult for him to express. They allow him to laugh and to be affectionate in ways that I imagine he wishes he could be with me and my brother: a person who feels comfortable giving his kids nonstop kisses and telling us over and over again how much he loves us. With his grandkids, my father is all of this and so much more. It's almost as if our children have given him permission to start all over again.

Mayela was the first of my father's grandchildren to benefit from my dad's always hidden mischievousness and childlike curiosity. From the first day they met, my dad would give her anything she wanted. While my mom likes to say, "What happens at Naná's house stays at Naná's house," my father takes it to a whole other level. When Mayela was a child, he would give her candy minutes before she went to bed, or buy her as many books as she wanted to encourage her love of reading. Let's just say that whatever Mayela wanted, Mayela got.

With his first grandson, Gabriel, my brother's firstborn, he was beyond ecstatic. I can't even put into words how it felt to see my father hold Gabriel for the first time. Around Mayela, you could tell that my dad was nervous, because he wasn't used to raising a little girl. But with Gabriel, the gloves were off. From day one, the love between the two of them was palpable. They have an undeniable bond, and like my father's relationship with his grandfather, there is something extremely special about their connection. To this day, they are inseparable, and Gabriel brings out a side of my father that is absolutely beautiful.

When Mio, my first biological child, was born, it was almost like my father was relieved and excited at the same time. People say that the gender of a child shouldn't matter as long as the baby is healthy, and while that's absolutely true, my father didn't hide the fact that he wanted me to have a baby boy. Call it a by-product of patriarchy or something else, but what I like to believe is that my father wanted me to develop a father-and-son relationship like he and I have been working to develop. And just like his relationship with Mayela and Gabriel, he absolutely adores Mio. He lets Mio do whatever he wants, from pulling his beard to eating anything, and I mean anything, he wants. My

SACRED LESSONS

father's love of Mio warms my heart in a way that I still can't put into words.

And finally, my brother's second child, Mateo, rounds out the tribe of children who give my father permission to be himself. Mateo's raspy voice always makes my dad laugh in ways I've never seen before. Mateo is probably the most rambunctious of all his grandchildren, and my dad gets a kick out of watching him try to beat up his older brother despite being just a baby. Mateo has my brother's fearlessness, which brings my father such happiness. It's like he gets to relive the joy of parenthood without actually having to be a parent again. Being with Mateo and the rest of his grandchildren is almost like a do-over for my father, allowing him the space and the opportunity to love them as freely and as openly as he wants without judgment or shame.

That's why two days before his surgery, I made sure to start the day by taking my father to the old Romano's Macaroni Grill on Telephone Road, one of his favorite Italian restaurants, to celebrate his sixty-sixth birthday surrounded by his grandchildren. I knew this would make him feel better and get him into the right mindset before going into surgery. Besides, it's always been a family tradition to get all of us together for birthdays. This, more than any other birthday, had to be a special one. So, despite my brother being out of town at his friend's bachelor party, we planned a daylong celebration complete with my abuelo and my niño coming over so we could all spend the entire day with my father.

Even though my father was in unbearable pain, he was determined to go. He wanted to spend as much time with family as possible before checking into the hospital. We decided to meet at my parents' house at 11:00 a.m. so we'd have enough time to get to the restaurant for lunch before it got too crowded.

In talking to my father during the week, I sensed that he wanted this day to go perfectly, so I made sure to arrive earlier than expected to maximize our time together.

At the restaurant, we had a great time complete with too much garlic bread, pizza, pasta, and more. My father even ordered a glass of wine. I smiled at the sight of him being so happy and content. As was customary, the moment we had finished eating, my mom brought out a big birthday cake and a couple of presents for my father to open. Right before we sang "Happy Birthday," I organized all the grandchildren to sit around him for a picture. I told the kids to smile big and say "cheese," and took the most wonderful picture of my father surrounded by his four beautiful grandchildren.

As we sang at the top of our lungs, some of the restaurant staff and people enjoying their lunch began to sing with us: *"Happy birthday to you / Happy birthday to you / Happy birthday, dear abuelo / Happy birthday to you."*

When we finished singing, Gabriel, my brother Albert's oldest son, looked at my father with a suspicious look on his face and said, "Abuelo, now close your eyes and make a wish."

Before he closed his eyes, my father looked at Gabriel and for some reason winked at him, then blew out all the candles with the help of his four grandchildren.

Right after my mom removed all the candles, my father unexpectedly thrust his face into the middle of the birthday cake. With a look of accomplishment, his face completely covered in frosting, he smiled at all of us. Stunned, my mom handed him some napkins to clean his face as the rest of us couldn't stop laughing.

SACRED LESSONS

With frosting still on his face, my father looked over to Gabriel who, still laughing, blurted out, "Good job, abuelo," and then proceeded to give him the biggest hug.

"Papá, why did you do that?" I asked, still laughing.

"Mijo, I always wanted to throw my face into a cake. So I just did it," he said matter-of-factly.

"So you had this planned all along?"

And with his *travieso* smile, my father simply said, "Well, Gabriel and I did talk about it."

It was a moment of pure bliss for my father, something he had wanted to do for his entire life. A moment of family, laughter, and dare I say, love.

Days after my father's surgery, I was working on his computer and noticed a paper that was folded in half. For some reason, something deep inside me told me to look at it. Following my gut instinct, I opened the paper and read a letter that my father had more than likely written the day before his surgery.

TO MY NUMERO UNO

I want to thank you for coming to my birthday party. You made my day. I am now sixty-six years old, but I want to live to see you graduate from college. I am going to try my hardest!

You are my sunshine and I love you very much... you are my NUMERO UNO. Your compassion makes me happy and gives me the strength to face my adversaries. I was numero uno with my grandpa and we had a lot of fun together.

Thank you for all the gifts…with all those socks my feet will not smell anymore.

Thank you for your coloring. I am going to frame it and put it in my room…it's beautiful!

I really enjoyed the cake in my face. I have never done that. I did not have that experience as a child and I always wanted to do it.

I really enjoyed swimming and the jacuzzi… best fun I had all week.

This was the best birthday I have had in a long time. I am sorry I could not spend more time with you, but I had to take care of my father and my sick brother. THEY LIKE TO DRINK.

Your grandpa that loves you a lot.

Abuelo

As I sat there reading my father's letter to his first grandson, I cried once again. I cried because within that one simple page my father was expressing himself in ways that I had rarely seen before. Here he was telling his first grandson that his picture was beautiful and that he was going to frame it and put it up in his room. Here he was telling his first grandson that he was his number one, just like he was his own grandfather's "numero uno." Here he was telling his first grandson that he loved him.

But I was also crying because I started to feel a weird sensation that my father wasn't telling me or anyone else the whole truth. I started to feel as if he was hiding how he was truly

SACRED LESSONS

feeling. As I read and reread his letter, I felt a sense of urgency in his words. I felt as if this was my father's way of telling not just Gabriel but all of us that he loved us. I felt as if this was my father's way of saying goodbye.

After finishing the letter, I sat for a few minutes in complete silence. I have no idea how long I sat there, but as time passed, the words started to disappear from the letter I was holding. It was as if I was looking at a blank piece of paper even though I had just read it over and over.

Without knowing what was happening or what to do next, I rubbed my eyes to try and stop the tears from flowing. And in that moment, all I could see, all I could remember, were my father's final words to Gabriel, to me, to all of us: "Your grandpa that loves you a lot."

Chapter 19
Why Can't I Ask for Help?

I had woken up early on a Sunday morning while Claudia and the kids were sleeping to drive to my parents' house. I wanted to surprise my mom by taking her out to breakfast and then surprise her even more by going to church with her.

It was a few weeks before my father's surgery, and I wanted to do something special for her. She had been so worried about the surgery that the only place that seemed to comfort her was church. Being the mamá's boy that I am, I knew that would bring her some semblance of relief and comfort.

As we passed the beaches that had been my place of solace as a child, and even today as an adult, I mustered up the courage to ask my mom the question I'd been struggling to answer myself. The question that had been haunting my father since he was a child and is at the root of so many of my problems.

"Mamá, why is it so hard for Papá to ask for help?"

SACRED LESSONS

Pondering my question, my mother said, "Mijo, your father is very independent. Growing up, he had to learn how to do things all by himself. His parents didn't support him."

"What do you mean they didn't support him?" I asked.

Without even hearing me, my mom continued, "In high school, when he was in college, nothing. They never supported him, so your father learned to do things all by himself."

"So, is that why it's so hard for him to ask anyone for help?" I said, hoping to get an explanation about why my father and I pretend to know everything when in truth we don't even have a clue about most things.

"Yup," my mother replied almost instantaneously.

"But that's not good for him, because he needs our help," I said.

"He never asks anyone for help. Even with me, he doesn't ask for anything. He never asks for money to pay the bills. He never asks me for money to pay the mortgage. So…"

"So what?" I asked.

"So I just put the money that I make from work into the bank and save it, so when we go on vacation I can buy the things that I want. Even though he buys me everything that I need, I still like to have my own money for things."

Looking out the window as if contemplating something deeper, my mother continued, "When there's an emergency and he really needs the money, I tell him that I have the money." Then she added, with a bit of sadness, "But your father won't take it."

Hearing the hurt in her voice, I said, "Mamá, I know that there's times when he needs the money to pay the bills and you give it to him. But…but I also know that it kills him to have to ask you for money."

"Oh, he can't stand it," she replied. "The few times that I do give him money, he always wants to pay me back. I know that he doesn't have the money, so I tell him, 'Hon, you don't have to pay me back. It's okay. You need the money. Just use it. That's what it's there for.'"

Looking at me as we passed the ocean, she said, "He never lets me pay for anything because he says that's what a man is supposed to do. He says that it's the man's job to take care of everything."

"And what do you tell him when he says that?" I asked.

"I tell him that if I have the money, then use it. But he always says, 'No, it's okay.' Your father just has a hard time asking for anything. It's how he's always been."

As we arrived at the Spanish-language Mass at San Buenaventura Mission Basilica, I changed the subject and hoped that Jesus would provide me with some answers. I hoped that for the next hour or so I wouldn't have to carry the heavy burden of masculinity that makes too many of us men feel as if we have to know everything, pay for everything, and be everything.

As I sat in the church, I started to get really angry. I started to curse the weight of patriarchy that contributed to my father having to go to the hospital again. I knew that if my father could have felt comfortable asking for help, maybe he could have prevented his back from getting worse. Who knows, maybe he could have stopped taking pain medication or found a nonsurgical way to handle his recurring back problems.

What I do know for sure is that the toxic myth of masculinity forced my father to act as if he had to endure his pain all alone. Like so many men, he felt emasculated when he had to ask for help. And yes, his pride and his ego definitely contributed to his situation, but I blame patriarchy for my father's poor health

SACRED LESSONS

because I know that it has caused nothing but harm, not just to my father but to all of us.

As I made the sign of the cross and sat down next to my mother, I began to reflect on my upbringing in the church and my complicated relationship with Catholicism and with organized religion in general.

My mom always hoped and prayed that I would be a practicing Catholic. I know that sounds stereotypical of Mexican mothers, but in my case, it's absolutely true. It's why my mother made sure that I made my first confession and took my first Holy Communion. It's why I became an altar boy and attended Catholic school for most of my life. And it's why I found myself at church once again. I needed some higher form of reassurance that my father's surgery would turn out fine.

As I got older, I started to veer away as far as possible from the church. The historical underpinnings of an institution that's been responsible for horrendous violence against women, children, and indigenous people are way too much for me to swallow. But while I stopped attending Mass, I never lost faith in a higher power. That's why I began learning African and indigenous practices that have connected me to spirit in very profound and deep ways. And, in a moment that may seem contradictory, I found myself once again in church praying to an unseen presence during a moment when I needed to find hope and salvation in something, or someone, outside myself.

That's why I was shocked, yet not shocked, when Virginia, one of my parents' closest friends, shared with me a story about my father a few days after he was admitted to the hospital. It was the Wednesday after his surgery when those prayers I said at San Buenaventura Mission started to ring true. The Wednesday when my father was supposed to be discharged from the hospital and allowed to go home. The Wednesday when my father's new life without back pain was supposed to begin.

That day, Virginia came to visit my parents at the hospital as she had every day since my father was first admitted early on that Monday morning. She would come to check on my father and to see if my mom needed anything.

As Virginia walked into the hospital room, my mother smiled at her as she always did and then asked, "Virginia, do you mind staying here so I can run and get something to eat from the cafeteria?"

"Of course not, Gloria. Mayo and I have a lot to catch up on," Virginia said jokingly as she looked at my father, who was noticeably irritable from learning that he had to stay in the hospital a few more days.

A few minutes after my mother left the room, my father looked at Virginia and quietly said, "Virginia, can I ask you something?"

"Of course, Mayo, what do you need?"

My father looked around the room to make sure that no one else could hear him, then said quietly, "Virginia, will you pray for me?"

My father was the last person Virginia would expect to ask such a question, but she immediately replied, "Sure, Mayo, I will pray for you. All of us are praying for you."

Uncharacteristically for him, or maybe showing his truest self, my father blurted out, "I can feel your prayers."

Without having to say the actual words, my father was asking for help in his own way. He wasn't just asking for help from Virginia, or from the doctors and the hospital staff, he was asking for help from a higher power. And in that moment, my father was not just baptized, he was healed.

SACRED LESSONS

As I said before, it was not like my father, a person who rejected religion for most of his life, to believe in prayer. If he had to choose a religion, he said that he would have converted to Islam because people often mistook my father for a Muslim because of his dark skin and his first name, Ismael. As someone who revels in identifying with the least of us, he relishes the fact that people think he's Muslim. He's always loved to stand alongside those who are demonized and scapegoated. Those of us who are forgotten and thrown away.

As soon as my mother returned, my father quickly changed the subject and the three of them talked for a bit. He didn't want my mom to know about his conversation with Virginia because he knew that she would start to worry. He knew that if she found out about him wanting to pray, she would know he wasn't feeling well. And that was something my father desperately tried to hide from both my mother and his doctors.

When Virginia left, my father looked at my mom, who was sitting at his bedside, and reached over and grabbed her hand. She immediately jumped up because my father rarely held my mother's hand.

"Hon, what's wrong? Are you okay?" my mother asked nervously, not used to this kind of physical affection from my father.

Here was the man who had difficulty asking for help, difficulty being emotionally vulnerable, holding my mother's hand. This was the moment when my mother knew that something was terribly wrong. This was the moment that would change our lives forever.

And with tears in his eyes, my father simply looked at my mother one last time and said, "I just want to hold your hand. I love you."

253

Chapter 20
Saying Goodbye

It was a Monday morning.

August 3, 2015, to be exact.

Community Memorial Hospital of San Buenaventura.

Unlike my typical Monday mornings, I found myself away from my home in Los Angeles. Having visited my father on Thursday, I'd decided to stay at my parents' house over the weekend so I could be closer to my papá in case he or my mother needed anything.

Despite being away from home, I found myself doing exactly what my father did every morning. I woke up before the sun rose so I could get some work done before the day began. I imagined that, just like my dad, I was struggling to sleep because I was worried about him not being able to come home yet.

After a couple of early morning work calls, I arrived at the hospital at 8:15. I parked my mom's blue Volvo on the second floor of the hospital parking garage and walked straight through the heavy hospital doors. I took the elevator up to the Coronary

SACRED LESSONS

Intensive Care Unit on the third floor where my father had been staying for the past four days.

I had a routine: Upon arriving, I'd check in with the nurses to see how my father was doing, then I'd ask my mom if she needed anything or wanted to go home and rest for a while. Next, I'd wait until the doctor came in to give us an update on my father's condition and, hopefully, tell us when we could take him home. Later, I'd attempt to get more work done at the hospital, but that was mainly to keep myself distracted from the fact that my father's condition had seemingly gotten worse.

On that Monday morning, I clasped my father's hands and told him that I couldn't wait for him to come home. As I looked at his wrinkled hands, I began to get very emotional. I didn't know what was happening. Despite his reliance on a respirator, and despite his being sedated, I spoke to him.

"Papá, I just want you to know that I love you so much, and that I can't wait for you to get out of this hospital and come back home."

Unsure of whether he could hear me, or whether my voice was merely a distant echo in his dreams, I continued to tell him how appreciative I was to be his son. I continued to pour my heart out and wanted him to know that I was there. I wanted him to know that I would always be there, that I would never stop loving him.

And just like one week before, when I held my father's hand before his surgery, I willed him to recover with every fiber of my body. No matter what happened next, I wanted him to feel my presence and to know that I would forever be by his side. I wanted him to know, without a shadow of a doubt, that he was loved.

Laughing as a way to deal with my anxiety and stress, I took out my phone to take a picture of my father as I said, "Papá, hurry up and get better. The kids are waiting to play with you. Plus, I want to take you to Barnes and Noble to buy some new books."

I desperately wanted everything to be okay. "I'm going to take a couple of pictures so you remember this day when you start exercising more and eating better. This is going to be the last time that we're both here together."

And then time stopped, or at least slowed down. Way down. It was at this exact moment that the nurses told me I had to immediately leave the room. It was at this exact moment that the doctors and nurses started rushing into my father's hospital room. It was at this exact moment that nothing would ever be the same again.

My father's body was succumbing to septic shock, a dire condition where everything starts to shut down. Intuitively, I knew something had gone wrong, so I didn't want to leave his bedside. I didn't want to leave the room. That's why I was holding his hand. That's why I was taking pictures of him. That's why I was telling him to hurry up and get better.

I did everything I could to stay with my father until a nurse gently pushed me outside and told me that she would let me know when I could come back to see him. Seeing the look of desperation on my face, the nurse reassured me that she would come and get me as soon as it was possible.

Minutes later, I found myself staring out the third-floor window in a state of complete confusion. *What had just happened? What were they doing to my father? When can I go back in to see him?* I couldn't make sense of anything. I couldn't concentrate. I couldn't believe that my father's health was deteriorating so fast.

SACRED LESSONS

As I stood there looking out into nothingness, my brother was frantically pacing back and forth in the hallway. He couldn't stay still, so he kept walking up and down, up and down. Just then, my brother saw the doctor push the door open, and for a moment, their eyes locked—and then the doctor mouthed the words, "I'm sorry."

My brother started to scream, "No! No! Noooooo!"

Hearing my brother slamming his fists into the wall and yelling from the depths of his soul, I immediately ran to my mother, who had jumped up once she heard my brother yelling.

"Mijo, what's happening? Why is Albert screaming? What's wrong with Papá?"

Without saying a word, I just held her tightly as the reality of the situation began to sink in. Then, like my brother, my precious mother started to scream. "No! No! No! This can't be true. God, please bring him back to me. Hon, please come back to me. Hon, please come back to me."

It's hard to put into words what happened next. It's hard to describe what happens when you can't do anything to stop the most important man in your life from passing away. It's hard to process the wave of emotions when you're holding the person who gave you life as she breaks down and tells you that she wants to join her partner in heaven. It's hard to recall all the details of the exact moment when I learned that my father had died.

That moment changed my life forever. For those who have lost a parent, you know how difficult it is to cope with the sinking reality of it all. The death of a parent is a club that inevitably every person has to join, and one of the most painful experiences that I've ever had to deal with. The minutes, hours, and days after my father passed, the air felt crisp, everything felt more vibrant, still, and dare I say, alive. And for those few days afterward, I felt as if I was in some kind of waking dream.

The loss of my father forced me to contemplate the fragility of life and my own mortality. It forced me to examine my childhood and the profound influence that my father had on shaping me and my family. It forced me to reevaluate my priorities and reexamine what truly matters to me. Even to this day, it feels as if it just happened yesterday. I can still vividly picture that fateful morning. Years later, I can still see the blank stares and the solemn gazes. I can still taste the overwhelming shock of it all.

I'm not going to lie and say that my father's death immediately propelled me to a deeper understanding of myself, because it didn't. The truth is that I was terrified and afraid. And at times, I still catch myself being too scared and too frightened. And like most scared and frightened little boys and men, I didn't know how to deal with my emotions. I didn't have the tools to process my sadness and my grief in a healthy way. So I did everything I could to run away from the reality that my father was gone.

In hindsight, even if I had known what to do after losing my father, I didn't have the time to think about it. I didn't have the time to process what had happened or to grieve because I was too busy planning my father's funeral. My mother was too heartbroken, and my brother needed the time and space to mourn. So I got into hyper work mode to try and distance myself from the avalanche of emotions I was feeling. I took on the lion's share of making the funeral arrangements to prevent myself from feeling. I wish that I could say I had it all figured out, but I didn't. I didn't then, and I still don't today.

That's why even today, I still find myself struggling to celebrate personal or professional accomplishments, because it's another reminder that my father is no longer with me. And

SACRED LESSONS

while I believe on a spiritual level that my father never left, it's still incredibly hard for me to accept that he's gone. I have a hard time celebrating, because it's another reminder that I'm not able to call him or see him. It's another reminder that I won't have the joy of physically holding my father ever again or giving him a kiss on the cheek.

That's why birthdays are no longer the same. That's why anniversaries are hard. That's why I continue to mourn. That's why I continue to cry. That's why I continue to grieve.

I didn't want to say goodbye.

Lesson VI
Faith

Chapter 21
Coming Full Circle

It was supposed to be a vacation of deep spiritual connection. A vacation of quality bonding time for my wife Claudia and me. And a much-needed time to release and let go.

Claudia had booked a healing retreat as a surprise for my upcoming birthday. She knew how hard birthdays were for me since my father's passing, so she wanted to plan something special. She knew that I really wanted to go on this retreat but that I was unsure whether we could make it happen given the five-day time commitment and our current financial situation. So, wanting to manifest a restful trip together without the children and without the pressures of work, Claudia took a giant leap of faith and made it happen.

Once I found out we were going on this retreat, I got super excited because the retreat was being facilitated by Ana Lilia, an incredible healer who specializes in breathwork and supporting people on their journey back home, back inward. She has become really close to both Claudia and me, and is a mentor, a teacher, and a friend.

I met Ana during the beginning of the COVID-19 pandemic when her free online "community gathering" classes helped me find sanity in the midst of a global crisis. As corny as it sounds, Ana helped me learn how to breathe again. She helped me feel less isolated and alone. She brought people together on a weekly basis to remind us, to remind me, that we are all spiritually wired for connection. That we all thirst for and need to feel connected because in the end, we are all energetically one.

After a few months of attending her online classes, I started to book individual sessions, and before I knew it, I was attending an intensive four-month, one-on-one master class. Once I completed this program, I started meeting with Ana every other Tuesday. And as the months and years passed, I finally found a safe space where I could be completely vulnerable. I finally found a safe space where I could just be me and not worry about the pressures I was putting on myself.

With Ana, I found someone who reminds me of my personal progress and helps me work through my trauma. With Ana, I have someone I trust and who supports me as I confront my shadows and teaches me the tools to deal with the ever-unfolding challenges of life. With Ana, I am certain that my father and all my angels and ancestors are smiling, because they wanted our souls to meet so we could work on healing ourselves and be of greater service to others.

So it was a no-brainer that Claudia and I wanted to attend an intimate spiritual retreat that Ana Lilia was putting together in Sedona, Arizona, one of the most powerful vortexes and energy centers on the planet. I was anxiously counting down the weeks, then the days, and then the minutes until the retreat would be

SACRED LESSONS

upon us. Two days prior to leaving was the Full Moon in Pieces, and during my early morning ritual, I pulled an oracle card that told me to expect something magical and unexpected very soon.

As Friday quickly approached, Claudia and I washed all our clothes and tried to get as much work done as possible so we could be fully immersed in the retreat. On Wednesday night, as we were about to watch a movie, we heard Mio get up and run to the bathroom.

Concerned, we both got up to see what was happening and noticed that his eyes were red from crying. "Mio, what's wrong?" I asked.

Without waiting for him to respond, Claudia asked, "Mio what's wrong? Does something hurt? Do you feel like throwing up?"

With tears in his eyes, Mio yelled, "NO!"

Calmly, Claudia said, "Mio, we're simply asking to find out what's happening so we can help you. We did nothing wrong. It is our job to make sure that you're okay."

And almost in unison, we both asked once again, "Mio, what's wrong?"

After a series of questions, some answered and some not, we chalked it up to a bad case of heartburn since Mio had eaten late and more than he usually does.

After he calmed down, we tucked Mio into bed and told him to let us know if he needed anything. Needless to say, Claudia woke up every hour to check on him and to make sure he wasn't coming down with a cold or flu.

With one day left before we were to make the seven-hour-plus drive to Sedona, both Claudia and I were frantically trying to complete our last-minute preparations. With meetings stacked on top of meetings, I got home later than usual and was grateful to see my mother, who had taken time off from work to watch Mio while we went on our vacation.

With too many things still left undone and packing not even close to being completed, Claudia and I were exhausted and irritable with each other. We were on the edge and wondering if going on vacation was worth all the trouble. As midnight fell upon us, we again heard Mio downstairs in the bathroom coughing.

Running to check on him, we asked the same series of questions as the night before. Seeing his eyes bloodshot yet again, I knew that our plans were inevitably going to change. And just like the Full Moon was asking me to do, I had to surrender to what needed to happen. I had to surrender to what needed to take place. I had to let go of my expectations for what I had wanted to happen over the next five days.

As I lay down to get a couple hours of sleep, I started to get upset. Even though I was on a spiritual path that teaches me to surrender, even though I knew that my ego was bruised because things weren't turning out the way I wanted, even though I knew all of this, I didn't want to accept what was happening. I didn't want our plans to change. I desperately wanted to go on this vacation with Claudia no matter what.

Sensing my frustration, Claudia looked at me before I fell asleep and gently said, "I can't go. I need to stay home and take care of Mio. Can you please find someone else to go with you?"

Pretending not to hear her, I closed my eyes and went to sleep. Three hours later, at 4:00 a.m., I woke up to meditate and take a shower so I could drive to Arizona by myself.

"Michael…? Michael…?" Claudia quietly said so as to not wake up my mother or the children.

"What?" I responded defensively because I didn't want to hear what she was going to say.

SACRED LESSONS

"You can't drive to Arizona by yourself. It's too dangerous. I found some flights that take you to Phoenix, and then you can drive two hours to Sedona."

"Claudia, I already picked up the rental car. I'm just going to go by myself."

"Michael, please do not go by yourself, it's too dangerous," she adamantly said again.

At that point, I had already walked out of our bedroom and started looking for flights on my phone. After finding one that would leave Burbank at 9:30 a.m. and get me to Phoenix by 1:00 p.m., I booked it and went back to bed without saying a word to Claudia.

Three hours later, I was up again, only this time Mio was awake. He was so excited to spend five days with his naná that he'd awakened earlier than usual. He hadn't spent that many days with my mom since before the COVID-19 pandemic, so he was absolutely ecstatic. Once he saw me, though, his heart shrank because he knew that his plans of spending time alone with his naná were over.

"You're not going on your vacation?" he asked.

"I'm not sure, Mio. I bought a plane ticket this morning, but I have to wait and see what Mamá wants to do."

Upset because I still wanted Claudia to go with me, it was time for my mom and me to walk Mio to school. As we were walking, Mio stopped me and said, "I'll be fine, Papá. Just go."

"I know you will, Mio, but we have to make sure that you're all right. It's not like you to wake up two nights in a row not feeling well. I'll talk to Mamá, and we'll make a decision."

Sensing his disappointment because things were now out of his control, I gave my son a kiss on his cheek and watched him as he walked into school. As I walked back home with my mother, she said, "I can watch him, Mijo. You and Claudia have plans. You two need to go. He'll be fine."

Reluctantly, I replied, "I know, Mamá. But I have to see how Claudia feels. She won't have a good time at the retreat if she knows that Mio is sick."

Hearing the frustration in my voice, my mom stopped talking as we walked in silence the rest of the way home. As the time got closer for me to go to the airport, Claudia and I began arguing over whether she should go to Sedona. I was adamant that my mom could take care of Mio, and she was adamant that he was our priority and that she needed to stay with him.

Long story short: I didn't get what I wanted. No matter what I said, Claudia was not going to go to Arizona. Not wanting to miss my flight, I quickly threw the rest of my clothes into a duffel bag and got ready to go. Pissed off, I asked my mom to go with me to the airport hoping that I could still make my flight. I ran out the door without even saying goodbye to Claudia.

Thirty minutes before my flight was to leave, I was frantically driving my mom's car to the Burbank airport. Breaking the awkward silence, my mother said, "Mijo, Mio is going to be upset if you and Claudia don't go on your trip. Just call Claudia and tell her that I can take care of him. He'll be fine. You two could still drive to Arizona."

Trying not to raise my voice, I replied sternly, "Claudia's not going to go. I already tried talking to her. She's staying and that's it. Mio's going to be upset, but I can't do anything about it. It is what it is."

"Mijo, you and Claudia can still go. I could watch him. He'll be fine," my mother, almost pleading, said once again.

"I know, but I told you already that Claudia won't have a good time if Mio's not feeling well. Plus, she's been texting with

SACRED LESSONS

his doctor all morning, who says that he probably caught a bug that's going around."

Sensing my disappointment, my mother surprised me and said, almost in a whisper, "I could go with you if you want."

As she said those words, my heart skipped a beat. My mom was the first person who came to mind when Claudia told me to ask someone else to go with me. I had wanted to ask her, but for some reason, more than likely because I let my anger get the best of me, I didn't say anything. Suddenly, with the possibility of my mom going with me to Sedona, I timidly asked, "Are you sure? You would want to go with me?"

"Yeah. If you want me to, I'll go with you."

Not wanting the moment to pass me by, I immediately called the airline to try and cancel my flight. But with a ten-minute wait time on the phone, and being only five minutes away from the airport, I decided to take my chances and see if I could pull off a miracle and get my money back, or at least get flight credit for a future trip.

I quickly parked my mom's car in the red zone and said, "Stay here. I'll be right back. Here's the keys in case you need to move the car."

I ran into the airport, waited in line, and finally got to speak with a person at the counter. After telling him the story about how Claudia had surprised me for my birthday by purchasing the retreat a few weeks ago, and then my son getting sick that night, the man at the counter took pity on me and was able to get me a full refund since I had booked the flight literally four hours before it was supposed to leave.

And with that, I drove home, threw my mom's suitcase into the rental car, and took off to Sedona. This was the first trip I had taken alone with my mom since I was a child on our family visits to San Jose to see my maternal grandmother. And this was the first trip we had taken together since my father had died eight years earlier.

Trying my best to make the 5:00 p.m. start time for the healing retreat, I raced down the 10 Freeway, zigzagging around cars as if I were driving on a motor speedway. When we got out of LA, I began asking my mom questions about her childhood, and about my grandmother.

For the next two hours, my mother poured her heart out recollecting stories, from working as an eight-year-old in the fields picking plums with my Naná Daria to the challenges she'd faced being married to my father to her difficulty accepting that he was gone. It was a special moment that we both had wanted and needed for quite some time. A moment of sharing and acceptance. A moment of revelation and connection.

And without warning, as soon as her tears dried and we crossed the Arizona state line, we ran straight into one of the biggest thunderstorms of the season. Unable to see a thing, and with the wind raging like crazy, I turned on the hazard lights so the cars behind us could see us through the pouring rain.

I was forced to go ten miles an hour as the rain and the wind continued to pound the car, making the situation extremely dangerous. It was yet another reminder that Mother Nature really does control my life, and that no matter how sure I am about the future or anything else, spirit always has other plans for me.

Despite the circumstances, there was no turning back now. We were in it. There was no way out, only through. We were entering right into the center of the storm, and whatever needed to be released would be released. And like my mentor Luis J. Rodriguez has always told me, the only way to truly heal and

SACRED LESSONS

move past our traumas is to go right through them, to go straight through the center of the wound.

We survived the thunderstorm, and after passing some of the most gorgeous red rocks in all of Arizona, if not in the world, we finally made it to the retreat at eleven minutes past 5:00 p.m. As Ana Lilia and the retreat staff greeted us, I introduced my mother to them, and then we made our way to our room. Having thirty minutes to spare, we quickly changed our clothes and got ready for the opening ceremony.

As we made our way outside to start the retreat, Ana smudged everyone with sage before they took their seats in a circle around a fire. Listening to the beautiful sound of indigenous flutes being played by Rita, one of the most pure and joyful souls I have ever met, I watched as my mom was smudged before entering the circle of women. And right before Ana broke our collective silence, the rain started to pour down on us once again.

"Welcome, everyone," Ana said as she smiled and looked at each one of us, reassuring us that we were exactly where we were meant to be.

With the rain clouds moving in closer around us, she continued, "My intention was that the first part of this retreat would allow us to release whatever we needed to let go of. And in true Full Moon fashion, the rain is reminding us that things may look different than what we had originally planned, but we are definitely going to get what all of us need from this retreat."

As we introduced ourselves to one another, I couldn't help but think about the last time I'd taken a trip alone with one of my parents. It was when I went on vacation to Reno with my father. And just like that time many years ago, I knew this trip with my mother would be life-changing. I knew this experience would deepen our relationship, and that the people, including myself and my mother, who needed to be in the opening ceremony were in the circle.

As the rain poured down, Ana asked us to close our eyes and think about what we wanted to release during the retreat. The smoke of the fire surrounded us, and I heard my mom start to cry. I heard her surrender to the unknown, to the unseen powers of the four directions and the four elements, and release years of emotions she had been holding on to since that fateful day when my father unexpectedly passed away.

After the beautiful welcoming ceremony, it was time for dinner. Given that I was the only man in a group of thirteen attendees, I purposely left my mother alone so she could connect with all the other women. As she got to know them, I found myself gravitating toward Wade, the only other man present, who was working as the retreat photographer and whose warm demeanor immediately welcomed me in. On top of wanting to connect with another man, I also wanted my mother to soak up all the female energy that she could since she's so used to giving and rarely makes the time to receive all the love she deserves.

As I ate my food, I overheard my mother's voice crack as she talked about the impact of losing my father: "I keep myself busy so I don't have to think about him. I hate silence because it reminds me that my husband isn't with me anymore."

And right at the point when she was about to break down, I heard, almost in unison, the women sitting next to her say, "Gloria, you were meant to be here."

When I looked back at my mom, I saw a smile on her face, a smile that I've grown accustomed to not seeing as much since my father died. Holding hands with one of the women, my mom simply responded, "I think so too."

SACRED LESSONS

That night, I intuitively knew that spirit wanted me to go on this retreat with my mother. As my body started to slowly drift off to sleep, I knew this retreat would be the catalyst for my mom to finally process and begin to release the pain of losing my father. I knew that the medicine both of us needed would be provided. Claudia had initially booked the retreat for us, but it seemed as if my father wanted my mother to attend so she could learn how to better cope with his passing.

In my heart, I absolutely believe there are no accidents in life. I believe that everything happens for a reason. It was written in the stars that Mio would feel sick and that Claudia would stay home with him. I was meant to go on this retreat with my mother, who taught me how to have faith in the unseen magic of God, Creator, source. I was meant to be here, now, with her.

By the next morning, my mom was making friends with every single person on the retreat. She was genuinely glowing and looked happier than I had seen her in years. Despite being tired, she made sure to get up early to read her Bible and say her prayers. Despite her aches and pains, she still participated in yoga. Despite her difficulty in processing the loss of my father, she seemed open to receiving the love of the land and of the people present.

By the third morning, I was overwhelmed with immense feelings of joy and gratitude. I was thrilled that I was able to participate in so many new experiences with my mother. I was studying every aspect of the retreat because I was determined to facilitate something similar for men—me being the only man on the retreat proved that we men really needed this kind of space for healing and connection. And that day in particular, I was looking forward to being with my mother as she participated in her first ever cacao ceremony.

In my ancestral lineage, cacao is known as the "food of the Gods." It's used in ceremonies to open up hearts and to bring people closer in alignment to their true selves. It's a powerful medicine, one that has given me a lot of insights in the past. As such, I knew that no matter what happened next, the cacao would bring me and my mother closer together, and bring us much needed clarity and peace.

Underneath the beauty of the Sedona sky, sitting in the shade of several beautiful trees, next to a creek where the soothing sound of the water caressed my soul, I let go of all my preconceived notions and expectations. I cleared my mind so that the plant medicine could provide me with the messages and the answers that I needed to hear.

As I introduced myself to the cacao, I thanked her for her medicina, and I put the cup of cacao next to my ear so I could hear what she was trying to tell me. As I listened with my intuition, I heard what I needed to hear. I finally understood what had been so hard for me to grasp. I was reminded that my life had always been a series of choices. I remembered that I would always have the ability to choose the direction of my life. I was reassured that my power, my divinity, my future, lies in the choices that I make each and every day.

After the cacao ceremony, I took some time to be alone. I started to reflect on Mariame Kaba's concept that "hope is a discipline." As I thought about the messages I'd received from the cacao medicine, I was reminded of the necessity of not losing sight of the fact that I, that men, are indeed changing. I had to remind myself that I don't have to succumb to the idea that people, and men in particular, cannot change. I had to remember, in the presence of my mother and all the women who had bravely

SACRED LESSONS

shown up for themselves, that we are all on an individual and collective journey to heal ourselves.

As the days passed, it seemed as if time had stopped. It was almost like we were living in an in-between space, a prolonged moment in time. And in this liminal space, I began to recognize that I wasn't the same man I was yesterday, and that I wouldn't be the same man tomorrow. And while this realization may have scared me in the past, at that moment I was okay. At that moment, I was finally at peace with myself. At that moment, I felt completely in love with myself and with all those around me.

Getting to spend quality time with my mother allowed me to see that there is no end, no beginning, and no finality to life. That once I think I have it all figured out, the Creator puts another challenge, another person, another test into my life to see if I've learned the sacred lessons I'm meant to learn.

As I spent hours talking to my mom, and even more time in deep meditation and contemplation, I realized that being on a spiritual journey doesn't mean that the hardships and losses will stop. On the contrary, it just means that I have to put into practice the ancient tools that are there to get me through these difficult times. It just means that I have to surround myself with people who love and support me. It just means that I am where I am meant to be on this sacred journey.

As the retreat slowly shifted to a time of rebirth and manifestation, I noticed that my mom was smiling more. I noticed that she was thoroughly enjoying our time together in Sedona. I noticed that she seemed more at peace and was even contemplating dancing, something that she loved but hadn't done since my father passed away.

As I marveled at my mother, I was enthralled by her beautiful childlike wonder and energy. She has always looked at life with eyes that see the goodness in every person. And although she was by far the oldest person on the retreat, she exhibited a childlike curiosity that was so special and uniquely her. She showed us all that we could still hold on to our innocence and purity. And while Ana Lilia was definitely the mama bear of the group, my mother became every person's favorite tia, auntie, and relative.

Listening to my mother speak with the other women made me laugh. She would talk for hours, or listen to the women as they shared their challenges, and then politely say, "I'm sorry, but I have to go potty." And I would sit there and smile because even her language was reminding us that we will always be that little child within us. That child that came into the world as pure energy and love. That child that still needs to heal so we can be who we were always meant to be, loving and free.

During our time together, the group instantaneously fell in love with my mother, and my mother instantaneously fell in love with them. As we went to bed that night, I put my arm around her and asked, "Mamá, have you had a good time?"

"Oh yes! It's been wonderful. A very different experience for me."

Laughing, I asked, "Have you ever done anything like this before?"

Stopping to think about it before she responded, my mother said, "Well, I have gone on religious retreats with the church before. But nothing like this."

"I bet that it was totally different from this retreat," I said with a smirk.

Then my mom looked right at me and said, "You know what...I have done something similar."

"What?" I said, now intrigued.

SACRED LESSONS

"I did that sweat lodge ceremony with you the week before you got married. That was really scary. But you know what, like this week, I survived," she said as we both started laughing.

As I kissed my mother good night, I said, "You did it, Mamá. I'm so proud of you. I love you."

On the last full day of the retreat, we hiked to a birthing cave for a sunrise ceremony. On the way there, we saw two deer crossing the street, perhaps a mother and a son or a husband and a wife.

In many cultures around the world, deer symbolize tenderness and strength, intuition and instinct, innocence and playfulness. It was the perfect animal spirit to see because deer encapsulate so many of the lessons that I was learning in Sedona. The deer were telling me to trust that I was on the right path, to trust my intuition. The deer were telling me, in fact leading me, back home to myself.

After making it to one of the most exquisite caves in all of Sedona, we sat on an overlook where the red rocks reached for the sun. We spent time reflecting on the deep healing work we had done together and envisioned lives that would be different from the ones we had left behind. Like the name of the cave itself, we were being reborn, giving birth to a new version of ourselves.

After some time had passed, we started to make our way out of the canyon without saying a word. The hike became a silent meditation so we could reflect upon and process all the insights that we had been given by the land. And just when we were about to leave the canyon, we saw the same two deer waiting for us. We were so silent that they didn't even know we were there until we were almost right next to them. It was the perfect way to conclude our walking meditation. The perfect way to remember our magical time together. The perfect way to say goodbye.

My time in Sedona, Arizona, once again reminded me of the transformative nature of relationships. The retreat showed me how, like a spider's web, we are all interconnected, how every person who comes into my life serves as a teacher, sometimes as a trigger, and always as an opportunity to learn and to grow.

As I got closer to concluding one of the greatest and most impactful times of my life, I knew that nothing would ever be finished. Nothing would ever be complete. Nothing would ever be the same again.

And through it all, my time with the healing powers of the Sedona mountains, sunsets, and sunrises reminded me to listen, to really, really listen. In silence. In nature. In the solitude of myself. The desert reminded me that the answers I'm seeking won't be found outside of my own self. In fact, the answers I'm searching for won't even be found through words but through feelings, sensations, and a quiet knowing.

This is intuition speaking to me. This is spirit speaking through me. This is my ceremony. This is my ritual. This is my higher calling.

Like Ana Lilia encouraged me, encouraged all of us to do during our retreat: "Breathe more. I am supported. Breathe more. I am blessed. Breathe more. I am worthy. Breathe more. I am loved."

Since the retreat, I've consistently said these affirmations out loud. I've consistently said these affirmations in silence. And like any powerful mantra, like any powerful prayer, the more that I say these words, the more that I repeat these affirmations, the more I'm starting to notice the daily synchronicities in my life.

As I left the healing energy of the desert, I understood that everything happens as it should. I understood that the more I count my blessings, the more I will attract abundance. However,

SACRED LESSONS

I also know that I must do this in the company of others. I must continue to address systemic inequities and institutional violence. I must be in service to others, and the broader world, if I truly want to live up to my promise and my potential.

This is my definition of self- and community care. This is my understanding of self-love. This is how I affirm myself and my purpose. And I urgently believe this is how I will heal. This is how we will all heal. One person, one family, one community at a time.

One week after returning home from my trip to Arizona, Claudia and I took a weekend vacation by ourselves to Ojai to make up for her not being able to go with me to Sedona. As we were eating dinner on our last night, Claudia started talking about how much I had changed since coming back from the retreat. Amidst some amazing food and wine, we laughed as I recollected stories of my trip and my desire to create something similar for men to come together in community to connect and to heal.

Just then, she looked at me with those same eyes that I'd fallen in love with so many years ago and said, "Can I share with you a text that I sent to Ana?"

"Ana Lilia?" I asked, wondering what she had said.

"Yeah," she replied.

"Of course," I enthusiastically said.

"Okay, here's what I wrote to her."

Hola Ana –

I wanted to send you a huge thank you for the sweet gifts that you sent along with Mike. I am so very sorry to have missed out on the retreat.

MIKE DE LA ROCHA

I was really looking forward to going and was sad to not be there. I send so much appreciation to you for hosting a beautiful circle of healing for Mike and my mother-in-law last weekend. He came back with an energy so full of love, appreciation, and gentleness. I haven't ever seen him this tapped into the power of vulnerability.

Thanks again!

After she finished reading her text, I smiled and finally said the words that had eluded me for so long: "Thank you so much for reading that to me. I really appreciate it. I love you so much."

Chapter 22
The Love of My Father

Years have gone by since the death of my father. Yet I'm still trying to accept the fact that he's gone. I'm still discovering new ways to support my mother, my brother, and myself. And the little secret is that there's no class, no book, no healing retreat that will ever provide me with all the answers that still escape my heart.

But one thing that does bring me joy and a sense of relief in these moments of despair is thinking about my father. And as weird as it may sound, in those moments when I feel lost or upset, a monarch butterfly always magically appears. I literally see a monarch butterfly circling around me when I go for walks or anytime I'm on the verge of tears or when I just need a little reassurance about a decision that I'm hesitating to make.

As I began to learn more about monarch butterflies, I found out that since precolonial times, monarch butterflies were believed to carry the souls of ancestors visiting their relatives. They are symbols of the connection between the living and the dead. And given my father's deep love and appreciation of Mesoamerican history, I know that every time a monarch butterfly visits me in person or in my dreams, it's him checking up on me.

Next to my children, this book is the greatest thing I've ever done. It's been my escape and my therapy. My church and my temple. My most intimate partner and my best friend. At times, I've felt as if this book was writing itself, as if I was channeling words from a place outside my own being, as if it was written in the stars for me to finish this book at this precise moment, at this exact point in my life.

But more than anything else, the signs that have appeared since the passing of my father, and definitely during the writing of *Sacred Lessons*, were the reassurance that I was doing what I was meant to do, that I was on the right path. It was reassurance that my father's memory would never be forgotten.

In many cultural traditions around the world, there is a saying that everyone is born with a sacred purpose. That we are born with a certain *ashe*, a certain reason for coming into this world. As I've gotten older and closer to my spiritual practices, I've come to realize this is as true for me as it is for you. As I look back on my life, I realize that I've always been a writer and that life has been a process of me remembering this truth and following this path to wherever it's supposed to take me.

Maybe it's because of the benefit of time, but at a certain point, I started to see parts of my life like one large puzzle piece or interconnected web of seemingly coincidental experiences that are anything but accidental. I began to understand that everything that has happened to me has happened for a reason, that it's been a test or a lesson in disguise. That every experience builds off a previous experience to bring me closer to myself, to my destiny, to my purpose. That even the death of my father

SACRED LESSONS

helped propel me to places within myself that I never would have had the courage or willingness to go to if he was still around.

Case in point: I decided to go on a weekend camping trip all by myself to El Capitán State Beach, a beautiful beach close to Santa Barbara where I recently found out that my Naná Daria loved to go camping, which probably explains why I've always had a desire to go there. However, I was nervous about going because I knew that I needed the space to confront parts of me that needed to be explored. As I've done my entire life, I decided to go to the beach alone so I could write about my relationship to water and, in the process, get close to finishing one of the most important chapters of my life.

As the day to leave drew near, I anxiously packed my bags and made a commitment to let go of anything that was holding me back, and to go deeper within myself by going deeper into nature. That Friday morning after my Jeep was packed and I was as ready as I would ever be to make this journey, I started to pull out of my driveway when suddenly, a big colorful monarch butterfly started flying around my car. I immediately stopped and knew that I was on the right path. I just sat there for a few minutes, thanking my father for giving me the sign that I needed to be strong enough to go on this camping trip alone.

Since I was driving through Ventura, I decided to stop to see my mom. As I parked in her driveway, I saw my mother was having a conversation with her next-door neighbor Sue. I got out of my car and gave both of them a big hug. As I looked behind Sue, what did I see? A monarch butterfly. Smiling, I knew it was my father once again pushing me forward and telling me that he was going to be with me on my trip. That no matter what, I would never be alone. That he would always be with me.

That weekend I wrote two more chapters, finished reading two books, and even wrote a new song. I battled the urge to go into town and instead walked to the beach every single morning and every single night. On that Saturday evening, sitting next to the campfire, I finished the chapter on my connection to the land and to the water. I had accomplished what I had set out to do, and was proud of myself for doing so.

As I wrote the last couple of words, the part where I prayed to God to take care of my dad, tears started to fall from my eyes. I had reached deep down inside and pulled out what needed to be pulled out. I had fulfilled my commitment to myself to dedicate the time to my own self-growth, and to finishing this important chapter. And I had succeeded in bringing to life the memories that needed to be remembered, and that needed to be shared.

As I sat alone around the campfire, I called my brother Albert. Since I started writing *Sacred Lessons*, I've found myself calling him when I'm at my most vulnerable. Given that he's the only person alive who would understand most of these stories, this entire writing process has brought us closer together. I called him crying, telling him that I had finally realized that my love of the beach was because it reminded me of the times when my father and I would go riding our bikes along the Ventura Pier. I was no longer alone with my tears but was now embraced by the heat of the campfire and the soothing voice of my brother.

I left that weekend refreshed and rejuvenated, ready to finish the book. I continued my early morning ritual of waking up before the sun rose to write for a few hours. I continued my daily ceremonies that brought me closer to myself and to my father. And I was committed now more than ever to doing everything I could to stop the cycle of harm that I had inherited from the

SACRED LESSONS

men in my life, and from the toxicity of our masculine-dominated culture and our male-dominated society as a whole.

The next weekend, I decided to go back to the same campsite with Claudia and the kids. We hurriedly packed our bags, threw some food into the back of my car, and rushed out to get to the campsite before it got too dark. It was surreal for me because I had been at the same spot seven days prior writing one of the most intimate chapters of my book. It was also surreal because I got to share this sacred space with three of the most important people in my life, my wife and my two children.

We spent the next day hiking and going to the beach, until the time finally came to get dinner ready. We cooked some carne asada, and I was beaming with pride as Mio started the campfire all by himself. As we sat around the fire making s'mores, the family next to us started playing some music. I was immediately drawn to the music, which was a mix of blues and soul and had an almost jam-like feel. I took out my iPhone and for the next couple of hours tried desperately to use the Shazam app to identify the band that was playing this enchanting music.

The next morning as I sat outside drinking a cup of coffee and reading a new book, I noticed the family next to us was starting to pack up to leave. Since I'd been unsuccessful in finding out the band's name, I asked the father, "Excuse me, what was the name of the band that you were listening to last night?"

"I'm sorry, was the music too loud?" he replied.

"Oh no, not at all. I was just trying to figure out what you were playing because I really enjoyed the music and wanted to listen to it again."

Excited to share the name of the band and the names of the songs he had been listening to, he took out his phone and said,

"It's from this app called Relisten where you can listen to live concerts from a number of different bands."

"Nice. What band were you listening to?"

"It was a live concert of the Grateful Dead. Since we were camping close to Ventura, I picked a concert that they did in 1984 at the Ventura County Fairgrounds."

Shocked, I said, "What?"

"Yeah. We were listening to a live Grateful Dead concert from Ventura in 1984."

Unable to process everything that was happening at that exact moment in time, I said, "You're not going to believe this, but I was staying at this same campsite last weekend, writing about my father and me riding our bikes along the beach during the same Grateful Dead concert that you were listening to last night!"

"What?" he said, "That's crazy."

"I was literally at that exact same concert that you were playing last night," I told him as I shook my head back and forth before finally saying, "I can't believe it."

After I thanked him for sharing the app and the music with me, I sat there no longer in disbelief but in awe. In awe of how my father continues to visit me. In awe of the thin veil between the seen and the unseen worlds, of the lives that we get to live, and the ancestors who continue to watch over us.

And just before I was about to go inside the cabin and tell Claudia what had happened, a beautiful monarch butterfly visited me once again. As I sat there thinking about my father, I felt an immense amount of gratitude at the fact that he decided to pay me another visit and, in the process, tell me, *Mijo, thank you for taking me camping with you.*

In that moment, like in every other moment, we were divinely connected. We were together once again.

Resources

The following resources are meant to assist you as you start or continue your healing journey.

Literary Resources

abdul-matin, ibrahim, *Green Deen: What Islam Teaches About Protecting the Planet* (Oakland, CA: Berrett-Koehler Publishers, 2010).

Anzaldua, Gloria, *Borderlands/La Frontera: The New Mestiza* (San Francisco: Spinsters/Aunt Lute, 1987).

brown, adrienne maree, *Emergent Strategy: Shaping Change, Changing Worlds* (Chico, CA: AK Press, 2017).

Buenaflor, Erika, MA, JD, *Cleansing Rites of Curanderismo: Limpias Espirituales of Ancient Mesoamerican Shamans* (Rochester, VT: Bear & Company, 2018).

Butler, Octavia, *Parable of the Sower* (New York: Four Walls Eight Windows, 1993).

Campoverdi, Alejandra, *First Gen: A Memoir* (New York: Grand Central Publishing, 2023).

Coelho, Paulo, *The Alchemist: A Fable About Following Your Dream* (San Francisco: HarperOne, 2014).

Dayal-Gulati, Anuradha, PhD, *Heal Your Ancestral Roots: Release the Family Patterns That Hold You Back* (Rochester, VT: Findhorn Press, 2023).

Haines, Staci K., *The Politics of Trauma: Somatics, Healing, and Social Justice* (Berkeley, CA: North Atlantic Books, 2019).

hooks, bell, *All About Love* (New York: William Morrow Paperbacks, 2001).

Kaba, Mariame, *We Do This 'Til We Free US* (Chico, CA: AK Press, 2020).

Kaur, Valarie, *See No Stranger: A Memoir and Manifesto of Revolutionary Love* (London: One World, 2021).

Kelly, Kerri, *American Detox: The Myth of Wellness and How We Can Truly Heal* (Berkeley, CA: North Atlantic Books, 2022).

Lee, Marisa Renee, *Grief Is Love: Living with Loss* (New York: Legacy Lit, 2022).

Lorde, Audre, *The Master's Tools Will Never Dismantle the Master's House* (London: Penguin UK, 2018).

Marcos, Subcomandante, *Our Word is Our Weapon: Selected Writings* (New York: Seven Stories Press, 2002).

Menakem, Resmaa, *My Grandmother's Hands: Racialized Trauma and the Pathway to Mending Our Hearts and Bodies* (Las Vegas, NV: Central Recovery Press, 2017).

Real, Terrence, *Us: Reconnect with Your Partner and Build a Loving and Lasting Relationship* (New York: Rodale Books, 2022).

Rodriguez, Luis J., *Hearts & Hands: Creating Community in Violent Times* (New York: Seven Stories Press, 2001).

Ruiz, Don Miguel, *The Four Agreements: A Practical Guide to Personal Freedom* (San Rafael, CA: Amber-Allen Publishing, 1997).

Tello, Jerry, *Rediscovering Your Sacredness* (Self-published, 2019).

SACRED LESSONS

Weller, Francis, *The Wild Edge of Sorrow: Rituals of Renewal and the Sacred Work of Grief* (Berkeley, CA: North Atlantic Books, 2015).

Healing Resources

Black Men Build
www.blackmen.build

Brotherhood of Elders
www.brotherhoodofelders.net

Brown Boi Project
www.brownboiproject.org

Coaching for Healing Justice & Liberation
www.healingjusticeliberation.org

David Lynch Foundation
www.davidlynchfoundation.org

Equimundo
www.equimundo.org

How Men Cry
www.howmencry.com

Man Forward
wwww.man-forward.org

National Compadres Network
www.nationalcompadresnetwork.org

National Queer and Trans Therapists of Color Network
www.nqttcn.com

Sacred Lessons
www.sacredlessons.com

Medicine
Author's Note

I like to believe this may be one of the greatest love stories ever told. I know this may sound funny, almost like a complete exaggeration, but I'm serious. This is by far the greatest love story of my life. It's not just a story about a father and a son. Not just a story about a husband and a wife. It's the story about all the relationships that are central to my life, and ultimately, my relationship with myself.

With the publication of *Sacred Lessons: Teaching My Father How to Love*, it's been almost a decade since I lost my father. It's been ten years of intense soul searching and trying to live my life without him. Some days are easier than others, and some days I feel crippled by sadness and grief. But like my dear friend Marissa Renee Lee says, "Grief is love," and she reminds me of just how much love I had, and still have, for my father.

Writing this book has been therapeutic, but it has also transported me back to very painful times. Reliving the trauma of my childhood and of losing my father were necessary steps toward me confronting my own wounds and having the courage to heal. This is something that I have accepted to be a lifelong process of unearthing the past and relearning the future.

By waking up almost every day before the sun rose, I got to examine the experiences that have made me who I am. I got to reconcile the reasons why I act the way I do. I got to realize that I am the manifestation of my father's hopes, dreams, and aspirations.

Through this process, I have freed myself from the limiting beliefs that have held me back from expressing my true self. And my greatest hope is that in telling my story, and the stories of the defining relationships in my life, others will feel less alone.

All of our healing journeys may look different, but one thing is certain: healing is not linear but cyclical. Healing requires us to believe in the unseen, in the supernatural, in the magic and assistance of people, past, present, and future.

But more than anything else, I have committed my life to working with others to build the bonds, the relationships, and the structures that will help us heal. Together, we are building inclusive and sacred spaces where we can individually and collectively take care of each other. We are building spaces where our ancestors are working alongside us to make sure that we can create a world of love and abundance.

I hope that anyone reading this book will have some sense of grace and patience with themselves, because healing is hard. Healing is painful. I wish there was another way, but unfortunately, there isn't. There is no quick fix. There is no magic pill. But I promise you that having the discipline to work on yourself, having the commitment to stay on your own healing path, will be one of the most rewarding things you will ever do in your life.

SACRED LESSONS

Healing the remnants of the past, oftentimes a past that we had no control over, is scary, shadowy, yet necessary work. But more than anything else, I have learned that our lives are made up of intertwining relationships that make us into the people we are and will become. That these relationships are sacred and important for the work we must do to build a society and a world that does not harm anyone, especially those who have different life experiences than ourselves.

Life, or more specifically the relationships in our lives, are central to our healing. But, as our cultural practices and traditions teach us, relationships are not just with the living but with the departed, with the oceans, with the animals, with the interconnected aspects of all our lives. That's why the phrase "life is magic" is so real, because we must be vulnerable enough to live the life that scares us the most. We must believe and step into our inherent magic that will provide us with the tools needed to truly heal.

My relationship with my father has deepened since his passing. I talk to my father every day because I know that, like the monarch butterfly, he's always with me. I share every intimate detail of my life with him because I know that he can see everything. I can no longer hide from him. And the truth is that I don't want to hide from him, from myself, or from my feelings any longer. And despite his sudden passing, I am now closer to my father than I ever was before because I know that we are both telling each other, in our own ways, "I love you."

That's why I make it a point to always share stories about my father with my son and my daughter. I make sure to keep his memory alive and to try and pass down his sacred lessons to my children. I want them to feel, like I feel, his presence and to include him in as many family moments and holidays as possible. I want them to remember their abuelo and not fear the unknown and the unseen. I want to normalize speaking with our ancestors and to help my children know that they will always have a guardian angel in my father.

One of the biggest revelations during the writing of *Sacred Lessons* is the fact that I'm not just healing for myself, I'm also healing for my father. Just because he's not physically present doesn't mean he still doesn't have work to do. I know this may sound weird and awkward to some, but this is my belief. I wholeheartedly believe that through my personal healing journey, my father, and his father, will finally be able to heal.

In short, I believe that I am healing for them, I am healing for generations long before me, I am healing for future generations, and I am healing for myself. I know that through my commitment to self-growth, to self-awareness, and to self-love, I am breaking the cycle of trauma and providing a different perspective and a different way forward for my son and for all the men that will come after us.

At least this is my hope, this is my purpose for writing this book. I want to incorporate the sacred lessons from my father into my own life. I want to provide another way for my son and for my family. I want to show my baby boy that he can indeed be vulnerable and express his emotions. I want us both to be more alive and more fully present with those we love. I want finally, after all these years, to be comfortable with being me, all of me.

I don't know what the future holds, but I do know that I am still a hopeless romantic and an eternal optimist who believes that I, that we, that men, can still change. Like the greatest organizers, we believe in the unseen, we make the unimaginable imaginable, and we make the impossible possible.

SACRED LESSONS

So, my story is my story, but it's also our story. It's uniquely mine, but it's also reminiscent of those of so many other men. I know. I wrote my story for all of us who want to share our feelings but are too afraid to try. I wrote my story for all of us who want to learn how to give and how to receive. I wrote my story for all of us who want to teach our fathers, our sons, and our brothers how to love.

I end this book with the hope that you begin to believe in yourself, because I believe in you.

I hope that you begin to truly love yourself, because the universe and I already do.

I pray that you learn to trust yourself, because that's God reminding you of your truth.

I hope you remember that life is all about the relationships you invest in, and that these relationships will bring you the utmost joy and blessings in life.

I hope you use your gifts and talents in service to others because that is your true destiny and your true calling.

I hope you remember that you are divine, you are human, you are healing.

And above all else, I wish you all the love and happiness that the universe has to offer, because you are more than worthy of receiving it all.

Remember, you are never alone.

You are connected to me, you are connected to all of us.

You are the manifestations of dreams.

You are special, you are sacred, you are a gift to the world.

Thank you from the bottom of my heart for being on this healing journey alongside me. Thank you for being an integral part of our interconnected humanity. Thank you for being my mirror, and my reflection. Tu eres mi otro yo.

As I, as all of us, continue to practice vulnerability, please be assured that you are taking an important step into the unknown, yet known, certainty that you and I are not only healing but that you and I are indeed loved.

So as I close another profound chapter in my life and open another, I want you to know that we are in a sacred community together. I want you to know that I am not perfect, but I am trying to be a better person each and every day. And I want you to know that I still tell my son, and I will always tell my son, that I love him every single day, because it's important for him to hear these words from another man, especially from his father.

And as I say these final words, I picture my father smiling. I picture him wanting to hold me. I picture him fighting the urge to hold back his tears. And, without hesitating, I always tell my father, "It's okay to cry, Papá. It just means that you love me as deeply as I love you."

And in my mind's eye, and in the deepest parts of my heart and my soul, my father just embraces me and says, *I know, Mijo. I love you too.*

Acknowledgments

Like any journey, healing doesn't happen in a vacuum but in the safety of a community. There are a number of people who made *Sacred Lessons: Teaching My Father How to Love* possible. Without you, this book, and my own healing, would not be possible.

I first would like to honor the Creator, Mother Earth, Father Sky, Grandmother Moon, and Grandfather Sun. Thank you to the Great Spirit for the ability to breathe and to be alive in this particular moment in time.

Thank you to my family: my father, Ismael "Mayo" de la Rocha, who was the catalyst for writing this book. Papá, I love you and I miss you so much. I think about you every single day, and I hope that these stories will make you feel all the love in the world.

I would like to thank my mamá for giving me life, literally giving me life, and for being my constant source of inspiration and hope. Mamá, you are the heart of this book, and more than anyone else, you have shown me the healing power of love and forgiveness.

I would like to thank my little/big brother, Albert. Bro, what can I say except that I am so blessed and thankful that I get to be your brother. I truly love you from the depths of my soul, and I'm so excited to share many more lifetimes with you.

I would like to thank Gretchen Young, my editor Caitlyn Limbaugh, my copyeditors John Mitchell and Jon Ford, and everyone at Regalo Press and Post Hill Press, especially Aleigha Koss, for your belief in this book. I am so grateful that the universe brought us together, because from day one you ensured that this book would not only be published but would be given the opportunity and support needed to impact as many people as possible. Thank you.

Thank you to my literary agents, Jan Miller and Ali Kominsky, for your willingness to take me on not only as a client but as a colleague. Your meticulous guidance and support throughout the entire process cannot be understated. Thank you so much from the bottom of my heart for all that you did to give light to my life, and to this book.

I also want to thank three incredible women who made this book possible. First, thank you to my sister Angela Rye. Without your encouragement, your support, and introducing me to Jan, none of this would have happened. I love you, sis, I truly do. Thank you. Secondly, thank you Alejandra Campoverdi for your guidance and insight throughout this entire process. I can't express enough how invaluable your input has been to making my dream of being a published writer a reality. I thank you from the bottom of my heart for everything you have done, and do, to enrich my life. Thank you. And thank you, Ana Lilia, for blessing me and my family. You are so important to Claudia and me. No words can express what you have given us through your presence and work. We love you.

Thank you to my mentors, especially those who are still physically present, including Daniel "Nane" Alejandrez, Bobby Arias, Aquil Basheer, Father Gregory Boyle, Tony Cárdenas, Dr.

SACRED LESSONS

John Carlos, Dolores Huerta, Blinky Rodriguez, Luis Rodriguez, and Trini Rodriguez. To those who have transitioned but are still very much with me in my heart, Harry Belafonte, Papá Rabbi Allen Freehling, Tom Hayden, and Wayne Kramer, I miss you all so very much and think about you regularly.

And to my community of friends who have been with me through thick and thin, I don't know where I'd be without you. Just know that I love you. I will surely miss naming every one, so please forgive me. Thank you so much to the following chosen family: Marc Abend, Jose Arellano, Fatima Ashraf, Alonzo Beas, Jake Brown, Audrey Buchanan, Sean Carr, Ben Gebhardt, Juan Gomez, Mark Gonzales, Kenny Green, dream hampton, Dave "Mo Dave" Johnson, Gaye Theresa Johnson, Ron Kurokawa, Carmen Perez, Ashlee Marie Preston, Alberto Retana, Fidel Rodriguez, Roy Rodriguez, Bamby Salcedo, Alex Sanchez, Carola Secada, Michael Skolnik, Sean Van Gundy, Hector Verdugo, Les Ybarra, Marselle Washington, Pete White, Cori Shepherd Whitten, Sabra Williams, Will O'Neill and the EqOp crew, everyone at 545 Glenrock, especially Eric, Josh, and Q, Athletes for Impact, especially Lindsay Kagawa Colas, Danielle Frost, and Jerry Sawyer, and everyone at Revolve Impact and Tepito Coffee. I can't express in words how much each and every one of you means to me. Thank you.

To the Torres family, thank you for accepting me into your wonderful Atengo y Nica family. I would be remiss if I didn't shout out into the universe, "Thank you, Marisol!" I owe you everything for introducing me to your sister. That moment altered my universe and gave me a life that I only dreamed of. Don Luis, you already know, but I will say it here, "I love you."

Thank you to the de la Rocha y Vasquez families, especially my niño, my Tio Cástulo, my Uncle Albert, my Tio Jerry,

Quinby and the boys, Gabriel and Mateo, Alexis, Milan, and Remi, Peter and Michael Chavez, Chato and Lisa Arias-Mora, my aunties Rose and Dolores, Becky, Buzz, Issac, Jeannine, Gina and George, Anthony, Steven, and Robert, Nellie, Tati, Lilian, and Melissa, and to all my uncles, aunts, and cousins, too many to name here, just know that I am blessed to be related to all of you. I love you from the bottom of my heart.

Thank you to the extended C.A.Ch.A. and Ventura College familia. Cliff and Karen Rodrigues, Antonio and Blanca Rueles, Peter and Virginia Aguirre, Fernando and Susan Elizondo, Yolanda Benetiz, Gary Johnson, Dr. Ola Washington, Joyce Evens, Michael Ward, Rubisela Gamboa, and everyone who made my father feel seen, included, and loved. Thank you so, so much for all that you did for my father, and for all of us.

To Tim Ngubeni, oh Tim, I love you, my South African brother, my South African king. Please know that you have made me a better person and given me a better life. Your presence has enriched me and countless others. Thank you for your vision and your guidance in building the CPO, and for holding us accountable when we were young student organizers in USAC and in the mother orgs. We are better because we have you and each other in our lives.

To Zack, you have literally changed the world through your music, and we are forever grateful for you and y/our familia. I don't know where to begin except to say that we have a very deep and special bond. You are one of the few people in my life who I feel completely comfortable being raw, honest, and vulnerable with. I have so much more to say, but I will end it here with a text message that we always send to each other: *I love you, sangre.*

To all my ancestors who continue to raise me, and guide me, I am so eternally grateful for your continued presence in my life,

SACRED LESSONS

especially my father, ibrahim abdul-matin, mi abuelo Alberto de la Rocha, Viva Liles-Wilkin, my Naná Cuca, my uncles Frank and Fernando Moreno, and of course my one and only Naná Daria. Te amo profundamente.

To all those who have chosen to read this book, thank you. My greatest hope is that *Sacred Lessons* will find an audience and inspire people to connect in deeper and more profound ways. You have motivated me in ways that I cannot express simply in words. May you know and embrace all the happiness and love that is already within you.

To all the men, fathers, brothers, trans, and nonbinary individuals trying to be better people, I will always walk beside you as we individually and collectively heal together. There are no accidents, just lessons to learn from. I know in my heart of hearts that all of us, no matter what we have done, are capable of healing and transforming for the better.

To my dear children, Mio and Mayela, I hope you know that you are by far the greatest thing that has ever happened to me. I am so blessed and honored to be your papá. You are my world, and I will forever be grateful that you are in my life.

And last but not least, to my first, only, and forever wife Claudia. What can I say except that I love you with all of my being. Thank you for your companionship, your friendship, and your love. You mean everything to me, and I am so thankful that we continue to choose each other in this lifetime. You are and will always be "my person." You are exceptional. You are exquisite. You will forever be my love. Te amo.

Ismael "Mayo" de la Rocha
(1949–2015)

Ismael "Mayo" de la Rocha, a beloved teacher and community leader, passed away on August 3, 2015. Mayo was a professor at Ventura College for over forty years who devoted himself to his family, friends, colleagues and students.

Mayo was born in Atascaderos, Chihuahua, México on July 25, 1949, and immigrated to the United States at the age of seven. The second oldest of five children, Mayo grew up in East Los Angeles where he graduated from Roosevelt High School before receiving his bachelor's and master's degrees from the University of California at Santa Barbara, with a specialization in the history of México, the United States, and Latin America. He also completed a considerable amount of postgraduate work at UCLA, becoming the first in his family to do so.

A passionate advocate for Latinas/os, Mayo played a significant role in the social movements of the 1960s and 1970s, taking part in the Chicano Moratorium, organizing with the United Farm Workers, and helping to establish M.E.Ch.A., where he served as a faculty adviser for more than forty years. He was involved in various community efforts, volunteering with Los

Amigos del Pueblo, Latinos for Better Government, El Concilio, and the Ventura College Foundation Scholarship Committee. He also worked with at-risk and indigenous youth through the Tezcalipoca Project and Mixteca Alta Formative Project, and served as the Scholarship Chair for the California Association of Bilingual Education for more than a decade.

Mayo began teaching History and Chicano Studies at Ventura College in 1974 and continued until he retired in December 2014. He also taught at UC Santa Barbara, Cal State University Northridge, Cal Lutheran University, and Cal State University Channel Islands. He traveled and taught extensively around the world, including lecturing in Cuba, Nicaragua, and Cuernavaca, México. During his time at Ventura College, Mayo also served as the Dean and Department Chair of the Social Sciences and Humanities Department. He received the Outstanding Instructor Award twice, the Academic Senate Award for Outstanding Service, the Latinos for Better Government Outstanding Service to the Latino Community Award, and was named the LULAC Outstanding College Educator of the Year.

He was an avid reader and runner participating in many 10k events, half marathons and marathons. He was a member of CAChA (California Association of Chicano Athletes), a local running group from Ventura County. Mayo's passion was sharing his rich heritage and culture with his family and students, and he absolutely loved being in the classroom.

Mayo was happily married to Gloria de la Rocha for forty-one years and was the proud father of two sons, Michael and Albert, two daughter-in-laws Claudia and Quenby; abuelo to four beautiful grandchildren, Mayela, Gabriel, Mio, and Mateo; and proud pet parent to his lovely dog Che, who passed away shortly after his death.